Joan Maynard

PASSIONATE SOCIALIST

Kristine Mason O'Connor

Foreword by

Tony Benn

POLITICO'S

First published in Great Britain 2003 by
Politico's Publishing, an imprint of
Methuen Publishing Limited
215 Vauxhall Bridge Road
London SW1V 1EJ

1 3 5 7 9 10 8 6 4 2

A CIP catalogue record for this book is available from the British Library

ISBN 1 84275 059 3

Printed and bound in Great Britain by
St Edmundsbury Press

CONTENTS

FOREWORD

by Tony Benn

This life of Joan Maynard is of the greatest importance for all Socialists, not only because it describes the work she did during her lifetime, but also because anyone who reads it will be able to appreciate the basis of her own deep political faith and commitment, and understand their relevance to the problems which we face at the beginning of the most dangerous century.

Her own experience fired her to do all she did – and did so well and faithfully – which is why she was loved and respected by so many people, including those with whom she disagreed most strongly.

As a trade unionist and local councillor she made a real difference to the lives of those she represented, and that too added to her faith in people and in what could be achieved by organisation from the bottom up, instead of expecting favours by pleading a case in the hope that the rich and the powerful would heed the cause of justice.

I saw myself, as a minister, the resistance put up by the Ministry of Agriculture to the proposals for the ending of the tied cottage system, and realised that if it had been left to the politicians nothing would ever have been done.

Speaking with Joan at Burston and knowing of her speeches at Tolpuddle, it was obvious that she had read and understood the history of the Labour movement far better than most of those who got very near the top of the ministerial ladder.

As a member of the National Executive Committee of the Labour Party I was able to see her in action when face to face with Labour leaders who did not really want to accept Conference policy, and it was that which made her such a formidable campaigner in the Campaign for Labour Party Democracy.

In particular I remember the valiant fight she put up to persuade the NEC to oppose the sale of council houses, and it is only now, many years later, that people are beginning to see that the property boom, which makes it so hard for young people to find accommodation, was in part because of that policy.

Then, as a Member of Parliament, it was a joy to hear her speak in the House with such depth of feeling and such a wide experience of life that it was impossible not to be moved by what she had to say.

As this book reveals, she was a passionate campaigner for Irish unity and independence at a time when even to meet the Sinn Fein leaders was seen by the establishment as an act of near-treachery, associating with 'terrorists'. But such a view never deflected her, and at her retirement party with comrades at the House of Commons she was given a letter of thanks written by an H-block prisoner expressing his appreciation for all she had done.

But my most vivid memory of her was when she was speaking at public meetings, and the clear way she explained the conflict in society, and the world between 'them' and 'us' – them being the bosses against the working class.

She never abandoned her socialism because she learned it by experience and not by reading some revolutionary texts as a student, whereas there were those who had done just that who then went into career politics and ended up with a peerage. That is why her life is still so relevant.

As New Labour moves further and further from socialism and the trade unions which created it and tries to reinvent itself as the party of big business, the unions and the public are looking once again at their own roots and finding inspiration from them which will help to tackle the problems of the future.

I was disappointed when Joan decided to leave Parliament and missed her greatly, but later visiting her at Thirsk I heard something of her work both as a carer and also back on the parish council, where she would have felt the same battles had to be fought.

Her funeral was intensely moving and very well attended, and the affection that she generated was absolutely genuine – as she was herself.

This marvellous book, which has been well researched, tells us all about Joan and it is good that future generations will be able, by reading it, to get some real understanding of what Joan Maynard was, what she did and why she did it.

September 2002

ACKNOWLEDGEMENTS

I am indebted to Carol Cartridge and Don Cartridge for introducing me to Joan Maynard; through their auspices this biography was undertaken. To Joan Maynard, Carol Cartridge was 'a Pearl of a Socialist'. In significant respects Don Cartridge reminded Joan of her father – perhaps the greatest compliment of all.

I wish to record my sincere thanks to the Hepburn family – the family of Joan Maynard – for their enabling support and encouragement.

The principal source for the biography is the series of discussions with Joan Maynard held over the four-year period preceding her death in March 1998. Joan gave me full access to her papers and presented me with a list of names of people to be interviewed (with the practical advice that I begin with the oldest). During the course of the research a number of other people agreed to be interviewed – both friends and opponents – and others gave me valuable material and advice. I wish therefore to acknowledge the contribution of Frank Allaun, Jack Boddy, Hans Breitenbach, Sid Brown, John Leslie Burnett, Doug Busfield, Olive Cartwright, Sister Sarah Clarke, Peter Consett, Jeremy Corbyn, Ann Cryer, Peter Chalk, Harry Cowen, Helen Dunman, Bill Eddison, Joan Addison, John Fry, John Gascoyne, Tony Gould, Stan Hayward, Bert Hazell, Bridget Henderson, Anne Hepburn, Helen Hepburn, Dennis Hodsdon, Paul Houldsworth, John Hose, Doris Hutchinson, Helen Jackson, Peter Jaconelli, Elizabeth Johnson, Chris Kaufman, Rosie Kett, Neville Knox, David Lawton, John Lloyd, George Matthews, Peter Medhurst, Chris Mullin, Marian Neville, Richard Neville, Daniel O'Connor, Wilf Page, Anthony Parkin, Charlie Pattison, Mollie Prendergast, Alastair Renwick, Sally Richardson, Liz Rolls, George Scales, Nigel Scotland, Pam Sellers, Mike Sellers, Dennis Skinner, Gladys Shears, Derek Stratton, Henry (Jock) Sturrock, Valerie Taylor, Brenda Thiede, John

Tubby, Lionel Twiss, Mary Watson, Audrey Wise, Harry Whitton, Jef Witham and Joan Witham.

Tony Benn is owed a particular debt of gratitude for his generous foreword to the book.

I gratefully acknowledge the professional expertise of Stephen Bird and Janette Martin of the Labour History Archive and Study Centre, Manchester University, and staff at the Working Class History Library, Salford, the Rural History Centre, University of Reading, and the Learning Centre at the University of Gloucestershire.

The biography has been supported by the Rural, Agriculture and Allied Workers' Section of the Transport and General Workers' Union, and by Rodney Bickerstaffe, who presented the Fourth Annual Joan Maynard Memorial Lecture in September 2002.

When so many publishers doubted the 'market value' of Joan Maynard's life (a concept which would have made Joan roar with laughter) Sean Magee, Publishing Director of Politico's, recognised her life as significant. For his perspicacity and good-humoured encouragement I thank him most sincerely.

David Boothroyd generously read the manuscript and proposed a number of amendments and improvements; the biography has benefited very significantly from his erudition.

In the final stages of the book's completion I was supported by the editorial expertise of Kevin Southernwood and Jonathan Wadman. Through their rigorous editing several points of clarification and detail were addressed.

With their enthusiasm for the project and many kindnesses my daughter Charlotte Davis and parents Christina and Leonard Mason have sustained me wonderfully during the research and writing, as have other family members, friends and colleagues.

Throughout the whole process Terence O'Connor has been my mentor. His cultural, political and historical insight and intellectual range permeate every chapter, in particular the penultimate chapter and the chapter on the land, so cherished by both Terence and Joan.

Whilst acknowledging the assistance and support of so many, the completed text remains my sole responsibility.

Kristine Mason O'Connor, March 2003

ONE

The ground on which she stood

Vera Joan Maynard – Joan – was born in July 1921 in Easingwold, the North Riding of Yorkshire, and died in March 1998 a few miles from there, in Sowerby, near Thirsk.[1] In her 76 years, having left school at the age of fourteen, she had become a parish councillor, a rural district councillor, a county councillor, a Justice of the Peace, Vice-President of the National Union of Agricultural Workers (NUAW), a member of the Labour Party National Executive, and a Member of Parliament. Her story could be written as the rise from humble obscurity to national prominence of an able person in an open society, achieving positions of grander and grander status.

True, but insufficient.

The significance of Joan's life is not position, but steadfastness. Whatever position she attained, it was to promote the moral and political principles that were her very being. Above all she argued for and demanded social justice with a characteristic directness and candour that is unfamiliar and not always admired in political circles.

Her beliefs were first and foremost from the heart, acquired in the home and homeland where she was born and died. This part of North Yorkshire has its own strong character – called nowadays the spirit of place. The plain to the north of York city is wide and fertile, cut by many rivers and streams, and bordered by the steep scarps and deep valleys of the Hambleton Hills and the North York Moors. Villages and towns have cobbled market places, and robust vernacular architecture in dark brick and stone, and names that speak of layers of settlement – Saxon, Norse, Norman – comfortably bedded down, orderly, ordered: Easingwold, Thirsk, Thornton-le-Street. The visitor has the impression of containedness. The mighty ruins of the Cistercian abbeys at Rievaulx, Byland, and Fountains are also eloquent witness to the centuries of competition for and parcelling out of this rich land.

British farmers, big and small, during and because of the First World War, had done rather well. This was true of the Joan's Parents, Effie (*née* Wright) and Matt Maynard, who were tenant farmers on 100 acres at Alne. Both were from smallholder families. After a shaky start on Matt's parents' smallholding at Upper Carr, they took the tenancy at Evergreen Farm, Alne, following the births of their first children – Elsie Mary, born in 1906, and Roland William (Rowie), born in 1908. Their third child, Edric Wright, was born in 1917. In those prosperous years, they were able to buy books and to contribute to the building of the Methodist chapel (Elsie's and Roland's initials are inscribed on the foundation stones).

The Maynards' prosperity and dreams of buying the farm ended with the end of the war. Evergreen's owner shrewdly sold off the farm in lots to neighbouring farmers, so the family moved to a rented house in Easingwold, where Matt took a job as a salesman for a corn merchant. Agriculture now entered a period of severe decline, experienced, as ever, most severely by the small farmers. Matt's customers were the big farmers.

There is much to indicate that the Maynard and Wright families were distinctive and thought of themselves as such. On Effie's side, the Wrights included coal merchants and Methodist lay preachers, as well as farmers. She was described as 'a good talker'.

Matt's mother, Polly Richardson, was a woman of considerable presence and independent spirit, who traced her forebears among the craftsmen 'from the Continent' who built Byland Abbey in the twelfth century. These two families were embedded in the land and culture of the area. But while for many, rootedness and community tend to a conservative mindset, for Matt they led with equal logic to a different conclusion. In a region where, it was said, 'you could hang a blue ribbon on a donkey and they'd vote for it', Matt Maynard was a Socialist.

He had been influenced primarily by the ideas of George Lansbury, whom he had heard speaking in Middlesbrough (influenced to the extent that their later home in Sowerby, where Joan eventually died, was named Lansbury House). Intelligent and widely read, Matt was also forthright in his opinions, and unafraid of offending his employer or customers. One can picture the farmyard scene in which the big farmer bitterly complains of low prices and fallen demand for wheat, so he won't be buying in as much seed; to which the salesman angrily replies that if workers were paid a decent wage, and if the Government created more employment, the situation would be different. In 1924, in the depth of the slump, Matt was 'let go' from the selling business for which he was ill-suited.

Thus, when Joan was three years old the family moved from Easingwold to the seventeen acre holding owned by Matt's parents at Carr Villa, across the road from Upper Carr where they had optimistically set out in marriage twenty years earlier. They were now truly immiserated.

Elsie was just nineteen, an intelligent, independent and educated young woman. Until the money ran out, Elsie was sent first to the Catholic convent in Easingwold, and when she was fifteen, to the grammar school in York. The family clearly placed great store on education. For Elsie it was also a way out; not for her the grinding poverty at Carr Villa. After brief spells in a draper's shop and domestic work in the home of Matt's sister Jinny in Coxwold, she left for London to train as a nurse.[2]

Unlike her brother Matt, Jinny possessed an excellent head for business and successfully developed the butcher's shop in Coxwold after her husband Herbert, 'a very kind man and enthusiastic drinker', died aged forty. As well as their approaches to business, the young Joan began to notice other differences between her Aunt Jinny and her father. Jinny was conservative and anxious to maintain appearances, always ensuring the front step of the butcher's shop was well scrubbed and polished, so the squire, Captain Malcolm Wombwell, on his way to church on a Sunday, could be assured his village was maintained in 'that perfect beauty and cleanliness, the keynote of the place' (Bogg 1926, p. 48).

Rowie went to the grammar school in Easingwold. He had the experience of the good years at Evergreen Farm, and for him farming was real; talk about politics and ideas he felt to be 'flimsy and facile'. Edric attended the Wesleyan Methodist elementary school in Easingwold and was only seven years old when the family moved to Carr Villa, so for him farming meant only hardship. Early on, he and little Joan made the mile and a half journey to the Church of England elementary school in Ampleforth, then he too went to the grammar school, where he was regarded as 'a brilliant scholar'. Temperamentally he was not suited to farming, and practically speaking, as a younger son, he would not have inherited the smallholding anyway. As Edric developed, he and Matt would engage in vigorous debate about politics and about ideas generally. Rowie kept his distance. Joan, initially uninterested, was eventually drawn in.

These were crucially formative years for Joan, and her memories of them have an almost cinematic quality. In one recollection, poignant and profound, she said:

> I think there is something about those early years which touched me deep down. I remember going to church we used to have to walk the mile and a half there and the mile and a half back, and sometimes I would get tired as a little girl, and me Dad would carry me. I can remember this as well as if it were yesterday. And he used to smoke a pipe and I remember the smell of his pipe. All this is somehow deep in my subconscious, and it's all connected with certain values in my mind.[3]

Joan's journies to school gave her a lasting love for that countryside. In summer the children enjoyed the walk but it could be treacherous in winter with deep drifts of snow and dark evenings with no light on the road – some of the children from nearby hamlets rode to school astride a huge log towed by a horse across the snow.

The school, now the village hall at Ampleforth, comprised three classes, infant, junior and senior. Joan remembers the junior mistress and the senior mistress (who was also the head) as 'exceptionally good' and considered herself extremely fortunate to have been taught by them. In later years, Joan, as a member of the North Riding County Council Education Committee, was thrilled to be invited to formally open the new school (though this occasion is not marked by a commemorative plaque).

Every day Joan and Edric would take cheese and bread made by Effie for their school dinner; this they ate in the Ampleforth home of Mrs Preston, whose three girls attended the school. Joan liked Mrs Preston, who gave them all cups of tea, but she had the strongest reservations about Mr Preston, 'a narrow-minded Methodist' who didn't allow any reading but the Bible on a Sunday. This seemed a strange injunction to a girl whose father read politics and literature at every opportunity – and especially on Sundays.

The school curriculum provided a grounding in the 'three Rs', Christian belief and the values of empire; Joan diligently learned 'the history of who won which wars and what was red on the map in geography'. Such views were challenged at home by her father in long discussions with Edric. Although becoming interested in such debate, Joan was far more concerned about the increasing rows between her parents. They were about debt. She was frightened that Matt or Effie would carry out their threat to leave home for good. Her mother 'used occasionally to walk out, but she didn't go very far, like'. Joan was to say her father 'would often upset folks without meaning to' and her mother 'was not level-headed and would give an emotional response rather than a reasoned one'. To an outsider, Effie's responses appear appropriate and understandable; she was a dedicated home-maker who took pride in the domestic labours of cooking, baking and home economy, yet she suffered ill health, raised children in penury and was married to a most attractive but financially utterly imprudent husband.

Carr Villa was typical of smallholding houses of the area and period. Its stone-floored rooms were sparsely furnished; in the downstairs room there was a chair and a sofa with a coat laid over it. There was no bathroom; the zinc bath was brought indoors and water carried from the beck running past the back of the house. Coal cost money and was therefore scarce but the surrounding woodland provided plenty of timber. In front of the fireplace, and elsewhere, were pricked rugs made from 'clips' of old clothes – each one having a dark border worked from wool habits of the monks of Ampleforth Abbey. Once a year habits were distributed to local women who queued at the abbey gate. The rugs, like the other domestic features, would be found in many of the local houses; what distinguished Carr Villa were the stacks of books on politics, on history and on literature.

As the years passed, the family descended progressively into debt. Effie toiled in the dairy milking the cows, separating milk and making butter to sell in Ampleforth. Joan assisted with the laundry and cleaning the house. Matt and Rowie worked with the cattle and grew vegetables for family consumption and sale in the local markets. Matt would take the horse and trap to Thirsk market on a Monday and Helmsley market on a Friday to sell anything they had: hens, eggs, rabbits, blackberries. But Matt was widely condemned as a spendthrift, 'no matter what he had, he wouldn't have any at the end of the week sort of business'. Joan, his loyal admirer, declared him 'not business-minded'.

The Newman family, who had employed Effie as a domestic servant in London, sent regular food parcels; on one memorable occasion an unknown fruit arrived – a melon. A friend of Effie passed on second-hand clothes for Joan. They were good quality and Joan didn't mind wearing them; 'I only learned later that you express your personality through the clothes you wear.' But the most generous help came from Matt's mother, Polly, 'Grandma Maynard', who yielded readily to her son's requests for money. But there was insufficient to stem the debt. By the time Grandma Maynard died it was said Matt had had all the money from her he was entitled to. Grandma Maynard had accumulated modest funds through hard work and careful accounting, the trait inherited by her daughter Jinny but not by her son. Matt's inheritance was Polly's direct and forthright manner and her capacity to express precisely what she thought – whether or not people agreed: 'I'd stick to my stall if I didn't sell a ha'p'orth.' As she grew up, Joan hoped she would have 'a bit of my Grandma Maynard in me'.

Reflecting on her childhood, Joan thought herself blessed to have been brought up in the countryside, despite the severe financial hardship. She loved the freedom of the fields and woodlands and endless outdoor fun with school friends. A favourite game was played on the steep hillside (carr) when a child climbed into a fox hole and had to be dragged out by the others. Cricket was played with a homemade bat. Woodlands were for hide and seek and exploration. Becks were for leaping and exploring the life in the clear waters. As a child, Joan appreciated the beauty of her surroundings, the crimson and white blossoms of the hawthorn trees, the primroses, violets and daffodils in the orchard.

She enjoyed going to church in Ampleforth; some Sundays it would be the Methodist chapel, others the Anglican Church, reflecting her parents' denominations. Sometimes they didn't go at all. An injudicious Sunday to be absent followed Joan's confirmation. It was Easter time, Elsie was visiting for a few days and Edric was home from grammar school, 'Well there was hell to pay about that. Apparently the great thing was that you were supposed to go to communion the first Sunday following your confirmation. I explained to the parson the reason why I didn't come; that was obviously *no* excuse'.

As well as the Church of England and the chapel attended by the Maynards, Ampleforth, famous for its Catholic college, possessed a Catholic church and yet another non-conformist chapel. Roughly half of Ampleforth was Protestant and half Catholic, 'everyone got along together, it wasn't an issue'.

By 1936 bankruptcy appeared imminent for Matt and Effie. Matt's father, William, had died and his mother, Polly had returned to live in Coxwold with Jinny; there was no more money to bale the family out. Effie feared the shame of bankruptcy. It would be known by all for miles around, not just through talk but through the press; a local expression was chilling: 'We all know what we're up to, but it's nice to see it in print.' The smallholding was sold to cover the accumulated debt and the family moved to work on Hall Farm in Shipton, a few miles from York. A few weeks later, on a visit back to Alne, Matt met up with James Hutchinson, an insurance manager. During the war, Hutchinson, whose parents lived in Alne, would return home on leave and work with the Maynards at Evergreen Farm. These respites from the horror of the trenches, the restorative power of nature and simple creative activity were significant memories, and occasion for gratitude.

Through his contacts in the insurance business, James Hutchinson knew the owner of a small farm with a sub-post office that was to be let in Thornton-le-Street, a hamlet near the market town of Thirsk. Hutchinson said, 'If you put in for this place, I know the people who own it and I will see you get a good reference'. With Matt's reputation, a good reference from a man such as James Hutchinson was invaluable. It was thus that the Maynards took over the lease of Post Office Farm in April 1936, bringing considerable improvement to their material circumstances. 'It were a good move for all of us.'[4]

Thornton-le-Street lies three miles from Thirsk

> half circled by the truant windings of the Codbeck... The prefix Tor, or Thor, denotes its Saxon occupier in pre-Norman days, and ton, or Toune, the hedged-in enclosure of the settlement by the road or street where the Romans

> of old, with measured and stately tramp, continually passed north and south. (Bogg 1906, p. 199)

When the Maynards moved into their new home it was still the main thoroughfare from Thirsk in the south to Northallerton in the north – an ideal location for a sub-post office. (Post Office Farm was literally open house with the post office being reached through the front door of the farm house).

Shortly after the Maynards moved in, the owner of Post Office Farm decided to put it up for sale and gave them first option to buy. Joan recalled:

> We hadn't a bean. But we went to see a solicitor in Thirsk, a wonderful chap called Arthur Walker and he managed to persuade the Bradford and Bingley Building Society to loan us, I think it was, two thirds of the price of the smallholding and of course the house went with it, a lovely old house because they didn't normally lend money on old property. I suppose land was the attraction, you can't go wrong with land. That's why they hang on to it, these landowners.

The rest of the money was borrowed from a friend of Elsie, so the family had a hundred per cent mortgage to pay off. Which they did.

The people of Thornton-le-Street welcomed their new neighbours, and, as was customary, local small farmers organised a 'ploughing day'. Each came with their own plough to work the Maynards' fields – 'It was a gift to help you get going'.

The smallholding was 28 acres, mainly dairy with a few sheep. In 1937 it was a propitious time to be a dairy farmer. As the country prepared for war, the Milk Marketing Board was established, providing dairy farmers with a regular monthly pay cheque. For the first time in many years Effie and Matt could afford to go away together on a short holiday. Matt wrote to Joan from Birkenhead:

> Dearest Joan and all
> We only wish you were here to enjoy yourselves with us. Uncle Arthur took us yesterday to Rhyll a seaside resort in Wales. Tell Rowie and Edric the scenery on the journey was magnificent. Mountains, the houses dotted along the route

> and the farms stock and corn stacks all intermingled were a sight never to be forgotten.[5]

At the age of sixteen Joan earned her first pay packet as 'sub-postmaster' of Post Office Farm. The family was very satisfied with the arrangement – Effie had always been keen for Joan to remain at home to help indoors, insisting that the entire house be frequently and thoroughly cleaned. Effie was expert in cooking and baking, skills she had developed in domestic service with the Newmans. During the evenings she would knit socks, mend clothes, read and listen to talks, plays and concerts on the wireless. She was not physically strong; typhoid in her youth had taken its toll, so she needed to rest in the afternoon and Joan's assistance with the housework – women's work – was essential. Although Joan suffered from minor ailments, described vaguely as 'liver problems', she was a strong young woman proudly able to lift a hundredweight sack of potatoes.

Joan relished working outdoors with her father, whilst Rowie often undertook contract labour for a farmer at the top of Hambleton; 'it all fitted in very well'. Except for the cattle, which were Matt and Rowie's domain, Joan worked at all the jobs on the smallholding. She stooked wheat and barley, hoed potatoes and sugar beet and pulled the turnips. Like all smallholders the Maynards kept a pig to be butchered, rendered and preserved for the months ahead.

An enduring memory for Joan was of her father, a tall, striking-looking man, striding across the fields, broadcasting seed with forefinger and thumb. This image startlingly evokes Millet's famous painting *The Sower*, which Joan, with her interest in art, would certainly have seen in reproduction. The spiritual and political resonances of the picture completely match the meanings which Matt and Joan found in such labour – heroic, primordial, honest. 'The earth is honest with you,' she said; 'it gives you back what you put in.'

Regular payments from the post office and Milk Marketing Board, and the combined efforts of the family ensured comfortable solvency, and eventually they were able to buy more land. The gradual improvement in material circumstances had a transforming effect on Matt's and Effie's relationship. The threats and rows diminished. In the summer evenings they would go for walks together across the fields 'looking like two love-birds, as Elsie would say'.

In summer the family enjoyed outings together to ploughing matches in the district, and in winter they went to the pictures in Thirsk. Joan retained fond memories of Christmas time at Thornton-le-Street; her mother baked Christmas cake and delicious spiced bread, and with other families they sang carols 'not just around the little villages and houses, but round all the farms on foot, on lovely starlit frosty nights'.

To begin with, the young 'sub-postmaster' experienced difficulties with accounting and had worrying moments when the figures didn't balance, but she was meticulous and determined, and soon began to enjoy the work and responsibility. Staff at the head post office in Thirsk, three miles away, were supportive of her efforts and she counted herself fortunate to have a good supervisor and head postmaster. She soon got to know the local people who used the post office and became very friendly with the 'outdoor staff' – the postmen and telegraph boys who called in for cups of tea at Post Office Farm joking and laughing at the latest gossip and goings-on.

The post office work was low paid – £2 a week – but not onerous, indeed, Joan appreciated the opportunities it offered to help people out in small ways. But she found it tying as she had to be available daily from 9.00 a.m. to 5.00 p.m. and on Saturday mornings. Some years later, however, she was to find the Post Office a very accommodating employer; unlike a private employer in a rural area, it allowed her to pursue political activity unhindered.

At the beginning of the war the postman who delivered in Thornton-le-Street was called up and Joan took over his round – three hours every morning between 8.00 and 11.00 'I delivered the letters not just in the little hamlet but in the parish. I went round on a bike and that was my first experience of the inequality of pay because they paid me less for doing the same job as they paid the man.' She vigorously contested this unequal treatment but didn't get anywhere. She had changed from the shy girl at school: 'I got this bug, you see. I think the thing that triggered me was injustice, I could not abide injustice.'

It was not only the injustice to herself which fired her. She had been a close observer of local culture and society:

> When we first moved to Thornton-le-Street I could see there were some people in society, richer people, who had a lot of advantages over other people who weren't so well off. I suppose I got to learn about land ownership

and the power and advantages that it gave people and the disadvantages of not having it.

In her early years at Post Office Farm, inequalities manifested themselves not only through the obvious distinctions of land ownership and housing, but also in numerous subtle ways. Though Joan was always deeply conscious that some families lived in tied cottages under the constant threat of eviction by their employer, she was also aware of the ways 'well-off people were very nice, quite often, to the people who weren't so well-off or high up in the pecking order. But they were only nice to them, generally speaking, if they were "down there". If they got within challenge of them, it was a rather different matter.' She remembered one woman in particular who would come into the post office:

> You could tell from talking to her that she thought you were a good deal lower in the pecking order than she was and she didn't like you saying anything that might indicate that you were going to challenge that situation; it's somehow related to my relationship with that woman.

Although the specifics of such encounters in the post office had been forgotten by Joan they evoked powerful feelings.

Recalling her daily postal delivery in the scattered parish Joan said:

> It was very interesting how different people treated you. Most people were fine, but sometimes, on Christmas Day [*sic*], instead of going round in the post woman's uniform I'd wear my own slacks and a nice Harris Tweed jacket. And I remember one farmer's wife actually fingering the jacket and saying, my word, fancy you… I mean, I read into that, fancy you being able to afford a jacket like that.

In the early months at Thornton-le-Street Joan attended church,

> but I gave it up because they say one thing on a Sunday but do something very different the rest of the week. For instance, there was a lady in the village, Mrs White, who was cross-eyed. They were prepared to let her scrub out the

> village hall and do the dirty work, but they wouldn't let her put the cakes on the table and things like that. I thought this has damn all to do with Christianity, so I packed it in.

Although Joan felt and perceived 'people being treated in a lesser way', others appeared to neither notice nor care, they just accepted it. 'Perhaps it's because of that something in me. What is that something in me? I think it is the feeling that we're all human beings and we should be thought of in an equal sense.' Increasingly Joan was relating her own experience to the theory and ideas discussed by her father and Edric. 'Originally I didn't agree with them, but the more I listened to them the more I thought there was something in what they said.' She began to join in the discussions; soon Rowie was resigned to 'those three being at it'.

Edric was an intelligent, scholarly and religious young man who had developed passions for music and reading. His second cousin Leslie Burnett has fond boyhood memories of Edric: 'He wasn't a weedy specimen, he was well built and very enthusiastic in everything he did. We played the sort of games we knocked up in the yard because in those days nobody had any toys.' Leslie's father was the blacksmith in Coxwold and the two boys would watch him shoe the horses or race across the yard with a red hot metal hoop to fix over the joiner's cartwheel. They laughed at the stories of Uncle Herbert's horse and trap returning home from the pub minus uncle Herbert. They played in the meadows and woods and jumped the becks; 'Who didn't?' There were voles to observe and trout to tickle; lampreys attached to stones swirled in the clear waters. These boys, so thoroughly versed in school about the kings and queens of England, knew that Henry I died of eating a surfeit of lampreys on 1 December 1135.

By the age of twelve, the boys began to lose contact. Edric was away from home at the grammar school and Leslie remained at Coxwold. From their shared boyhood idyll their lives were to diverge further in the future, Leslie to fight in the war and be imprisoned by the Japanese, Edric to become a conscientious objector.

As Edric grew older he began increasingly to suffer bouts of mental illness. It was scarcely talked about at the time, 'things in those days were not known like they are today'. Even when Edric was to die of peritonitis as a young man, Great Aunt Lena would always maintain 'he was too intelligent and his brain was so brilliant that it killed him' – the kind of family myth-making that recoups a socially 'unacceptable' condition.

Whilst Edric loved the countryside he was not in the least interested in farm work. He moved to London in 1936 and secured employment in a world he valued – a bookshop. He aspired to combine this work with part-time study and to enter academic life. Joan longed for the day he would become a professor.

In London Edric became friends with like-minded young men who were anti-war and espoused left-wing politics. They were also passionate about art and music. A leading figure was the composer Michael Tippett, who took an interest in Edric and offered to accompany him and the young writer Douglas (Den) Newton to their conscientious objector tribunal in Fulham. Jailed for his pacifist beliefs, Tippett was something of a hero. For a time Edric, along with other conscientious objectors assigned to land work as an alternative to military service, worked on a smallholding in East Grinstead owned by a friend of Tippett who had purchased a plot to be a commune for this very purpose. Working on the smallholding with Edric was Bryan Fisher, whom Edric had met in London at Toc H.[6] Tippett, who had undertaken psychological self-analysis, felt he could help Edric with his problems. However, he was soon convinced that professional help was needed, for which he and others would pay. Tippett records that Edric 'uttered a gnomic remark that stuck in my mind – "It'll all come. These are the laughing children"; I used this (in modified form) later, for the final lines of Act One of Midsummer Marriage' (Tippett 1991, p. 122).[7]

From 1944 to the end of the war Edric worked for W. H. Smith in Carfax, Oxford, undertaking fire watch duties and undergoing psychotherapeutic treatment. Any spare time was devoted to the study of theology and philosophy in Pusey House Library. After the war he returned to London, to live in Notting Hill, sold books and commenced part-time study for university entrance worried that university places would all be offered to returning ex-servicemen. He went to the theatre and ballet and, by invitation from the composer, performances of Michael Tippett's work at Morley College. These concerts, broadcast live on the wireless, were listened to attentively by Joan in North Yorkshire.

Joan and Edric inhabited contrasting worlds but they were not separate; politics, books and domestic arrangements nurtured the deep bond between them. From his digs, Edric posted clothes home to be laundered each week. They were duly returned together with news from the family and produce from the farm; safely parcelling up the eggs required much dexterity. From time to time Edric received second-hand clothes from home. Accompanying a pair of shoes, was a letter from Joan explaining that a neighbour had brought them to Effie:

> Mother said she thought they would be useful for either you or Rowie. Unfortunately they are nines. I have put a sole in for you and perhaps if you put in another (a good thick one) and a bit of cotton wool in the toes they might do; if not please return them.

Other letters from Joan to Edric share life on the farm:

> After all the rain we have had lately the wind is more than welcome to dry the corn up. Dad has finished thatching the clover stack today and I have been setting up corn, wheat and barley that had been blown down with the wind or knocked down with the rain. Then in the evening we weighed 1 ton 4 cwt of potatoes up, so I am now feeling pretty tired. We have finished the potatoes now except for the harrowings. Altogether there has been 9 tons 12 cwt off 2 acres. Tomorrow we hope to get the last three loads of wheat if it's fine. Rowie is pulling turnips today, last Saturday we had another cow calf and another bull calf, another heifer is due to calve a week on Monday. The cowhouse is finished now. Mother is knitting you another pair of socks, grey ones. Sorry to have misquoted Voltaire.

Effie, Matt and Joan listened to the wireless with discernment, enjoying the plays of Ibsen and Shaw and a wide range of classical music. Joan loved Bach's *Jesu, Joy of Man's Desiring*; it was played at her great-niece's wedding. Edric loved it too: 'there is something delightfully simple about it, like a small child repeating something again and again; say polishing a door knob.'

Edric's influence on Joan's reading was immense. He sent her copies of the *New Statesman*, the *Listener*, and the *Manchester Guardian*. Joan responded:

> You will be glad to hear the *Manchester Guardian* has come at last, I'm enjoying reading it very much. Am also managing to read Plato's 'Republic' in bed at night.
>
> I am reading, in fact I hope to finish it tonight, Russell's book 'Problems of Philosophy' which I enjoyed very much. It's written very concisely and in plain language for an intricate subject like philosophy.

Joan's language was itself plain, both in form and in words used, but the weight generated could give complex meanings a centrifugal charge: 'Last night it was a wonderful sky, red with the setting sun and the clouds were racing across the sky with the wind. I thought of Vaughan's poem "I saw Eternity last night" and I also thought of you, and how you would have enjoyed it, it was really exhilarating.'

While her use of language was a matter of temperament, she would certainly have been encouraged by tutors encountered through the Workers' Educational Association (WEA) such as J.F.C. Harrison. A discourse had emerged in educational and literary circles which privileged language rooted in Anglo-Saxon for its immediacy in expressing the experiences of ordinary people. Leeds born Richard Hoggart, a contemporary of Harrison, writes of his grandmother's speech at times having 'the elemental quality of Anglo Saxon poetry' (Hoggart 1958, p. 49). In contrast, Latinate English was by usage the language of professional and academic distancing, of pretended neutrality.

Joan took the bus to Northallerton every fortnight. There she chose books from the library for herself and her parents and, for Edric's birthdays, bought volumes of poetry and theology. She kept him informed of their parents' reading, and when he could afford it, he sent books for their birthdays – on political issues, *Economics for Democrats* for his father, and about the Yorkshire Dales, and short stories, for his mother. Rowie's reading was mostly confined to Hammond's book on cricket. One Christmas Edric gave Joan Aristotle's *Politics*.

As the war ended and the General Election was imminent, Edric feared the return of a Conservative Government. Despite the widely held belief the Conservatives would win, Joan urged her brother not to be despondent:

> Please don't lose your enthusiasm dear, some great man (I can't remember who) said 'Nothing great was ever achieved without enthusiasm'. Personally I agree. We shall need all our enthusiasm to win the election and the peace of course. We shall need other things too, but nothing can stop us doing it if we really mean it with all our hearts, and of course I think with God's help too.

On 26 July 1945 the result of the General Election was declared. An enormous swing in votes had swept into power the country's first majority Labour Government.

Over the next two years Joan's and Edric's correspondence continued to traverse political, economic, artistic and family matters. Joan wrote to Edric:

> Last night we listened again to Kingsley Martin and the others after the 9 o'clock news, and it was very interesting. The Tribune must be very left wing. I was also interested to hear the report of the Communist Party Conference, which was given on the wireless the other day. About the tobacco tax I know it's unfair on working people, but Dalton and Co. have gone very thoroughly into the question of rationing it . . . Yes I enjoyed Dalton's budget talk very much, and John Anderson the next night was very dreary and still of course trotting out the old stuff.

In 1946 Edric was preparing for the University Special Entrance Exam and seeking another job. In June of that year Michael Tippett's reference stated:

> I have no hesitation whatsoever in recommending him to any post or job in the book trade, because I have always known him to be a person of integrity and quality. I personally have a great respect for him. As far as I am aware he has always been a fully responsible person in any work he has undertaken. I am prepared to answer further enquiries concerning him at discretion because I know him very well indeed.

The following year Joan had planned a summer holiday with Elsie and

Edric, walking in the Lake District. Rowie was busy, as ever, with farm work. During the war, although she had managed short holidays visiting friends and relatives in Edinburgh, Nottingham and Oxford, it was always difficult for Joan to get away because she was responsible for finding someone to take over her daily postal delivery round. Now she could enjoy a good break with her brother and sister; the three of them were excited about the prospect. It was agreed the two sisters would remain in the Lake District whilst Edric returned to the Dales to walk and reflect alone (Elsie and Joan were great talkers). Walking in the Dales Edric suffered agonising stomach pains but managed to reach home. The doctor was called but misdiagnosed the symptoms. Shortly afterwards, on 23 July, Edric died in hospital of peritonitis.

Joan was inconsolable. A friend wrote to her: 'I know you will miss your brother. He was not an ordinary young man, studious and rather shy, and the bond between you and him was not an ordinary one. It was lovely to see it. Accept my sincere sympathy in your great trouble.'

A passage in one of Joan's letters to Edric in 1945 expresses with moving simplicity her great love for her homeland and for her brother:

> The countryside is beginning to look really wonderful round here now, the hedges trees and grass are all a lovely green. It is warm at last, the day a lovely blue, the wind is soft and caressing, the tractors hum and the birds sing. Rowie is up working on the land, I took his tea up at about 8 last night. I wished you had been here to go with me, it was such a lovely evening.

Like the recollection quoted earlier of her father carrying her home from Ampleforth, the words are spare, but suggest oceans of feeling, 'and it's all connected with certain values in my mind'.

TWO

Education – breath of life

The WEA, founded by Albert Mansbridge in 1903, aimed to provide educational opportunities for men and women who hitherto had been denied access to adult education. In Yorkshire the WEA enjoyed a close relationship with the University of Leeds Department of Extra-Mural Studies whose bright, committed tutors sought to make available university standard education for WEA members. For Joan:

> The WEA opened up a completely new world for me.

Whilst Matt and Edric stimulated her early thinking and encouraged her reading, Joan's enrolment at classes in Thirsk with the WEA presented opportunities for sustained study and debate, extending and challenging the ideas with which she had grown up. She was prompted to think about her future: 'I wondered if I should do something practical in politics. This was the first time I began to think about what I should do.' Two possibilities emerged – to pursue her studies, and perhaps follow Edric's dream of becoming an academic, or to undertake political work. 'I don't know whether, in the end, I made a clear decision or whether I just drifted into going for the practical rather than the academic approach.' For Joan, the 'practical' was the political option. Politics meant action; this was fundamental to Joan's conception of politics.

Some years later, in 1953, attending the WEA Jubilee Conference at

Harrogate, Joan heard the Vice-Chancellor of Leeds University, Dr Charles Morris, former Fellow of Balliol, argue elegantly for the value of life experience in learning. The WEA was

> greatly interested in the great subjects – history, literature, philosophy, economics. They are not subjects where you can shine in the limelight of the world at the age of nineteen or twenty-one, but where accumulated learning and wisdom tell; subjects which need deep study by grown and mature people with a wide variety of experience. These subjects went to the roots of a man's mind, to the roots of his experience and to the roots where emotions were deeply involved.[1]

During the 1950s, in the depths of the Cold War, the struggle for hearts and minds extended to education, and the WEA was seen by the Conservative Government as a loose cannon. When the Minister for Education, Florence Horsbrugh, threatened to cut grants for adult education, the *Manchester Guardian* joined the public outcry:

> Adult education as run by the universities and the WEA is one of the great fertilising agents in our culture . . . it reaches thousands who are reached in no other way. In the circles in which the Minister (and her Parliamentary Secretary) moves all this may seem but a pale and needless echo of the real thing, of education as enjoyed by the elite; as a superfluous 'frill' which would be better replaced by evening classes in plumbing or French. To many of those who share in it, it is the breath of life.[2]

Joining the WEA in 1945 was for Joan 'a sheer bit of luck really'. Her interest had been aroused by a small advertisement in a Thirsk shop window, inviting members of the public to an evening class on *Social History Through Literature*. Joan enrolled and thus began a lifetime association with the WEA, which saw her becoming branch secretary and vice president of the district: 'The life of branches depended on a very small number of dedicated enthusiasts who took upon themselves the burden of getting together the nucleus for a class.' (Harrison 1995, p. 124) Some of the tutors were organisers for the WEA and others academics at the University of Leeds Extra-Mural Department. 'An extra-mural department is like the off-licence of a pub.'

When she first enrolled, 'all of the tutors were Socialists' – rare phenomena in the area. One tutor, J. F. C Harrison, described an experience in North Yorkshire: 'On polling day when our car appeared displaying a Labour poster the lady of the manor was so surprised that she almost drove her car into a ditch while craning to get a closer look at this unheard-of abomination.' (Harrison 1995, p. 132)

Clearly not all Socialist adult educators had forsaken the WEA to teach with the National College, which refused state funding – contaminated by capitalism. In *Beyond the Walls* (R. Taylor ed. 1996) contributors from the University of Leeds describe the controversies fermenting in the world of extra-mural education at the university in the early 1950s. Much of the debate was about standards and objectivity with the young tutor E. P. Thompson vigorously arguing:

> To prescribe an attitude of calmness, or moderation, or tolerance towards a society or social problem is to pre-judge that this attitude is an appropriate one. The exponents of this theory of 'objectivity' are not only agreeing to make available facts about society to their students, but are also claiming to dictate the student's response, and therefore, behaviour in relation to those facts . . . The nature of this indoctrination is to deny the validity of the student's experience and prescribe an attitude (usually of 'tolerance' or some associated response) to situations that might well demand an attitude of militancy or indignation.[3]

J. F. C. Harrison, who became Professor of History at the University of Sussex, writes in his autobiography how nowadays

> it is difficult to appreciate the passion with which we debated the issue of objectivity in our teaching. But in the Cold War atmosphere there were genuine fears on both sides: the right suspected Communist infiltration; the left complained of discrimination and harassment… It was essential to avoid fuelling the suspicions of critics of the WEA that 'education for social purpose' meant socialist purpose (Harrison 1995, p. 122)

The WEA helped Joan 'understand that there's more than one kind of democracy':

There isn't just political democracy, putting a cross on a ballot box every four or five years, there's also economic democracy. In other words what do you own? Because it's only when you own it that you really control it in a positive way. I think that was an invaluable lesson which I learned, and I'm sure that I learned it through the WEA. I began to realise that a very small number of people own the real wealth in society and the majority of people didn't own very much at all. Nevertheless, the majority were the people who created the wealth for the minority; those ideas have never left me. I'll tell you that changing society is a great deal harder than I thought it was then. I also think that perhaps one thinks one's own contribution and life span is a great deal more important than it is. You don't realise that your lifespan is a very short period really in the scheme of things.

For Joan the 'Social History through Literature' class was 'absolutely fascinating, and I'll never forget it. I'm sure that it widened my interest in reading and certainly taught me there was all this wonderful history of working people which went with the politics I was getting interested in'.

At her first class Joan befriended Doris Bendelow who worked in the bookshop in Thirsk and, according to Joan, was the only one in the shop who knew anything about books. Like Joan, Doris and her husband were interested in Socialist ideas. After the evening class in Thirsk, Joan and Doris would buy fish and chips, with extra newspaper wrapping for Joan's portions, and she would carry them on her bike the three miles back to Thornton-le-Street for her parents and Rowie. Then, the part of the evening she enjoyed most – discussing the class with her Dad.

Her appetite for learning was not satisfied with one course. She enrolled on other evenings to study social philosophy and political theory and was so enthralled by political theory that she repeated it. The WEA provided the class members – they weren't called students – with book boxes from which they borrowed the works required to write their essays. It was also possible to purchase books through the Association at a reduced rate. Members were expected to read in advance of the class and produce written work, a requirement that could make recruitment difficult. Whilst the 'Social History through Literature' course had recruited well, an economics course had to be cancelled after three sessions because fewer than the required twelve members had enrolled. Undaunted, Joan asked for the syllabus and book box and established a reading group. As well as reading and discussing macroeconomic theory and the big economic issues of the day, members acquired information to answer those niggling little questions; what, for example, is the difference between hard and soft currencies? Left unanswered they could block further understanding.

In her holidays Joan attended WEA summer schools and weekend schools, occasionally getting a small scholarship to assist with the living expenses. At a Whitsun weekend school in Matlock, Derbyshire, she listened to lectures on politics and religion, enjoyed the sessions on musical appreciation and between classes joined other participants for hikes in the Peak District and further lively debate.

Joan delighted in the information, the facts, the debate, the arguments and the theories but felt the need to improve her basic literacy skills. She discovered that Ruskin College correspondence courses, in conjunction with the WEA and the Workers' Educational Trade Union Committee, aimed, 'to equip the student with a clearer understanding of human affairs, a more competent grasp of economic and political facts, and a better capacity to express himself in writing.' Since her concern was to develop her writing skills she enrolled on 'English Composition and Grammar' which demanded a solitary and diligent commitment to writing grammatical exercises and essays every month and posting them to Ruskin. Deconstructing tutor feedback could be quite a struggle:

> Both 'lie' and 'lay' are verbs, but 'lie' is intransitive and 'lay' transitive.
>
> This is the man who, he understood was a Socialist. It should be 'who' not 'whom' because the subject is in the Nominative Case, and 'who' is the relative Pronoun in the Nominative Case.

On completion of the course Joan received a certificate headed: 'The student has completed his course for which he enrolled under the General Scheme on 2.7.51.' It continued: 'Miss Maynard has responded readily to tuition during the course and has taken a very thoughtful interest in the work. Her progress has been very satisfactory.'

How Joan preferred the communal comradeship and curricula of the Leeds WEA classes. In 'Social History through Literature', for example, she could choose one of the following assignments:

> 1. Read Cole and Postgate: *The Common People*, section viii, especially chapters thirty-eight and thirty-nine. Then describe the increasing use of violent methods in English political and social life in the period 1910–1914. Note the resort to syndicalism, the suffragette movement, armed force in Ireland, and unconstitutional methods in the House of Lords struggle. How do you account for this unparliamentary and undemocratic development? Consider how nineteenth century liberalism could no longer meet the needs of the times.
>
> 2. TS Eliot's '*The Waste Land*' expresses much of the dissatisfaction and disillusionment of the years following the First World War. Read the poem through several times (you will not grasp it all on a single reading) and then try to describe in your own words how the poet feels about the civilisation of his time. Note the references to aridity, deserts, lack of water, crowds, the sordidness and cosmopolitan nature of modern life and comparison with the past.
>
> 3. Compare the years after the First World War with our own times; note the contrasting economic conditions and the contemporary writers and poets.

Joan chose to write her essay on the third topic and developed a comparative analysis of the prevailing economic conditions following the two world wars. Towards the end she wrote:

> The most striking similarity I see between things after the two world wars is the general apathy amongst the workers. This I think is due to various things, amongst them, unemployment and poverty, which is soul destroying and mind destroying. Too much hard work, combined with the idea inculcated a good deal from the top that what we need is a leader, someone to think for us.

A precursor of Joan's oft-repeated dictum 'never put your faith in leaders'.

Towards the end of her essay Joan refers to the work of contemporary writers and poets but admits: 'I do not know a great deal about it.' She writes of the 'frustration, cynicism and disillusionment of Huxley and Eliot' and sensibly concludes: 'We are perhaps a little near our own time to judge.'

J. F. C. Harrison's assessment of Joan's essay is comprehensive, considered and formative, written to develop the student's own thinking – no indoctrination here:

> (1) Note the extent to which ideas (such as nationalisation of basic industries, far-reaching social service schemes, improved educational opportunities, etc) which seemed revolutionary in 1919, gradually became accepted in some measure by all parties and by all thinking people in the inter-war period, and that this was utilised by the Labour Government as a capital fund of goodwill on which to draw for their reforms. No such situation existed in 1919.
>
> (2) After the Armistice of Nov[ember] 1918 everyone tried to forget about the war and foreign affairs: even the negotiations of the Peace Conference in 1919 created little stir and were soon forgotten. The main interests of the people turned immediately to home affairs and little attention was paid to external events. Compare this with our own times, when the world situation is on everyone's lips and when our home economic position can only be explained in terms of world affairs.

Breath of life indeed for the young woman who had left school aged fourteen.

In September 1947 Joan joined the National Union of Agricultural Workers (NUAW) at the invitation of its district organiser, Jack Brocklebank. Together they would work to forge ever stronger links between the Union and the WEA with the aim of opening greater educational opportunities for farm workers. Such activity was viewed by some with suspicion. J. F. C. Harrison recalled:

> [the] owner of the village shop and petrol pumps suspected that I was a communist agitator as I used petrol coupons stamped "JTCCOMM" (Joint Tutorial Classes Committee). Such suspicions were confirmed by my efforts to organise WEA classes for agricultural workers (I was at the time a paid up

> member of the National Union of Agricultural Workers). Farm workers were the lowest paid workers in the country and farmers bitterly contested any attempt by the National Union of Agricultural Workers to raise their wages. (Harrison 1995, pp. 131–132)[4]

The joint WEA and Union initiative which Joan remembered with warmth and pride was the course for farm workers which ran annually over eight residential weekends between 1952 and 1955 at Grantley Hall, a local education authority centre near Fountains Abbey. The course 'Life and Labour in Rural England' was led by W. P. (Bill) Baker from the University of Leeds, author of *The English Village*.

Joan recalled: 'in those days most of us didn't have any cars but Bill had a van so he used to pick us up.' On Saturday mornings, eight weekends between October and March, Bill Baker would leave home in Ebberson to collect Joan and drive around the scattered farms and villages to pick up the other class members; 'there were twelve of us and we became known as Baker's Dozen'. Today, in the common room of Grantley Hall, this unique class is commemorated by an oak plaque carved in the shape of the Union badge.

When the class began, the WEA reduced the fee for the weekend from seven shillings and sixpence to five shillings. If, because of work, members could only attend on a Sunday their meals were charged at half price. Bill Baker was careful to arrange the classes at intervals that would not exclude any member having to work alternate Sundays. The subjects addressed included the workings of local government, beginning with the parish council, 'potentially the most democratic institution', debates about 'the comprehensive school', and 'economic divisions in the countryside – Big House, Little House . . . the Tied Cottage'. After the formal sessions sometimes there was country dancing at Grantley Hall but usually class members would repair to the pub to continue vigorous debate before returning to the common room to make tea and talk into the early hours.

William Cobbett's *Rural Rides* was a principal course text. Joan became so interested in Cobbett that Bill Baker asked her to give a talk to the class on her essay 'An Appreciation of William Cobbett'. Whilst critical of some aspects of his work – Joan was a good student – the following extracts from her essay suggest not only her regard for Cobbett but an unwitting prescience about her own future:

> His style of writing must surely be a delight to any radical, it is direct and forceful and shows vividly his independent mind; he was an agitator rather than an administrator; he lacked the ability to compromise. In the end however on Parliamentary Reform he did compromise in order to get a little rather than get nothing. But he was very clear in his own mind what he was doing, the compromise did not corrupt him, and once in the reformed Parliament he continued the campaign for full Parliamentary Reform with all the vigour that his failing health would allow.

Sympathetically, Joan describes the strain on Cobbett of being elected as a Member of Parliament in 'his latter years', rising early in the morning and working late into the night.

The essay concludes with comment on Cobbett's virtues:

> I would put first his spirit of fearless independence, second he was a Countryman, who loved our beautiful Countryside, and the people who worked in it. This he demonstrated in a practical way by devoting so much of his life, and his great ability, in order that working people and particularly those in the countryside should share in the good life.

Until she entered Parliament in her own latter years Joan remained actively involved in organising and participating in the WEA, even making her own front room available for classes. The tutor of 'The History of the Agricultural Worker' was Leeds academic and National Union of Agricultural and Allied Workers (NUAAW) branch secretary Roger Fieldhouse.[5] Weekend schools took place in Scarborough and Harrogate and half-day schools were arranged in Lansbury House on Sundays from 4.30 p.m. to 9.00 p.m. Class member John Gascoyne remembers Joan

> rounding people up and their squashing into her front room on a chair, on a stool, on a bedroom chair or whatever. If you got in first you got an easy chair, or if you were young you just sat on the floor and Roger would do the

class bit. It was Joan's enthusiasm that got people there and kept these things going.

Despite her efforts Joan remained very conscious of a lack in her own formal education, an awareness that drove her to progress the education of others. For Joan, 'education is about helping each individual to express their potential to the full'. In a debate about the 1944 Education Act at the WEA Jubilee Conference in Harrogate she had told delegates: 'A very small percentage of the children in this country are really educated. We talk about education for responsibility, but in the field of public education there is still much to be done in the field of emancipation.'[6]

THREE

The Labour Party from below

The 1945 General Election Labour victory had come as a shock to both the Labour and Conservative parties (Dorey, 1995), and, indeed, to the nation – a shock that translated to jubilation for the whole Labour Movement (Shaw 1996, p. 20). Opinion polls, which had been pointing to a Labour victory, were dismissed or ignored. Attlee and Bevin had even considered Churchill's offer to form a coalition, believing his wartime leadership would assure him of success.

When Labour won 393 seats it became the first majority Labour Government in history. It has been argued that the war helped to establish 'a new political consensus and that the leftward shift in popular attitudes began as early as 1940 with the appointment of Labour ministers to the Coalition Government'.[1] The perception was that 'the trade unions, as well as the Labour Party, were involved at the very heart of government' (Dorey 1995, p. 2).

The Labour Government ministers, 'represented before the war as red revolutionaries' (Hattersley, 1997, p.3), had become widely respected:

> Ernest Bevin had been transformed from the aggressive union leader of the General Strike into the much-loved Minister of Labour. Herbert Morrison – before the war, the tyrant of the London County Council – was the Home Secretary who had been photographed in the ruins of every blitzed city in Britain. Attlee himself – excoriated by Tory newspapers during the Spanish

> Civil War for giving the clenched-fist salute to the republican international Brigade – had become Churchill's deputy in the victorious coalition. The newspapers which had once denounced him as a Communist stooge spent the war years extolling his virtues as the essential partner in the triumph of a united nation. (*Ibid.*, pp. 3–4)

More important than this depiction of Labour's leaders was the lived experience vivid in voters' minds, of the pre-war years of poverty, bad housing, mass unemployment and the advent of war itself. As Butler (1995, p. 8) observes, 'The *Daily Mirror* sustained a notable pro-Labour campaign on the themes "Don't let it happen again" – war and unemployment – and "I'll vote for him" – addressed to the wives of soldiers still serving overseas'. Laybourn (1997, p. 139) argues that by 1945 'the Labour Party was demonstrably the party most likely to introduce the social reforms that were essential if Britain was to avoid the economic and social mistakes of the interwar years'.

The prominent role of the Red Army in the defeat of fascism promoted a sense that Socialism was both heroic and successful. In the heat of the conflict, previous social status was made irrelevant. Yet again, all that was solid, all the frozen relationships of the pre-war era, melted into air. For the time being.

The Labour Party manifesto, *Let Us Face the Future* committed the party to 'jobs for all'; public ownership (of fuel and power industries, inland transport, iron and steel); a housing programme; further or adult education and free secondary education for all; the National Health Service and social insurance 'against the rainy day'. The Conservative Party manifesto, *Mr Churchill's Declaration of Policy to the Electors*, emphasised the maintenance of high and stable employment; mutual cooperation between industry and the state; a large house building programme, a nationwide and compulsory scheme of national insurance; a comprehensive health service and an education system 'to produce the good citizens of tomorrow'.

Clearly there were several points of similarity in the two manifestos but one obvious point of difference was the the issue of nationalisation – embraced by Labour and shunned by the Conservatives.

Labour's *Northern Voice* proclaimed the Labour victory to be 'The revolution without a single cracked skull. The pioneers' dream realized at last. Nothing to stand in the way of laying the Socialist foundation of the new social order'. A Gallup poll revealed 56% wanted 'sweeping changes such as nationalization' (Heffer 1993, p. 35).

The return of Conservative MP Robert Hugh (Robin) Turton in Joan's constituency of Thirsk and Malton came as no surprise; 'even the grass was blue'. The big surprise was the seat being contested at all – by the Common Wealth Party candidate Edward Moeran.

Joan described the Common Wealth Party as a 'wonderful party' and the man who established it, Sir Richard Acland, as 'a true Socialist', an opinion she formed about most of the Common Wealth people she met. Common ownership of land was the feature of Common Wealth policy that particularly appealed to her. As she saw it:

> Their idea was that you would pay the person who you took the land off, but when that person died you didn't pay any more. Which was quite a good point of view and quite a good easy one to argue for logically as well as morally. I later came to see the Common Wealth Party as being to the left of the Labour Party.

The launch of the Common Wealth Party election campaign at Malton was an inspiring occasion with over two thousand people gathered in the market place for the open-air meeting. J. B. Priestley's address made a searing impression on Joan, 'For we are the people of England, that never have spoken yet'.[2]

Enthralled, Joan volunteered to help during the three week campaign and to billet Common Wealth canvassers at Post Office Farm. She was one of only a handful of local campaigners for the Common Wealth Party; most she described as 'imported'. When the Common Wealth campaigners spoke at Thirsk market place quite a crowd turned out to listen – it was a novelty. When Robin Turton spoke in Thirsk almost every sentence was laced with Churchill, 'he said something about free enterprise and then about six words, then Churchill, and another six or seven words and Churchill again. From the crowd a heckler yelled out, "Churchyard! Churchyard!"'

For Joan the campaign was 'a tremendous experience; listening to them I thought, well this is marvellous, it sounded like sanity after listening to all that Tory talk'. It was Joan's first taste of campaigning. As well, as polling over 13,000 votes the Common Wealth Party had presented voters in Thirsk and Malton with their first opportunity to vote for a candidate of the Left.

At the 1946 Labour Party conference Attlee emphasised the party's commitment to nationalisation; the Government was 'resolved to carry out as rapidly and as energetically as we can the distinctive side of Labour's programme: our Socialist policy on nationalisation'.[3]

According to Peter Dorey, Labour's nationalisation programme achieved through the establishment of semi-independent boards was 'something of a messy compromise, representing a half-way house between autonomy and accountability'. In Alec Cairncross's view the nationalisation programme was introduced 'by a set of rather conservative politicians whose main anxiety was to secure efficient management and give it a fairly free hand provided it followed commercial precedents'.[4]

Reflecting on Labour's victory of 1945 Joan remained convinced:

> So much good will amongst people was even more important than our huge majority in the Commons. We could have done really anything if we'd had the confidence in ordinary people and been straight and honest with them, and determined to help them to change society. We could have done anything. I think if ever we could have brought about a revolution in this country, peacefully, 1945 was it, because the Tories were reeling. They didn't reel for long because they soon realised that there wasn't going to be any real threat to their bastions of power like land ownership and money and the City, and of course industry.

Trade union leaders were disinclined to urge the Government towards greater worker control – a point never forgotten by Joan. Union leaders were also key to maintaining wage restraint in the 1940s. Describing the response of union leaders to left-wing criticism of Government policy displayed at the popular 'Brains Trust' meetings held by constituency parties across the country in the late 1940s, Jones (1994, pp. 186–187) states:

> Angriest of all were the trade union leaders for whom – as for Ernest Bevin in his day – loyalty was the supreme virtue and any dissidence was a stab in the

> back. Bevin's successor at the head of the Transport and General Workers' Union was Arthur Deakin, a man who had inherited all of Bevin's intolerance and ruthlessness. Shoulder to shoulder with him stood a group of union bosses – the word is fair, considering the absence of democracy in their organisations – including Sir Tom Williamson of the General and Municipal Workers, Sir Will Lawther of the Miners, Sir Lincoln Evans of the Steel workers and Sir Tom O'Brien of the Cine-technicians.

Whilst historians have highlighted the achievements of Attlee's Labour Governments, particularly in social welfare and education, for Joan, as for other Socialists, 'nationalisation was and is a litmus test of the Party's commitment to Socialism.' (Dorey 1995, p. 7) Joan would always maintain that Attlee had failed the test. Even after reading Robert Pearce's 1997 biography of Attlee and 'learning lots of things I didn't know about him', she remained convinced that under his leadership the Party had missed its best opportunity for Socialist transformation.

Reading The *Darlington and Stockton Times* at Post Office Farm one freezing January evening in 1946, Joan noticed an advertisement inviting anyone interested in forming a Thirsk Labour Party to come to a meeting in Church House, Kirkgate. The advertisement had been placed by the Thirsk and Malton Divisional Labour Party Committee, which itself had only been established at York in February of the previous year by the Northern Regional Council of the Labour Party. The new Committee with its Chairman, National Union of Agricultural Workers (NUAW) delegate Jack Brocklebank, set about forming local Labour Parties across the Division.

Edric, home for the Christmas holiday, accompanied Joan to the meeting in Church House. Although Thornton-le-Street is barely three miles from Thirsk, Joan and Edric didn't really know any of the people present – Thirsk was outside Joan's postal round. She did, however, recognise Jack Brocklebank, who had caught her eye giving the Conservatives a hard time at election meetings in Thirsk marketplace. The seven or eight people, encouraged by the enthusiasm and arguments of Jack Brocklebank and Jimmy Aldous, member of the Transport and General Workers' Union, decided that night to form a local Labour Party. In Joan's view, 'They thought this was a sensible and appropriate time to form a Labour Party, which was a jolly good idea. They were right about the timing, and that's how the meeting came to be called. There was national euphoria'.

The regional secretary, W. B. Leurcock, addressed the meeting on the position, aims and constitution of the Labour Party and moved the officers be elected. The Reverend E. B. Storr was elected president and Mr Boyes treasurer. Joan recalled:

> They could get a chairman and a treasurer but couldn't get anyone to be secretary. Nobody was willing to do the secretary's work, I think because they knew more about it than me. They realised the amount of work entailed in that side of the job. Eventually they asked me if I would do it and I said I really haven't any idea what it amounts to but I am prepared to do my best. Anyway, I got the job and somebody else wrote up the first minutes for me. I couldn't have known less about it because I remember arriving at the next meeting without an agenda. I didn't know what an agenda was, so you couldn't be greener than that. I might say I never did that again.

And so, on 24 January 1946, this handful of people, inspired by the Labour victory and the promise of Socialism, established the Thirsk Labour Party. Its new secretary would devote her energies to the Labour Movement for a further fifty years. It is interesting for a moment to compare the nascent Thirsk Party with the Labour MPs voted into power the previous year. In a Labour Party 'dedicated to the overthrow of the old Tory ruling class and to the primacy of working class interests and needs [it] was in its composition less proletarian than any of its predecessors... The middle class orientation applied to the left as much to the right, if not more so' (Jones 1994, p. 136). What could those on the left in Parliament, who lunched at the Savoy Grill with Richard Crossman, possibly understand about the poverty and insecurities of rural workers?

Jack Brocklebank, was struck by the enthusiasm and energy of the new secretary at Thirsk. In his job as organiser of the NUAW in North Yorkshire he was always on the lookout for committed and 'lively spirits' to enthuse the membership; within a year he invited Joan to join the NUAW. Brocklebank was to become her lifetime and 'dearest friend' and the Union her 'greatest love'. He was to write of Joan: 'A smallholder's daughter in a truly rural area, she had all the ingredients for going the other way, yet she undoubtedly found the outlet she was looking for through her work for this Union.'

The other outlet was the Labour Party. Soon after the Party was established at Thirsk Joan began to be selected as its delegate to regional Labour Party Conferences in Northallerton, York and Gateshead.

The Party in Thirsk resolved to fight the local elections 'if a candidate could be found'. One member was willing to stand for the parish council, but as an Independent. This offer got very short shrift; Joan's minutes record that 'it was resolved Mr Myers be pressed to come out as a Labour Candidate for the Parish Council Election as we cannot give him official backing as an Independent'.

Two members were persuaded to stand for the county (Carlton Miniott ward) and the rural district council (RDC) elections. For the county contest the Party was delighted and relieved to be informed that the National Union of Railwaymen (NUR) would adopt the Labour candidate, Cliff Megson, defraying his expenses and those of printing election addresses. Labour was heavily defeated in the county election but the new Party had made its mark; it also succeeded in winning seats on the rural district and parish councils. As well as seeking election, the Party was committed to representation on local bodies (one of being the Post-War Planning Committee in Thirsk) and the Party delegates were mandated to work particularly for the accommodation of 'aged people'.

Party meetings took place in Church House, Thirsk, through the auspices of the Reverend Storr. When it was unavailable, meetings were arranged in members' houses or the Black Lion Hotel. The business meetings were followed by talks and discussion to promote political education. Topics included 'Are all Men Equal?' presented by Reverend Storr and 'Party Organisation, Questions and Discussion' led by W. B. Leurcock. On 29 June 1946 Joan gave her first talk, 'Rural Life and Conditions'.

In planning Labour Party meetings Joan worked closely with the chairman, Reverend Storr, who, in his youth, had attended public meetings addressed by Keir Hardie. Storr's views were reported in the local press under the heading 'Socialism and the Christian Ideal':

> Expressing his firm conviction that Socialism was a way of communal life nearer to the Christian ideal than capitalism, the Reverend E. B. Storr, Chairman of the Thirsk Labour Party, declared... 'I believe Atheism to be a wrong creed, but I had rather stand before the Judgement Throne as an Atheist who had spent himself for human causes than a believer in God who had lived selfishly in his own interests' . . . When a person reached Socialism through Christianity as he did, he honestly thought that Socialism was the social application of the Sermon on the Mount.[5]

Such views accorded strongly with Joan's Christian upbringing and 'burning desire to help to build Socialism for Britain'.[6]

The successes in the RDC and parish elections boosted the Party's confidence and they set about arranging public meetings. Resolutions were passed to invite national figures such as J. B. Priestley and Harold Laski to speak at Thirsk. Efforts to get Professor Laski to Thirsk continued Godot-like for several years; whilst indicating he was willing to speak, he was always prevented from doing so at the last moment. On one occasion Joan had even booked him a room at the Golden Fleece and advertisements had been placed in the local press – a major drain on scarce Party resources and another disappointment.

The Party managed to obtain the services of Labour MPs from the Northern constituencies and it was Joan's responsibility to contact them and make the necessary arrangements. Occasionally the Party secured a Government minister. The Minister of Pensions, Wilfred Paling, spoke for the Party at Thirsk Town Hall on 18 October. Sitting beside him on the platform Joan noted with satisfaction his message hitting home with the audience:

> One of the most dreadful fears in the mind of the average working man is the fear of sickness overtaking him as the father of a family, the fear of old age when he is no longer able to work, or perhaps more common still, not be allowed to work. In the first year of this Government's life they brought in schemes of social security which are the biggest thing that the world has ever known. It is the first time we have had a comprehensive scheme bringing in everybody.[7]

Arranging public meetings and contesting elections demanded considerable financial outlay, as did defraying the expenses of councillors and contributing funds to the Divisional Labour Party. The relentless task of raising money, described by Joan as 'grim and gruelling', was to consume much of her time and energies over the next thirty years.

Socials, quizzes and whist drives were organised in Thirsk and the surrounded villages. For the Thirsk Christmas Party of 1946 it 'was resolved the charge at the door would cover refreshments too and that people, when getting refreshments, should hand over admittance tickets – so as to avoid them coming twice'.

Dances were arranged at Thirsk Town Hall with buses organised to pick up people from the villages. It could be a risky business though, with dance bands coming from as far away as Leeds costing up to 25 guineas; the winter weather could prevent buses running to the villages so only a few tickets would be sold at the door, making a loss for the night. But the dances were fun, 'the more we are together the merrier we shall be'. There were 'novelty dances' and 'competition dances' in the florally decorated hall; a coveted prize was a bunch of Thirsk-grown grapes. Refreshments were served by the Ladies Committee.

Joan established the Ladies Committee to support the activities of the Social Committee; the women met in each others' houses, preparing for their greatest fund-raising successes – the 'Sales of Work'. Joan preferred to organise than to sew preserve and bake, and relied on her mother's famed plum cake to make a good bit in the raffle.

Although Party funds came from trade union affiliation fees, principally the NUR, the National Union of Public Employees (NUPE) and the NUAW, the main source of funding was members' contributions. In the evenings, in all weathers, Joan would cycle into Thirsk and meet up with Party members who had changed out of their working clothes to canvass in the town and adjacent parishes. Often she would be given a lift by NUAW activist Bert Waind. She proved to have a natural flair for canvassing and her direct and friendly disposition usually secured her an invitation into people's homes. What she said made sense; people related it to their own experiences of work, housing, education and health. She had always done her homework – not to mystify others or aggrandise herself, but to enable her to explain clearly and to have facts in support of what she was saying. This commitment and capability was to take her into literally thousands of homes in the division and result in over two thousand members. She wrote of her early experiences:

> Dear Ivy
>
> I feel I must write and tell you of the fun I and a Labour Party friend are having canvassing for Party members in the villages round here. Not only are we having fun but we are getting new members and gaining experience. Recently we have canvassed four villages. In the first we got eight new members, and the amusing incident there was that a fairly well to do woman, not realising we were canvassing for the Labour Party, asked us in. As we entered the house she was apologising for having the washing round the fire, and when she got into the room she started taking the clothes horse away from the fire. By this time I had got round to letting her know what we had come for and the change of attitude was immediate. Back went the clothes round the fire and she said, 'Oh, that's different. I'm a Conservative'. We had the greatest difficulty to stop laughing until we got outside, but managed somehow. The next village we did, we met a woman who nearly spat on the floor when we told her what we had come for. She proceeded to tell us that the landed gentry were the backbone of the country and nothing was worth anything but gold. Gold had always been valuable since Solomon's time. We thought we were flogging a dead horse talking to her and after trying to talk reason for a while, we left. We have often gone a long way back, but never as far as Solomon's time before.

It wasn't always fun. Joan remembered canvassing a village in the old Thirsk RDC area 'I was asking a working man if he would be voting for the Labour candidate. He thought for a while and said, "I should like to." The village and surroundings were owned by one family who took people to vote in their car. The lady from the big house checked everyone off at the polling station. So it was not strange that this man was nervous of voting for the Labour candidate.'

The Thirsk Party had been in existence for two years and had recruited over one hundred members when the treasurer, Mr Boyes, announced his resignation because he was moving out of the area. He wrote to Joan:

> I cannot sever my connections with Thirsk and our local Labour Party without letting you know how much I have enjoyed working with you for the cause that we both thought well worth working for. I think it was only your example that has kept me up to scratch when sometimes I felt like slacking off when I saw the slow progress we were making in breaking down the apathy which is the biggest stumbling block to progress in this backward and benighted area. Well cheerio. All the best to you and a special message to Mother and Dad – that is 'Keep smiling'.

As secretary of the Thirsk Party, Joan was a delegate to the Thirsk and Malton Divisional Party chaired by Jack Brocklebank; in August 1946 she was voted on to its executive and three years later appointed press officer. Members of the Thirsk and Malton Divisional Party referred to each other as comrade and meetings commenced with a lusty singing of 'The Red Flag':

> Though cowards flinch and traitors sneer
> We'll keep the Red Flag flying here!

Motions put to the Annual Conference of the Labour Party reflected the Divisional Party's commitment to Socialism and internationalism. Relations with the national Labour Party were characterised by policy and organisational tension.

On foreign policy, Jones (1994, p. 137) states:

> [For] many Labour activists and some MPs, adherence to 'socialist objectives' meant primarily friendship with the Soviet Union. Indeed, the Labour leaders had given this impression at the election campaign. Cripps had promised that a Labour Government would be 'in broad sympathy with the views of the Russian people' . . . For those who saw a comradely relationship with the Soviet Union as the litmus test of a 'socialist foreign policy', the assumption was that there were two, and only two, political forces in the world in 1945, one seeking the maintenance of capitalism and the other aiming to abolish it. In the latter the most important element was obviously the huge nation in which capitalism had been abolished since 1917.

However, as Dorey (1995, p. 20) writes, it soon became clear that Attlee was unwilling to adopt a 'fraternal' stance to the Soviet Union and instead looked to the United States to develop political and military links:

> The surprising appointment of Ernest Bevin as Foreign Secretary in 1945... actually served to strengthen Britain's 'Atlanticism' and its concomitant antipathy towards the Soviet Union. Bevin himself was profoundly distrustful of the Communists generally, and the Soviet Union in particular'. This distrust was fuelled by his being 'bombarded from the Foreign Office with pessimistic diagnoses of the long term ideological roots and urge for world expansion of the Soviet leaders, inherent in their Marxist-Leninist philosophy'.[8]

According to Shaw, credence should not be given to the idea of the Soviet Union being bent on world conquest, an idea contested by Left critics at the time. The crippling losses suffered by Russia during the Second World War had rendered it incapable of such a move. Further, Shaw argues, along with others, the 'decisive consideration was Labour's insistence on upholding Britain's status as a world power rather than fear of Soviet expansionism' (Shaw 1996, p. 23).

The Marshall Plan, announced by US Secretary of State George Marshall in June 1947, was intended to provide financial aid to reconstruct and regenerate European economies after the war. Although the policy was declared as 'directed not against any country or doctrine, but against hunger, poverty, desperation and chaos' (Hattersley 1997, p. 33), the strategy was to ensure Europe would be less susceptible to Soviet expansionist ideology.

On the morning of 25 June 1950, North Korea invaded South Korea across the 38th parallel. 'Under the auspices of the United Nations Security Council [which Stalin was boycotting at the time] American troops, with a British contingent, were sent to repel the invasion.' (Shaw 1996, p. 41)

At Thirsk and Malton Labour Party, Tom Gascoyne explained the situation to members who then passed an emergency resolution, proposed by Gascoyne and seconded by Joan 'This Divisional Party urges that a meeting of the four great powers, Russia, Britain, America and France, should be convened as soon as possible in an attempt to arrest and reverse the present drift towards world war.'

During its brief history, the approach of the Thirsk and Malton Divisional Labour Party towards Communism and the Soviet Union had shifted. Immediately after the war it had opposed any move by the Communist Party to affiliate to the Labour Party. Under the powerful intellectual influence of Tom Gascoyne, the Thirsk and Malton Labour Party was to develop a pro-Soviet Union position. In 1947 Joan spoke to members about 'The Differences between Western Democracy and Soviet Democracy'.

On the question of arms the Divisional Party grew increasingly at odds with the Labour Government, sending resolutions to annual conference for reductions in the level of armaments. On its own domestic front the Divisional Party ensured survival by the incessant round of canvassing for new members and organising fund raising events. In 1947 it had not been able to pay the expenses of its own delegate to the Labour Party Annual Conference. It was even in regular receipt of food parcels from Australia, which it distributed to local parties across the division. In seeking a grant from Head Office in London to appoint a part-time agent they were informed grants were only available for full-time agents, which they could not afford.

*

The task for the Divisional Labour Party was to find a Parliamentary candidate to contest the seat for Labour. There was only one nomination, this being from Thirsk – Edward Moeran. Moeran was the Socialist who had fought Thirsk and Malton in 1945 for the Common Wealth Party and Joan was a prime mover in his selection at Thirsk, having campaigned for him in 1945. Others at Thirsk had hoped that a 'local man' would stand and tried to persuade E. B. Storr and Jack Brocklebank – both of whom declined. After some consideration, and despite pressure from the local Party, Moeran declined the nomination, concurring with the view that the division needed a 'local man' to fight the seat. The Party placed on record its appreciation of his services to the constituency and obtained the official list of candidates from the Area Office.[9] Three people were selected to address a meeting in York in January 1949 and on a card vote Ivan Geffen secured the nomination as Labour's prospective Parliamentary candidate.

Geffen, a young solicitor to the Durham Miners, had lectured for the Workers' Educational Association and Durham University. Joan accompanied him to his first public meeting in the division, held in the Red Cross hut at Easingwold. She always enjoyed public meetings; a favourite story was of Ellen Wilkinson goading a farmer to remove his waistcoat after he'd asked her the number of ribs in a fat pig. Geffen was in for a similarly rowdy time. He told his audience, 'This is a new experience for me, because I have never been a Parliamentary candidate before, and a new experience for you because you never had a Labour candidate before.'[10] His listeners were out to enjoy themselves and to embarrass the young candidate; what did he think about the weevils in the barley at Tholthorpe Aerodrome? There were protests shortly after 9.30 p.m. when Councillor Patterson, chairman of York Labour Party, who presided, proposed the meeting be brought to a close. 'I have to be up at 5 o'clock,' he said, promising the boisterous questioners they would have other opportunities of meeting Mr Geffen in the near future.

The Party arranged numerous opportunities for constituents to hear from Geffen. In the period between his adoption as Labour's prospective Parliamentary candidate for the division and the General Election, he addressed over two hundred meetings across the constituency. The one that Joan relished was the open-air meeting in the village of Upsall where, at the castle, the sitting MP Robin Turton had his home.

The Party was determined to appoint an agent to support the new candidate, and on receipt of a development grant of £100 from Head Office, to be repaid, advertisements were published and interviews held. In October 1949 Irvin Denny was appointed as secretary agent. As Joan was later to observe, the young man 'was faced with a General Election in February 1950 – almost before he had found his feet'. By September 1950 the finances meant that Denny's appointment had to terminate and he offered his services free to the Divisional Party.

Joan's response to Attlee's announcement of a January 1950 dissolution of Parliament and February General Election was fear that winter weather would produce a low turnout of Labour supporters across the country. In rural constituencies the problem was exacerbated. Already the Party locally had been campaigning for more polling stations to increase the turnout by reducing the travelling distance for voters.

A further worry for Joan was finding accommodation for the Labour Party Committee Rooms in Thirsk. Whereas rooms had been secured in Easingwold, above a cobbler's shop in the market place, it became clear that whilst Thirsk might tolerate Labour rural district and parish councillors it was not in the business of contributing to the unseating of its Conservative MP, who had served the division since 1929. There was nowhere available save the living room of Labour councillor W. Stephenson. Ivan Geffen told the press, 'We have tried several times to rent vacant rooms in Thirsk. We have been unsuccessful, and no reasons have been given. There seems to be a definite effort to keep us out of Thirsk Market Place.' He still remained hopeful that the campaign in the division would be 'fought fair from now on which is the way we intend to fight it'. As well as fighting fairly, the Party, under Jack Brocklebank's admonition, was 'to fight upon constructive principles, what we have done and what we are preparing to do, rather than upon the record of our opponents'.

The Labour Party manifesto *Let Us Win Through Together* called for the nationalisation of further industries: steel, sugar and cement. The overall tone was cautious and characterised by Herbert Morrison's slogan of 'consolidation' (Butler 1995, p. 10).

Commentators (Jones 1994) have described the result of the 1950 general election as a victory for the two-party system. The two Communist MPs disappeared from Westminster and 319 Liberals lost their deposits. For the members of the Thirsk and Malton Divisional Labour Party, the result of the General Election nationally was a profound disappointment, with the Labour majority reduced to five seats. But for their own constituency there were feelings of satisfaction: in a three-cornered fight – the Liberals put up a candidate for the first time in twenty years – the result was Conservative, 26,324 votes; Labour, 11,480; Liberal, 2,441.

*

On her 29th birthday, Joan was sworn in as a magistrate at the North Riding

Quarter Sessions in Northallerton. Her WEA tutor John Harrison was thrilled:

> Heartiest congratulations – I read of your election to the bench in the Yorkshire Evening Press and had no idea that 'the youngest JP in the North Riding etc' would turn out to be yourself. I'm delighted, I really am.
>
> I hope you won't feel like a trade union leader who has been given a seat in the House of Lords! After all, the struggle for social justice can well be combined with the administrating of legal justice.

The letter closes with Harrison looking forward to seeing Joan at the forthcoming joint tutorial class on 'Tito and the Comintern'. The other magistrate to be sworn in was Major Peter Bell, Lord of the Manor of Thirsk.

Both the Thirsk and Malton Labour Party and the NUAW had encouraged Joan to be put forward as a magistrate. The Divisional Party had resolved in July 1949 that all local parties be asked to submit names for magistrates. It was the declared policy of the NUAW to nominate members for the bench:

> The farm workers were conscious of the power of tradition in rural areas and sought to influence the appointments made to public bodies and in particular the magistrate's bench... we got to know our (Labour) nominees on the advisory committee and made sure that they knew when our people were going in. It really was amazing the number of people who managed to get through on to the benches. Joan Maynard, for instance, was only twenty-nine when she was appointed to the bench. (Jack Brocklebank in Grayson 1991, pp. 75–76)

As the first 'Labour magistrate' in Thirsk Joan received a most grudging reception from the chairman on arriving at her first morning in court: 'Well, I suppose I shall have to welcome you.' Later Joan became aware that many on the Left, usually in urban areas, refused any involvement with the appointment of magistrates. In Sheffield, for example, 'they wouldn't have anything to do with nominating anybody for the bench'. Yet, in the rural area where Joan lived, becoming a magistrate was regarded by both trade unionists and Labour Party members as important. 'If Joan was doing the job she was keeping somebody else that was maybe a lot stricter than her out of it. It was our Union policy to try to get farm workers on as magistrates for that very reason. Obviously if we were up there it was good education for us, but we were also maybe keeping Lord So-and-so off who could whip you off to jail if you looked sideways at him'.[11]

When Joan was appointed as a magistrate there was scant training for the work, but NUAW members considered that being a JP in itself offered excellent training for its members:

> Joan and Jack and Union officers recognised that if you could get up there – it wasn't the social thing – it was the fact that that it was good training for meetings with the farmers. It was damn good training to be able to listen and speak your mind and stand up to them. It gave you the backbone to stand up to them on other occasions; it's done that for me. When, as a Union official, I meet them across the table they all try the old upper crust lark on you and it doesn't work; they can't pull that stunt on you.[12]

Joan was troubled by some people's behaviour towards her when they learned of her appointment. 'The working-class people in Thirsk and Malton were just a bit different to me for a while. And I realised that they thought that if you became a magistrate you'd joined the other side. Well, they soon found out that wasn't right; but I didn't appreciate that they might think it.'

Joan was usually on the side of the people in the dock:

> I tried to leaven the bread. I tried to get the other magistrates to see that people were usually there because of the circumstances under which they had been brought up. Because most of them were there for that reason... I always tried to vote against anybody being sent to prison.

The only people she had no sympathy for were drivers under the influence of drink or drugs: 'I would give them some hammer if I could.'

Reflecting on her work as a magistrate, Joan said:

> I always try to say that the important thing when you're on the bench is not to become too judgemental and to realise that it's very different to be sitting there than to be on the other side. And to realise that there but for the grace of God go I, kind of idea. And I don't think I ever lost that. One of the things that kept coming up was I'd be criticising the law instead of implementing it. And they'd be saying, but we're here to implement it, Joan, you'll have to go somewhere else if you want to alter it! So I got there eventually (laughs) but didn't find it any easier when I got there.

Years later, in the miners' strike of 1984 there were calls for Joan to resign or be dismissed as a magistrate. 'On television's *Question Time* I said that I believed that there are occasions when people have to break the law if they feel the law is unjust and against their conscience. I still do'.

*

In May 1950 the Thirsk and Malton Labour Party received a letter from Ivan Geffen recommending that a local person be the Party's next Parliamentary candidate. Once more Jack Brocklebank's name was proposed by a number of the local parties but he declined. Irvin Denny reported that some twelve people on the national panel had been approached but none would allow their name to go forward. Not only was the seat regarded as 'hopeless' but to most aspirant Labour MPs its rurality and vast territory made it a very unattractive practice ground.

Eventually the Divisional Party found a candidate in John Parkinson. Unlike those who had refused to be considered, he knew he would be assured of a good campaign. Though not a 'local man' he was familiar with the constituency having assisted with Ivan Geffen's campaign of the previous year; he had known Geffen from Durham University days when he was president of Durham University Labour Club. Now a lecturer at Darlington Technical College he was secretary of the Northern Region Fabian Society and member of the Management Committee of Darlington Labour Party.

By the General Election of October 1951 membership of Thirsk and Malton Divisional Labour Party had increased to such an extent that it was presented with the Regional Membership Shield at Easingwold Labour Party's festival and sports day. Yet despite such growth finances were in a dire state. In June the local Party was informed by Morgan Phillips that it was in arrears with its national affiliation fees and until the amount was paid it could send neither delegation nor resolution to the Annual Conference. In September 1951 one hundred collecting boxes were bought at sixpence each for the election fighting fund.

At national level 'the main issues of the campaign were the cost of living and the danger of war: the Conservatives concentrated on the former, the Labour Party on the latter' (Pelling and Reid 1996, p. 99). The Conservatives criticised Labour for the devaluation of the pound; 'the Labour Party, for its part, maintained that the Conservative attitude on the Persian question showed that they were "warmongers"' (Ibid.).

In 'Election Day in my Constituency' Joan wrote:

> In Thirsk and Malton a large rural constituency in the North Riding of Yorkshire, we in the Labour Party were glad it was such a fine day on October 25. We were glad because it is difficult often for our people to get to their various polling stations on a wet day, as we are usually short of cars, and the distance sometimes to be covered is 2 miles or more. The day was on the whole quite uneventful. I spent the day working at Thirsk and Sowerby, the main centres in the Thirsk Rural District. Voters came in very steadily all day at Sowerby, and the pace only quickened slightly in the evening. At Thirsk polling was slightly heavier. At lunchtime we had a call to take a Thirsk voter by car to Northallerton to vote, as she should have voted by post, but the necessary papers hadn't come through. She was therefore taken the 9 miles to Northallerton to the County Hall and duly registered her vote on the appropriate form. We were short of people to man the polling booths during the day, owing to our people being at work and we who were on duty often had to do 3 hour spells. In the evening, however, we were soon reinforced by willing helpers who had hurriedly had their teas, changed, and come along to do their bit. After the poll closed at 9 o'clock tension relaxed in the Committee Room, and we all went off to a nearby café to have hot coffee, cheese and biscuits, and to watch the results coming in on television.

The turnout in Thirsk and Malton was a high 77.4% and the result was that Turton received 27,854 votes; Parkinson 10,692. John Parkinson thanked the Party for the splendid spirit shown during the campaign. The national result gave the Conservatives an overall majority of seventeen.

Pelling and Reid (1996, p. 100) state:

> In the succeeding years the Labour Party paid all too little attention to the business of winning future elections. Instead, controversy within the ranks, already launched when Labour was in power, came to dominate its activities, absorbing much of the energies of the members; and Party organisation, both at the centre and the local level, suffered in consequence.

Pelling and Reid's assessment of the Labour Party's lack of attention to winning elections hardly applied to Thirsk and Malton Division. There the 1950s and 1960s would be characterised by meticulous planning and a concerted fight for Labour representation at national and local level.

FOUR

Joining the Union

'The Union and Yorkshire – what could be dearer to my heart!'
(Joan, the *Land Worker* August 1969)

Though the grass is blue in rural North Yorkshire the NUAW attracted and encouraged members who contested the social order. It educated members to speak for themselves, to wrest power through local government and to question the very basis and legitimacy of power and land ownership.[1]

With comrades in the Union Joan developed her political praxis. Opposition was not enough – 'it is easy to be against things but more difficult to be constructive and work for something.' She would remain indebted to four members of the Union who shaped the direction of her life 'Jack Brocklebank, my dearest friend; Tom Gascoyne, county chairman for a period, who taught me all I know about politics and how to fight the battle; Jack Bowen, life member of the Union whose wisdom, kindness and shrewdness was a lesson to all; and last but not least Bert Waind, county committee member.'

Joan had joined the NUAW at the invitation of Jack Brocklebank, organiser for North Yorkshire in September 1947. Through their work together establishing the Thirsk Labour Party he recognised in her a 'lively spirit' to advance the cause of the Union. For Joan, Brocklebank's

> warmth, enthusiasm and genuine love of people fired my imagination. He had a more moderate approach to things than me, although sometimes we'd agree

> very strongly. I think he appreciated my personality and my commitment to the members. He was like that. Whereas some Organisers went about knocking the lively spirits on the head because they thought they're going to be a bloody nuisance to them, Jack didn't do that. He encouraged the lively spirit with the result the organising area was really successful.

Jack Brocklebank was born in Leven, near Hull. His father, a country bricklayer, instilled in him values of citizenship through local government, and his schoolteacher emphasised the importance of public service. On leaving school at fourteen he began farm work and joined the farm workers' union becoming Chairman of his local branch. He took a keen interest in Union work; 'I realised it was our only salvation to get us away from the very low wages of agriculture.'[2]

During the inter-war years of the depression, agriculture had suffered with farmers being bankrupted by the thousand; there was little farm work and wages were terrible. In August 1937 the entire county of Yorkshire with its mighty 3.8 million acres had only 600 members of the Union.[3]

In 1942 Jack moved with his wife Ada and family to Dishforth to work full time as district organiser for the Union. During the war the country was put to the plough and as prices of agricultural products rose so did the number and wages of farm workers. Jack Brocklebank was the first to admit that when he started organising in North Yorkshire, there were so many farm workers, that recruiting them was like picking cherries off a tree. 'I was anxious that, no matter how isolated the area, the flag of the Union should be shown, so that in the hills and dales, as well as the arable areas, the members had somewhere to go for help and advice, and for them, too, to unite with their fellow workers.'[4]

Taking his father's and teacher's principles to heart he served on numerous public bodies, representing Dishforth on Wath Rural District Council, chairing Dishforth Parish Council and being elected to the North Riding County Council. As union organiser he would attend branch meetings across north Yorkshire and encourage members to stand for local government elections. 'It is essential for every farm worker to see that they are well represented on the Parish Council, the RDC and the County Committees to enable us to get better housing conditions and water supplies.'[5]

Ever mindful of the Labour Party's foundation in the trade union movement, Jack Brocklebank was committed to forging links between industrial and political action, between the Labour Party locally and the Union. As Union organiser and chair of the Divisional Labour Party he was in a strong position to build an active and integral relationship.

Joan said of Jack Brocklebank: 'He was never a trade union bureaucrat, he was a trade unionist with a human face.' He had observed wealthy farmers gathering for formal dinners and social occasions, and determined that farm workers and their families should enjoy similar congenial opportunities to get together – and develop their political awareness. In 1947 he organised the first Union district dinner in Northallerton and invited as speaker George Brown, then Parliamentary Secretary to the Ministry of Agriculture. Within a few years District Committees were holding dinners across Yorkshire. Other social events were organised during the course of the year. A favourite occasion for Joan was the Great Yorkshire Show where the Union would have a stand – along with the National Union of Farmers and the Country Landowners Association. Visitors were encouraged to 'be thrilled by the gaily-painted pavilions and restaurants, marquees, flags, bunting, music and the largest show-ring in the Kingdom. Fill your lungs with the tonic of Harrogate's pine woods – go home exhilarated and refreshed'.[6]

The Union stand served to recruit new members and provide a relaxed meeting place for members and their families from across Yorkshire, and beyond. The beer ran freely, but it frequently befell Joan to organise the tea making.

Across the county, branches and districts organised dances, darts matches, personality contests, outings and rallies. Joan recalled: 'the opportunity to get over the Union message at such events was never neglected. We tried to spread the political message and never miss the opportunity to get the Union's message to the Labour politicians.' The message was clear – do something about low wages and the tied cottage.

Occasionally, to Joan's irritation,

> branches would have a dinner and wouldn't have a Labour MP – they couldn't run to that – and they would have a farmer and of course it was always one of

> these good ones, you see. I used to say to Jack, all it does is to confuse our people. It did annoy me the patronising way they used to talk to our people, I said to someone recently I wish the farm workers would get as steamed up about the injustices as I do!

The focus on community was crucial to effective Union organisation. Even today, according to farm workers' leader Barry Leathwood,[7] 'most industrial groups are workplace based. In our case it's the community rather than the workplace; it's fundamentally different. We believe that we are community based rather than work based'.

Throughout its history the NUAW had recognised the importance of education for its members. 'The problem as far as agricultural trade unionism is concerned has been to raise the farm worker's consciousness of his position and then to persuade him that such a situation is not his fatalistic "lot" but is amenable to change through socialism.' (Newby *c.*1974, p. 7)

Like Joan, Jack Brocklebank was highly conscious of the limitations of his formal education; he would spend hours discussing with her the worries and nightmares of being an organiser. It had not been easy to leave the plough and farm work and, with little training and education, organise members and negotiate with employers and officials who were far more educated than him. His strong encouragement of Union involvement with the WEA had 'one objective in mind – to improve the self-expression of our members and enable them to play a richer and fuller life in the world around them'.[8] WEA and Leeds tutors would be invited to speak at branch meetings and many tutors played a full part in the Union, accepting Jack's invitation to join.[9] For Joan, the purpose of the WEA classes was to broaden the minds of members and encourage them, 'to know more and be able to do the job we needed doing in the Union'.

Though farm workers' formal education was limited, they possessed a depth and range of recondite knowledge and skills, from mechanics and environmental management to animal husbandry. If anything was guaranteed to provoke Joan's fury, it was referring to farm workers as labourers:

> It's a term that makes me feel very hot under the collar; it denigrates farm workers because they have always been very skilled. Anybody who doesn't

> believe it wants to try building a haystack or a corn stack, or cutting and laying a hedge, or ploughing a furrow. All these things are very skilled; try using a scythe, that's very skilled too. They are all skills you have to learn. It was a way of denigrating these people who were so important, I mean we all need food, don't we? You couldn't think of anyone more important than the farm workers who produce it. Unfortunately not very many of them felt as angry as I did about the injustice. When you went to shop at the end of the week you couldn't pay with fresh air and sunshine.

She was angry the Union had such a struggle to obtain decent wages and conditions for such skilled and productive workers. A book she read and re-read was Reg Groves's *Sharpen the Sickle,* an impassioned history of the Union completed the year after Joan joined. It opens with the six Tolpuddle Martyrs of Dorset and closes in praise of union members, 'who manned the thinned ranks in the bad years and who filled the branch offices – the humble heroes of rural England'. (Groves 1949, p. 240)

Twenty years later she met one such hero at the opening of the Union offices, Headland House, in London. As a young man Herbert Harvey had joined the new Eastern Counties Agricultural Labourers' and Smallholders' Union. George Edwards, its founder, had warned him: 'Well, we've started the Union. You will be up against fearful opposition. You will be held up to ridicule and persecution and probably prosecution. I am not sure you will be able to stick it'.

Another hero was Joan's friend Jack Bowen whom she met when he was secretary of a grouping of Union branches covering Northallerton, Thirsk and Ripon. He was elected as chairman of the Union's Yorkshire County Committee in 1929 and his life in the Union is commemorated in a publication edited by Roger Fieldhouse (*c.*1977). In the foreword Joan wrote:

> I was very privileged to know Jack Bowen. He was a great inspiration to me. I valued greatly his friendship, his wise counsel and his shrewdness, his sense of humour but most of all his complete dedication to rural workers. Jack always knew which side he was on...He stood out as a union man and was victimised for it by the farmers. In particular he vowed never to live in a tied cottage and he never did... his example gives me confidence in working people and their ability to build a Socialist society.

Jack Bowen was born in 1893 and remembered seeing bonfires on the Hambleton Hills signalling the relief of the siege of Mafeking. As a lad he was taken to the hirings in Bedale where his father would haggle for hours with farmers about his wages and board. In later life, when his family was suffering terrible financial privation, he refused any work paid below the union-negotiated rate; word got around and none of the farmers would employ him:

> in the paraffin lighted living room in the Bowen's council house... men in difficulties turned in their distress. Talk was often about evictions from tied cottages the next Saturday noon, with nowhere to go. Tears were not uncommon at these meetings, and no wonder, for eviction sometimes meant permanent separation, with the wife and children being sent to Bedale or Ripon workhouse. (*ibid.*)

Joan delighted in Jack Bowen's gift for capturing political and economic essentials, 'the minimum wage deserves the minimum work'. As sole worker member on the West Riding Wages Committee – when wages were calculated on a county basis before the war – he had listened whilst the great and good ruminated about the wages needed to sustain a farm worker's family. Pondering the sum required for food, one member extolled the nutritious value and cheapness of a sheep's head, prompting enthusiastic contributions about its tastiness. Observing Jack Bowen's silence, the chairman enquired: 'Have you got anything to add, Mr Bowen?' 'I'm thinking, who's going to eat rest of sheep.'

The Union Executive Committee member for Yorkshire, Frank Robinson, has written movingly of the early days of the Union in Yorkshire and of farmers' victimisation of Union members – 'one had to have the courage of a Daniel to be a trade unionist.' The *Wages Board Gazette* recorded how farm workers and their families would be evicted from their tied cottages solely on the basis of Union membership.

Unlike workers in other industries farm workers were employed in small numbers in close proximity to their employer. As Joan wrote: 'Farm workers therefore lack the feeling of strength, solidarity and confidence which numbers bring. The boss is not some remote figure it is easy to dislike, he is the man who works beside you most days of the week.' (Maynard *c.*1974, p. 3)

The scattered nature of farm workers' employment presented problems for NUAW organisation. Because Union activity could not be organised at the workplace, NUAW members would cycle or walk long distances in the evening or weekends to branch meetings. Postal communication was risky; the Union's name was not printed on envelopes lest it be noted by the farmer. Monthly Union contributions were collected in person with the branch officer covering long distances to farms and hamlets. Little wonder being a branch secretary required a 'hard head, tough neck and skin like an elephant'.[10]

Harassment and intimidation were not confined to the Union in Yorkshire. Retired Dorset farm worker John Fry told of a farm where 'anyone who was a member of the Union would get the sack eventually. I couldn't even let the Union collector come round'. Referring to Norfolk, former NUAAW General Secretary Jack Boddy recalled:

> When I first became associated with the land when I was about 11 years of age, the farm workers never got holidays in those days, even bank holidays. They could be paid for a bank holiday if they went to church and the boss would stand outside the church to make sure his workers went. If they didn't go they didn't get paid. So to that extent their political influence would be brought to bear on the workers.

In Leicester, when Union organiser Tom Mackley arranged meetings of farm workers in village halls to publicise the Union and recruit new members, farmers would turn up and sit around the edge of the room to ensure the farm workers 'did nothing rash'. On one occasion a meeting was held in darkness because there were no supplies of gas or electricity and the oil had run out. The only light came from candles on the table so the speakers were visible but not the audience. Such was the thunderous response of clapping and cheering, unlike any previous meeting, that Mackley joked afterwards that all union recruitment meetings should be held in the dark.[11]

Intimidation, sackings and evictions allowed branch officers and members of the NUAW to be employed in occupations other than farm work. As an employee of the Post Office, Joan was eligible for full membership of the NUAW. Union activists were employed in occupations as diverse as railway work and university teaching. Joan recalled:

> Because of the oppression of the farm workers and the tied cottage, if you look at our history lots of non-farm workers have been members because in the old days when it was really bad it was very difficult for a farm worker to be a secretary of the Union because if the farmer found out he'd get the sack. So we had lots of railwaymen who were members of our Union as secretaries. They were a great help to us in the early days. My affinity went with my connection with agriculture and the Labour politics. One, or maybe more, of the WEA tutors became a branch secretary. Another thing that happened, lots of people finished their ordinary day's work and then went to work on a farm in the evenings in the busy periods like hay time. I used to say, I don't know what a railwayman would think if you just jumped over the fence to do their work; wasn't it a bloody cheek, like. They never saw it, did other workers. It was a way of undermining our people. But we weren't organised enough to stop it. The railwaymen would have stopped it immediately. They would have said, we're not having that, like.

Jack Boddy has described how county council roadmen were a powerful influence in the Union:

> In the 1926 strike hundreds of farm workers in the Eastern Region lost their jobs. They couldn't get a job so they became roadmen, what we call in the country lengthmen. Now a lengthman worked on his own and was responsible for a length of highway. Having lost his job because of his trade union activities in the agricultural industry, they became trade unionists in an industry where he could use his spare time to assist those he used to work with and so became a branch secretary.

Asked if this situation was unique to the farm workers' Union Jack Boddy replied:

> I would say so, yes. I doubt whether any other industry has the problems of the agricultural industry in their employer–worker relationship; compare it with the

> miners – several hundred people under one employer, as they used to be in the old days. The employer in those circumstances couldn't influence the individual worker in the same way the agricultural worker is influenced by his employer.

Joan's devoted Union comrade Bert Waind was employed outside farm work selling Kleen-ezee brushes from door to door. Tall with wispy hair, he looked as if he was still wearing a demob suit, and might have passed as a farmer down on his luck, yet, 'he was a man and a half'. Joan appreciated his stalwart reliability and impenetrable Yorkshire accent: 'He would use every ounce of energy to help a member or fellow worker. His Yorkshire was very broad and he didn't even know he was.' On a Union delegation to the USSR Joan had to translate Bert's Yorkshire into English for the Russian interpreter.

In a letter to the *Land Worker* (June 1953) Bert Waind wrote:

> When I took over the Great Ayton Branch it had about twenty members. I felt it should have one hundred. So I set to work on six and even seven nights of each week and unaided enrolled sixty-five members in twelve weeks. We soon reached my target of one hundred members. I should like to ask if my appointments as a voluntary worker in the Union constitute a record. I am a Branch Chairman and also a Branch Secretary – two different branches, of course. I am also a District Committee Chairman and Secretary and a member of the County Committee. I am wondering if there are any other local officers of the Union serving in these dual capacities.

Joan would talk for hours with Jack Brocklebank, Jack Bowen and Bert Waind about their experiences of inequality, the experiences of fellow members and their studies of labour history with the WEA. But it was Tom Gascoyne whom Joan credited with teaching her, 'all I know about politics'. They were introduced at a Thirsk and Malton Divisional Labour Party meeting in York. On the drive home, Joan recalled, Jack Brocklebank had asked her: 'Well, what do you think to Tom? I said I thought he was pretty good.'

Through Tom Gascoyne Joan learned Marxist theory:

> the need to understand how capitalist society is structured. How all the structures in society are there to maintain capitalism in the same way as if you had

> a Socialist state, if you had any sense you'd make structures to maintain that state – which we've never got round to doing. First of all because we never accepted that the present structures were there to keep capitalism going. When I met Tom I had this idea that the educational system and the legal system were all independent. Tom tried to knock that out of my head. In the end I said, oh I see what you mean! And he said, Oh bloody hell, I thought you'd never see. It's so deeply ingrained.

Tom Gascoyne was conveying the classic base–superstructure model commonly espoused by British Marxists in the 1950s. According to that theory, all aspects of culture and politics were ultimately subject to the controlling influence of the 'base' – the economic organisation of society. This led to an emphasis on oppositional action focusing on the workplace. Notwithstanding Joan's seeing the light, her actual praxis exemplified more closely a Gramscian idea of counter-hegemonic process – controlling ideology was contested in the field of education, in the conduct of the law, in the constitutions and cultures of political parties and unions.

Tom Gascoyne was a formidable, charismatic figure as well as being an articulate exponent of Marxist economics. Born in Malton, he had been apprenticed to his father's tailoring shop. Joan was always fascinated by his colourful accounts of travelling tailors seeking casual employment in his father's shop and bringing 'all sorts of tales and knowledge'. Listening to their ideas made him think and see things differently. These travelling tailors had heard the 'eloquent fury' (Groves 1949, p. 101) of the Socialist tailor, Charles Mowbray, speaking in Norwich. Like weavers and watchmakers they were a classic example of the self-taught, independent artisans of earlier times.

At the outset of the First World War Tom Gascoyne incurred vicious public opprobrium by declaring himself a conscientious objector. Women spat on him as he was marched through Malton. Incarcerated in Dartmoor Prison he received his political education from Marxist and other left-wing prisoners who organised classes and lectures. They would open the governor's mail before he did. Tom Gascoyne's son John has a photograph of him among the eighty members of the Dartmoor Socialist Society.

Between the two wars Tom Gascoyne concentrated on tailoring. The trade all but ceased at the commencement of the Second World War so he took a job as a warden in an agricultural hostel. The hostel housed Irish men hired out by the day to local farmers, and British people devoting their holidays to bringing in the harvest. It was through his work in the hostel that Tom Gascoyne met Jack Brocklebank, who came knocking at his door wanting to set up a branch of the NUAW in the village of Aldburgh St John. Thus began Tom Gascoyne's involvement in the Union. His son recalls: 'They set up the branch and Jack rekindled my Dad's desire to be involved in politics and so they established Union branches all over and they set up the Labour Party, and this lass Joan Maynard got involved.'

Tom Gascoyne was elected chairman of the Yorkshire County Committee of the Union; according to John Gascoyne: 'They elected him Chairman of Durham as well – and there was a big fight on because they said he couldn't be Chairman of two County Committees at once. He said show me the rule that says I can't – so they made one.'

In 1950 he stood against the revered long-serving president of the NUAW, Edwin Gooch, and received a fifth of the votes. Earlier in the year Gooch had retained his Parliamentary seat in the General Election with an increased vote. Joan's involvement in Tom Gascoyne's campaign for the presidency, against a seemingly unassailable opponent, made a powerful impression on her; the membership could challenge the leadership – it had no God-given right to rule. How different from the assumed seigneurial rights of the ruling elites of rural North Yorkshire.

Joan was becoming popular with Union members. During visits to their homes collecting monthly Union contributions, they told her of their problems – fears of eviction from the tied cottage if the member was ill or too old and infirm to work; constant worries about managing on low wages; having to use equipment and chemicals they knew to be dangerous. Joan listened attentively to these accounts, month after month. She was an active participant in NUAW branch and district meetings having been elected as Thirsk branch delegate to the District Committee, later becoming its secretary. She travelled to NUAW meetings in Jack Brocklebank's car giving talks about the WEA, the Trades Council (of which she was also secretary) and Labour Party policy. She loved these evening meetings, held in smoky rooms in public houses. Joan really was a breath of fresh air – a bright, forthright, knowledgeable young woman. She brought vitality and warmth; never mind that 'up here the members are dour, hardworking, shrewd, forthright and know what brass is all about'.[12]

Minutes of a Northallerton branch meeting (10 January 1959) record Joan giving a talk criticising the Labour Party's superannuation scheme. Afterwards, 'Bro[ther] Jack began his address by attacking some of the points made by Miss Maynard to which she retaliated and a very lively and instructive discussion began'. The members loved it.

With encouragement and support from friends in the Union, Joan began to be nominated for election to represent Yorkshire on the all-powerful NUAW Executive Committee which met in London. Many members considered her nomination audacious; Frank Robinson had represented them on the Executive for decades, and always with a huge majority.

In 1954 Tom Gascoyne and Joan were elected as Yorkshire delegates to the NUAW's Biennial Conference in Cheltenham. Here officials of the Union and its Executive Committee would meet with over 200 delegates, coming from 'the seat of the tractor, milking sheds, the stables and the fields to express their opinions and formulate the policy which will form the basis of the Union's work for the next two years'.[13]

Summary accounts of Biennial Conferences are published in the *Land Worker*, but as a delegate from Northallerton reported to branch members, 'every spare minute of the time and every chance was taken up (even at the concerts) in debate, argument, plotting, and counter plotting by delegates'. It was a great experience to attend. County Conferences seemed so tame by comparison. Delegates at the Biennial Conferences were 'more vigorous and vicious'. He described scenes following a resolution on working hours, 'delegates were walking towards the platform shaking their fists demanding a recount'. He concluded, 'there were great men on the floor, better than on the platform' and warned the branch to word all resolutions very carefully, as 'a word could be chopped in two to alter the meaning of the resolution'.

'No Gathering of Rustics' was the ironic depiction of the Union conference in Cheltenham's local paper. Joan was thankful to attend her first national conference of the NUAW in the company of Tom Gascoyne. Through contesting the presidency in 1950 and moving radical resolutions at conferences he was well known and respected, even by his adversaries. He was a persuasive and passionate orator, leavening hard economic argument with thundering Socialist rhetoric: 'If there remains on earth a slave, are we truly true and brave?'

In Cheltenham delegates warmed to his (astute) magnanimity in nominating Gooch for the 26th year of his presidency. During the conference he introduced 'Sister Joan Maynard' to delegates and officials. Through his sponsorship, five of them were to become her close comrades in the Union: Wilf Page from Norfolk, Les Shears and Ted Sales from Dorset, Jack Dunman from Berkshire and the organiser for Dorset, Arthur Jordan. They were all delighted to meet with Joan, author of the provocative article published in the *Land Worker* the previous year, 'Why Nationalise the Land?'. Wilf Page, Jack Dunman and Arthur Jordan were active in the Communist Party as well as the Union and though remaining Joan's loyal comrades they, like Tom Gascoyne, could be critical of her approach. In Wilf Page's view, 'Communists' actions are usually based on deep theoretical studies first, then we arrive at a decision and then we take action. Whereas with Joan and the Socialists, 'they see something wrong and it's got to be put right'. Alleging the superiority of 'rigorous theory' over intuitively held beliefs is a commonplace of Left politics. (The gendered basis of such a distinction might also be interrogated.)

Joan was no stranger to speaking on national platforms. As delegate for Thirsk and Malton she had spoken at the Labour Party's annual party conferences. Only the previous month, as a delegate of the Union, she had delivered impassioned speeches at the Conference of Labour Women in Eastbourne. Margaret Herbison, Edith Summerskill and Clement Attlee had heard her moving an emergency resolution against West German re-armament and a resolution demanding the prohibition of children working in agriculture: 'In principle we object to children working, whether it is in agriculture or any other industry. They should be at school being educated.'

In Cheltenham Town Hall, under the plaster gaze of Kings Edward VII and George V, and watchful eyes of the Executive Committee, Joan took the podium. She wowed her audience in speech after speech, calling for the Government to speed up the school-building programme in rural areas and demanding the nationalisation of land. On education, where she was seconded by Ted Sales, the motion was carried. However, the Executive was worried by her radical proposals for land nationalisation. Frank Robinson argued in an amendment that all-out nationalisation of the land would mean a huge upheaval and would not increase production. The amendment was carried; but Joan had undoubtedly made her mark.

She returned home confident that beyond her close union comrades in Yorkshire, Jack Brocklebank, Jack Bowen, Bert Waind and Tom Gascoyne, there was a powerful network of progressive members in other counties. She had also noted at first hand the pragmatic conservatism of the union leaders. And they had noted Joan.

FIVE

First contests

In February 1952 the Thirsk Labour Party proposed Joan as candidate for Thirsk in the forthcoming county council elections. Her opponent, Ben Foggitt, was the sitting Independent county councillor. The Foggitt family had long occupied the seat, with Thomas Jackson Foggitt representing it from 1912–1931 before serving as an alderman for a further six years (Ashcroft 1974). He was an active Methodist who had retired in 1936 from the century-old family chemist business in Thirsk.

Joan's campaign declared: 'Socialists believe in progress, not in stagnation; in how to do it, not in how not to do it'. Education was the focus. 'If we are ever to have real democracy education must be a top priority. If our people are to live really full lives, education must not be neglected. We hear a lot about waste from the Tories. By that they always mean monetary waste. They never seem to be concerned about wasted lives.' (*Ibid.*)[1]

Church House Committee members were excoriated for allowing Joan to rent a room for the campaign – Foggitt was right, party politics had no place in local government! Joan retaliated; the opinions of everyone on the council were determined by political belief. While canvassing as the Labour candidate she would be asked, who is the Conservative candidate? When she told them Foggitt was standing as Independent, their response was, oh well, that's the same thing. 'It seemed plain that the electors were clear about the position, whether Mr Foggitt was or not. Perhaps he was working on the assumption that Conservatism in this area was not politics, but just the status quo.'[2]

The election took place on 8 April 1952. Joan lost, but she had made a deep impression on her opponent. In a prescient declaration speech Ben Foggitt said many would live to see 'MP' after Joan's name, but not in the Thirsk and Malton Division. Rallying her supporters Joan told of her longing to win the seat for working people: 'To our people, I would say, don't be despondent. The fight will go on.' Jack Brocklebank, who had won the nearby seat of Topcliffe, considered Joan's fight well worthwhile. 'If we have not gained sweeping successes, we have shown the Tories that we are very much alive.'

Joan was persuaded by Party members to contest South Kilvington for the RDC election of 6 May 1952. South Kilvington lies a couple of miles from the hamlet of Thornton-le-Street. The campaign was planned meticulously with election addresses, canvassing teams, promises of car loans and a request to extend the poll until 9.00 p.m.

> They wanted me to stand because the bloke who was on, a farmer, was a dead loss; he didn't go to meetings so we thought there'd be a bit of a chance. It would be easier to shift him than most people. So that's what we did – called at every house. At that point we were standing against this rubbish that there's no politics in local government. They got a shock, first of all because it was an election, they hadn't had an election for quarter of a century. This had gone on for years in rural areas. The people who stood carved the areas up for themselves. So first of all there was the shock of the election, then the shock of a Labour candidate, and then, damn it all, a woman. Polling day arrived eventually and at the count – I think they threw out two of my votes, spoiled papers – I still won by two votes after a number of recounts. After all the recounts the clerk said to the man I was up against, well are you satisfied? Well I shall have to be he said grudgingly. The thing that really annoyed me was next day the local paper, instead of saying Labour wins by two votes it was She wins by two votes. They played the political down and the feminine up.[3]

Carried away by its theme the local paper reported under 'Election Reflections':

> Thirsk Rural Council will no doubt welcome with its customary gallantry its first woman for six years. Many members of the Council will not favour the

> party which Miss Maynard adorns, but few would deny that she will be a useful asset to the Council even if it were merely to brighten with her feminine presence a chamber hitherto all too drab in its unrelieved masculinity.

Heartened by Joan's success, the Party nominated her for the county by-election at South Otterington. Her opponents were G. A. Hill-Walker, Conservative and Lieutenant Colonel Montague Charles Warcop Peter Consett of Brawith Hall, Independent. With 985 votes Colonel Consett was delighted to poll more than the two 'political parties' put together (Conservative 461; Labour 375) – it was a victory for independence. But Joan and her supporters were buoyant, judging the campaign to be very encouraging; nearly 400 votes for Socialism was very good at the first time of asking in a rural division. 'We shall continue to contest all elections, local and otherwise because we feel this is only the beginning and that Socialism and all it stands for will triumph in the end.'

Thirsk Labour Party was adamant its councillors on the parish and district councils would be accountable. In March 1952 it resolved: 'The Executive Committee would like the three RDC councillors to meet together before council meetings to discuss the business and to try to form a united policy on matters arising. As a last resort it is agreed that all councillors should vote and speak according to their conscience.'[4]

Further, all councillors should report back to their branches. Councillors who did not contribute effectively to council business were reprimanded; the message was unequivocal – they were in local government solely because of the policies and efforts the Party. This was at odds with the prevailing ethos of local government with its emphasis on the personal qualities and individual judgement of the councillor and the playing down – or disavowal of – the political. In the years ahead, as the Party gained strength in the constituency, Joan kept firm tabs on Labour councillors:

> At the meeting we had in Skelton the other night I was asked to write to you and say that we are perturbed at your non attendance at Party meetings, and that you have so far been unable to help with any canvassing. The Committee members feel that it is unfair that they should be expected to canvass and that the councillor is either unwilling or unable to help. In the Labour Party we do

expect councillors to do some of the hard work, because if it were not for the fact that the Party had selected and worked for you as a Labour Candidate you would not be on the Council. In other words you have a responsibility to the Party. I should be glad if you would write and give me an explanation, or if you prefer it I will come and see you, on some day which you name.

Hoping to hear from you soon
Yours fraternally
Joan Maynard

*

In September 1953 family life at Post Office Farm was to end for Joan and her parents. Her brother Rowie married Florence Bainbridge, a widow and mother of Anne, who at nineteen was a student at university. Rowie was in his mid-forties, and as Joan acknowledged, could not afford to have married any younger. By 1953 Rowie's work at Post Office Farm and his local contract farm work had yielded financial security. He'd work all hours of the day, 'I bet you've got a good best suit, Rowie, you never get a chance to wear it'. Like Joan he had experienced the privations of poverty as a young man and was determined to provide well for his new family. Joan and her parents accepted they should leave Post Office Farm to make way.

They found a house to rent in Sowerby, 76 Front Street. The red brick Georgian terraced house was small, run down and dark, but the Maynards were pleased with its location, a short walk from Thirsk, and its low rent. The weekly rent was controlled at 15 shillings but the Maynards agreed to pay £1, almost half of Matt's and Effie's pension, the family's sole source of income. Matt lifted Joan's spirits by proposing a name for their new home – Lansbury House, the name it retains to this day. It certainly marked out the new residents of Front Street. Joan had grown up listening to Matt speaking of the passionate convictions and ideals of George Lansbury, of whom Harold Laski wrote:

> There are abler men in the Labour Movement; minds more subtle and distinguished. But George Lansbury is its soul. He is the incarnation of the fellowship in the Labour Movement. He represents, as no other man repre-

> sents, its faith in the common man, its simple and kindly altruism, its genuine indignation at the existence of unnecessary pain. Other men may see farther or more clearly; no man sees more justly . . . He is a genuine egalitarian, because he genuinely respects his fellow-men for themselves…[5]

In Lansbury House Joan's convictions developed.

> The first of my guiding principles was that I saw a lot of injustice going on and I felt I couldn't accept it. That's one of the things that made me a Socialist. Perhaps it is just in my make up more than anything, the fact that I have always been outspoken and said what I have thought, truthfully, about things.

Yet the move to Front Street signalled a very low point for Joan. She had given up the sociable job in the post office and the farm work she loved – no more the deep satisfaction of shared labour in the fields. She was now thirty-three and as the unmarried daughter at home resigned to her duty to take care of her elderly parents, 'I took on a big responsibility taking on those two old people. If you're a daughter, and you're the youngest and single, it's inevitable, I'm afraid'.

Matters were made worse by shrill letters of advice from her sister Elsie in London, now pursuing her career as a hospital almoner. Joan remembered with some bitterness her mother being unwell and having no appetite and Elsie writing, 'silly letters about you should get Mother a chicken or something. Chickens were a bit of a luxury, like. I felt like writing back and saying, you send me the money and I'll get the chicken.'

Joan had discussed the impending move to Sowerby with Jack Brocklebank and Tom Gascoyne and they came up with a proposal. For an initial three month period she should be appointed as part-time agent for the Thirsk and Malton Divisional Labour Party. It would take her away from the house and ease the wrench of leaving the farm. But the financial basis of the arrangement would be precarious:

> I started off on £5 a week and it was a terrible struggle. The Party hadn't got any money. It was a terrible struggle to get enough money to keep the job

> going. You never knew whether there'd be enough money in the kitty. We didn't get any help at all from regional or national level.

The mainstay of the job, canvassing for Party members, required Joan to go out every evening. Her mode of transport was a heavy, black sit-up-and-beg push-bike. Whilst she enjoyed cycling in the spring and summer evenings it was tough going on winter nights. As she pedalled along the unlit country lanes, she would sing 'The Red Flag' to lift her spirits against the wind and rain:

> Then raise the scarlet standard high,
> Beneath its shade we'll live or die...

Such was Joan's success in recruiting new members that the Party agreed to extend her appointment as agent. Her energies and output were prodigious. Within three months she reported to the Thirsk and Malton General Committee 'a further increase in membership of 189, total increase over the 12 weeks of my appointment 454, total membership in the Division approximately 860'. She expressed heartfelt thanks on behalf of the division to all the members who had given her hospitality, food and lodgings whilst she had worked across the local Party areas of the division. In February 1954 Douglas Busfield stood down from the post of divisional secretary and Joan was elected to the position – one she would combine with Party agent, Party secretary at Thirsk, branch secretary of the WEA and Trades Council, NUAW district secretary and magistrate. Plus caring for her parents.

*

Fighting local elections in the period between the General Elections of 1951 and 1955 was combined with close scrutiny and debate about national politics and international events. Churchill's Conservative Government with its small overall majority was pursuing many of the social and economic policies of Labour. As well as retaining most of the nationalised industries, except iron and steel and road haulage, 'economic policy in general remained broadly similar to that pursued by the Attlee Governments, with Keynesian techniques of demand management being retained, along with a period of full employment'. (Dorey 1995, p. 43).

In contrast with the apparent policy consensus between the two major parties nationally, the Labour Party in opposition was increasingly riven by open conflict amongst its leaders, with the National Executive Committee (NEC) becoming a 'cockpit of conflict' (Pelling and Reid 1996, p. 27). The conflict was not solely between left and right in the Party, the left itself was split with Laybourn referring to ten Labour left groups in 1952. The previous year Nye Bevan, together with Harold Wilson and John Freeman, had resigned from the Labour Government over its introduction of prescription charges and involvement of Britain in the Korean War.

Whilst historians tend to agree Conservative policy was not markedly different from that of Labour, and that nationally Labour was focused on internal disputes, Thirsk and Malton under its chairman Jack Brocklebank lambasted Conservative policy, and thought the divisions among the Conservatives were greater than those within Labour, 'but weren't being ventilated'. Jack and Joan emphasised the Party's duty to oppose the Conservatives on education, health and housing. In February 1952 they moved a whole raft of resolutions attacking Government policy.

The Thirsk and Malton Labour Party was deeply opposed to Government proposals to end the Utility scheme in March 1952. Joan was concerned the existing guarantees would be destroyed to the detriment of the poorest sections of the community. Guaranteed prices and quality, within the reach of people on low incomes, were essential and safeguards should be assured into the future.[6]

The local Party continued to approach national speakers to address their open air public meetings – Nye Bevan, Barbara Castle and Alice Bacon – but with little success. They particularly wanted Konni Zilliacus (expelled from the Labour Party in May 1949 and readmitted in 1952). He represented 'a genuine international perspective towards peace and [was] hostile to the Atlantic Pact'. (Laybourn 1997, p. 127). In May 1953 the Northern Regional Labour Party succeeded in getting Harold Wilson, Hilary Marquand and Dai Jones to do a 'Brains Trust' in Thirsk. Later that year, on 17 October, Michael Foot spoke at Thirsk market place.

On matters of foreign policy, many in the Thirsk Party were very critical of the Labour leadership. At a meeting in May 1952 Joan's minutes record:

> The majority of the members regretted what they considered our too close links with the USA and considered the rearmament programme too high. Some members said they would prefer Britain to be in the Soviet block rather than the USA block. There was a minority opinion which supported the late Labour Government's foreign policy and rearmament programme which followed from it.

Resolutions on a range of foreign policy issues were sent from the Thirsk Party to the Foreign Secretary Anthony Eden and Opposition Leader Clement Attlee. Joan and the Party members were frustrated by the lack of response. In July 1952 Joan wrote to Attlee demanding to know, 'why our resolution on Korea hadn't been acknowledged and if there were any points upon which he disagreed'. Still no response.

The Thirsk and Malton Party was generous in its support for oppressed groups and individuals, donating funds to, for example, the defence of Seretse Khama (April 1953).[7] The previous year the Party had forwarded a resolution to the Secretary of State for the Colonies, 'not to press through the federation of Southern Rhodesia and Northern Rhodesia and Nyasaland against the wishes of the 6 million Africans in these territories'.

In October 1953 the Thirsk and Malton Party was 'unanimous in its support for a national day of protest against continued repression in Kenya and to send a resolution on the subject to the colonial secretary with a copy and message of thanks to Fenner Brockway MP'.

*

On 17 January 1955 Matt Maynard died. Joan would forever speak of him with deep love and pride as the Socialist who had instilled and nurtured her Socialism. Matt died in hospital in Thirsk, where he had been for some months following a stroke; he was a big man and Joan and her mother were unable to lift him. There had been little choice for the troubled Joan: 'I could have stayed at home to look after him, but how was I to earn a living?'

Joan arranged for her father to be buried next to Edric in the country churchyard of St Leonard beside their former home, Post Office Farm. Here she would come in her grief to tend their graves and remember Rowie's good-humoured complaint, 'it's them three at it, always politics'.

Matt would have relished his daughter's victory for Labour when in the April 1955 local government elections she won a seat on North Riding County Council. Under the banner 'A vote for Joan Maynard is a vote for progress' she set out Labour policy on education, roads and rural water and sanitation 'I am very proud and happy to once again have the honour of being your LABOUR CANDIDATE. I am strongly opposed to people standing as Independents, there is no such thing as an Independent. I prefer to stand under my true colours.' Again she was criticised for contaminating local government with politics. Her response was always: 'It is not the Labour Party that has brought party politics into local government. They have always been present.'

Joan won the seat with a majority of 144 votes. For the first time Thirsk had returned for Labour and Joan became the first woman Labour member of the county council. She was ecstatic to have 'won the seat as a Socialist under my true colours'.[8]

Congratulations arrived at Lansbury House:

> Dear Joan,
> Congratulations – a wonderful achievement and under your TRUE colours too!! with all the self styled elite running around helping the 'Independent' you beat your man hands down.
> Jean (Ward)

Joan's diligent and effective work as member of the RDC had clearly earned her votes in the county fight:

> Congratulations. Your record on the RDC is magnificent and something that the ratepayers should be grateful to you for.
> A Smelling.

By now Reverend E. B. Storr had retired from office in Thirsk Labour Party.

He wrote to Joan:

9 April 1955

Dear Miss Maynard,

Let me add my belated congratulations to the many you have no doubt received on your splendid victory. I am reminded of one incident in the khaki parliamentary election of 1918. Every ILP [Independent Labour Party] candidate in that election lost his seat or failed to win one (including MacDonald and Snowden) with one exception. My friend Ben Spoor won Bishop Auckland for Labour for the first time, running as an ILP candidate. So, when Labour seats have been falling all around you, you wrest from the Tories (miscalled Independents) the seat they have held for so long. Your joy will be tempered by the fact that your friend Mr Brocklebank lost his seat. I am sorry for that.

I hope you will enjoy your new duties and that, with your colleagues, you will be able to put up a good fight for Socialist principles.

With warm regards

Ernest B Storr.

The Labour Group of North Riding County Council met at 10.00 a.m. on 27 April at the Harewood Arms, Northallerton, immediately prior to Joan's first council meeting. Because Jack Brocklebank had lost at Topcliffe, Joan would be the sole Labour member representing a rural seat. She was to retain vivid memories of her first meeting of the Labour Group:

There were Labour Councillors on, but they were all from Teesside – Teesside was taken away later – and most of them were just Labour people. They weren't Socialists. All these Teeside wallahs were just Labour people, apparatchiks really. The first Labour Group meeting I went to I was stunned because I was talking about some Labour Party policy or other, and they said, we're autonomous on here. They meant they could decide what was going on irrespective of the Labour Party. I said, how can we be autonomous? We wouldn't be here if it wasn't for the Labour Party. They put us up, paid for the election, did the work. We're supposed to be carrying out Labour Party policy *I* thought.

An exception on the group, 'a true Socialist' was the Labour councillor who chaired the Children's Committee:

> All of the chairmen of the committees had to move the minutes. They would get up and say – there were a few lords – My Lords, Ladies and Gentlemen, I beg to move these minutes. But Gordon used to get up and say, *Mr* Chairman, Ladies and Gentlemen, I *wish* to move these minutes. He never referred to the lords like. He used to say, I'm not begging those buggers for anything. It never failed, the officers always looked round with a little smile, they got the message, like.

Joan made her mark on Labour, Conservative and Independent members and began creating headlines in the local press. The hitherto bored reporters were delighted. The year after her election she astounded the council by moving a motion of no confidence in the chairman and members of a council committee. This was unprecedented and Joan was approached by all sides to withdraw it, 'in her own interests'. Her response was vigorously asserted in the council chamber: 'I did not come on the Council to further my own interests, but to represent the electorate.'[9]

The motion of no confidence was directed at the chairman, Colonel Slingsby, and members of the Highways and Bridges Committee of the County Council for lack of attention to North Riding roads during the severe winter snowstorms. Rejecting the motion, Colonel Slingsby (supported by the entire council except Joan's seconder) blustered that he could not remember a motion of no confidence in the chairman and members of the committee 'It smacks rather of the House of Commons than of the County Council!'[10]

As a member of the Education Committee Joan upset the social order. County councillors nominated school managers (governors); Joan was soon removing managers whose own children were privately educated and replacing them with parents of children in the county schools. On 20 June 1955 the chairman of the committee, Ralph Butterfield, OBE., MC, wrote:

Dear Miss Maynard

Appointment of Managers

I should like to discuss with you, sometime in the near future, the nominations for appointment as managers of primary schools which you have submitted for the Thirsk Area. It has been the policy of the Committee to preserve continuity in the management wherever possible. Your nominations would obviously run most drastically against this idea. Before, therefore, having this matter raised in the appropriate sub committee I feel it would be more friendly if we could talk about it beforehand.

A brusque and unfriendly Joan pointed out 'there has been a bit too much continuity' and stuck by her nominations, knowing they had to be accepted.

In council meetings Joan cut an imposing figure, tall and confident with a strong voice and fearless in the face of opposition. 'I didn't have to steel myself. I didn't always realise the fury I was going to run into [laughs]. I just had a commitment to the issue and the people. That was how my mind worked. My friend Jack Brocklebank used to say, now don't get too far ahead of the troops, like!'

*

The 1955 Labour Party election manifesto *Forward with Labour* promised a return to a free health service, the abolition of the eleven-plus exam and further nationalisation (Butler 1995, p. 14). But at national level the Labour Party was ill-prepared for a General Election. Though old and tired Attlee resolved to retain the leadership to unify the Party and prevent his old rival Morrison from succeeding him. In contrast, the Conservative Party had recently appointed a new leader in Sir Anthony Eden, who was to lead the Conservatives to another victory, with an overall majority of sixty. It was the first time in almost a century that a party in government had increased its majority. Labour's previous warnings that a Conservative Government would herald a return to mass unemployment had clearly not been realised. For Labour, following the 1951 defeat, the 'election setback in 1955 came as a shock. On a lower turnout, Labour lost almost 1.5 million votes, its percentage of the poll fell from 48.8% to 46.4% and lost twenty seats' (Shaw 1996, pp. 50–51).

Labour's NEC set up a committee chaired by Harold Wilson to inquire into Labour's defeat. Its report revealed 'serious faults in the work of full-time employees of the Party and in the use of the Party's funds. The report recommended forming a special sub committee of the National Executive to supervise the work of the organisation; special help in future for marginal constituencies; and a decentralisation of organisation to regional offices' (Pelling and Reid 1996, p. 106).

In contrast with Labour disorganisation nationally, the Party in Thirsk and Malton increased the Labour vote for their candidate George Mitton. This was the first General Election Labour had fought with Joan as agent. Acknowledging her exceptional work George Mitton said Thirsk and Malton should no longer be considered an unwinnable or hopeless seat. Determined to build on the experience, Joan set up a review of the election campaign which concluded that planning could have been more effective, with a greater concentration on public meetings to raise awareness of the political issues. Butler (1995, p. 14) has pointed out that this General Election was the last, 'to be left uncovered by the broadcasters'). The postal vote had not been organised systematically and more posters should have been displayed. Joan would ensure such matters were addressed.

Joan and the Party grew increasingly frustrated in their dealings with both the regional and national Labour Party organisations. The Thirsk and Malton Party wanted to make Joan's appointment full-time, yet in the General Election year when the NEC acceded to the request, the national agent, Len Williams, advised against awarding them a development grant. A rule specified that Thirsk and Malton Labour Party was not entitled to a grant for a full-time agent until four years had elapsed since the last appointment of Denny. It counted for nought that as part-time agent, Joan was significantly increasing Labour Party membership against the national trend and winning for Thirsk and Malton the Northern Region's Membership Shield.

Joan undertook her activities across the vast rural division without a car and with growing concern about her mother's health. When canvassing the York area (then part of the constituency) she would cycle to Thirsk station, take the train to York and catch a bus to her destination. Towards the end of an evening's canvassing she would become anxious about reaching home: 'I had to make sure, especially when my mother was bedfast, that I got the last train home. Otherwise she would have been stranded. She couldn't have coped without me.' Sometimes Joan used her meagre pay for a taxi home and could only be refunded if there were sufficient funds 'in the kitty' – which was not always the case.

In winter months she canvassed the more urban regions of New Earswick and Malton, and on summer evenings she worked in the villages. Canvassing on Saturdays was unproductive because people were out shopping, and whilst canvassing and collecting subscriptions was occasionally undertaken on Sundays, some members frowned on the practice and even resigned over it.

The agent's report of 6 November 1955 indicates the scale of her activity:

> Over the past 7 weeks the following places have been visited, Malton, Kirbymoorside, Helperby, Easingwold, Clifton Without, Rosedale, New Earswick, Haxby, Bedale, Middleton and Wrelton, Helmsley, Ampleforth and work done in the Thirsk area. It was proposed to hold a jumble sale at Kirbymoorside in November, a whist drive at Easingwold in December, a jumble sale at Thirsk in November and a whist drive in December, a concert in early January.

A single event would require Joan to arrange

> a reception centre for goods, seven tables for stalls, three teapots for Mrs Brocklebank, pots for Margaret Stephenson, tea urn and plates. Arrange for three women to look after the tea, two for the jumble sale, five for other stalls. Get white paper for the tables. See the treasurer about 100 whist score cards, fifty mens and fifty womens.

Joan made heavy demands on others as well as herself. Tom Gascoyne's son John remembers lying in a hospital bed recovering from an operation:

> This bloke came in and said, John Gascoyne? I said yes. He then dumped this big box on my bed and said, Joan Maynard sent you these, something to do while you lie in bed. I opened the box, which contained a huge number of election envelopes to address. He said, I'll bring you some more tomorrow. I

> said, how the bloody hell did you find me? He said, Joan's boys are everywhere. That was Joan, nobody should have any time wasted.

Resolutions to the Northern Region Conference seeking financial assistance to fight elections in rural constituencies went unheeded. To Joan's irritation too much of her time, in addition to canvassing and fundraising, was spent collecting Party subscriptions. Although there were 'collectors' in the local parties they could not all be relied upon. There was no question of members paying by post or standing order; subscriptions had to be collected in person. John Gascoyne remembers his aunt and uncle anticipating Joan's visit:

> They lived in Fulmer, which is near Castle Howard, and Joan went to collect their subs on the bus. She would have gone to Malton and stayed with us and then got on the bus to Fulmer and get their subs. Then I don't know how she would get back, there might not have been two buses a day. It would never have occurred to them to put it in the post. If you wanted money they had to see your face, they weren't going to post any money to a faceless entity.

*

People in Sowerby and Thirsk were suspicious of Joan reading the *Daily Worker*. They assured her, 'there aren't any workers round here, you only read that if you live in towns like Sheffield and Leeds'.[11] She had been following an argument by G. D. H. Cole concerning the need for Labour to make links with the Communist Party. In 1954 NUAW activist and Communist Jack Dunman had put her in touch with Bert Ramelson, secretary to the York District Committee of the Communist Party, and Joan subsequently arranged for him to come to Lansbury House to lead discussions about Marxism. She thought Labour Party members could benefit from the Communist Party's approach to educating its members in understanding political theory. She felt the Labour Party was too much of an electoral party, rather than one that educated and campaigned. Furthermore, Lansbury had described Communist 'philosophy' (as against 'method') as 'sound' (Shaw 1988, p. 304, note 34).

In the discussions in the front room of Lansbury House Tom Gascoyne and Bert Ramelson were the main protagonists. John Gascoyne remembers how his father

> would argue with Bert, which was something none of us could do. He had a background in Marxism, we hadn't; all we could do was listen to what we were told and then go home and try to make sense of it. When somebody is telling you what Marx said or what Marx meant, if you hadn't studied it before, you can't offer an opinion. But my father could give a different interpretation to Bert and he would raise issues about how the Communist Party had let the workers down and all the shenanigans going on in the Communist Party. It was part of our educational process. Between my father and Bert Ramelson we learned our Socialism, our Marxism. Jack Bowen would say his piece as Jack always did.

Arranging such meetings was dangerous in the climate of Labour Party proscriptions and expulsions. The Cold War was being waged and whilst the Communist Party was

> no longer interested in infiltrating its Labour rival (most of its efforts were now expended on strengthening its industrial base) . . . it was with the utmost mistrust that Labour reacted to Moscow's various peace campaigns in the early 1950s, in particular its efforts to woo non-Communists by encouraging the formation of 'peace' and 'friendship' societies. The NEC denounced them as 'front' organisations 'set up for the purpose of enticing non-Communists to support policies and activities in harmony with the Communist Party line' (Labour Party Conference Report 1953, p 12). Within the context of the social-democratic centralist regime this provided adequate justification for the proscription of such groups and the expulsion of those who persisted in participating in them (Shaw 1988, p. 59).

In Yorkshire alone, 221 people were expelled for membership of peace groups. Shaw says this 'disproportionate number... may well have reflected the priorities, energy and influence of the Regional Organiser John Anson' (*Ibid.*, p. 61).

Anson had succeeded Len Williams as regional organiser in 1946 and was 'noted for his fierce "loyalist" stance. He became closely identified with the Gaitskellites in the battles of the 1950s'. (Grayson 1991, p. 58).

Joan and the Thirsk and Malton Party Executive were firm supporters of Bevan. Unsurprisingly Joan fell under John Anson's scrutiny and he warned her about involvement in activities whose organisers had links with the Communist Party. Such activities were characterised as 'efforts through a pseudonym to divert our people away from the Party'. One event which Joan planned to attend was a Peace Conference in Halifax in April 1956. But she felt vulnerable, and after much heart searching and consultation with friends decided against going to it. For the first time she was making a sacrifice of principle, yet if she were expelled from the Labour Party what would be gained? Her first loyalty was to the rank and file of the Rural Divisional Labour Party which she considered to be utterly neglected by urban-centric regional and national Party officials.

Having warned Joan not to attend the Halifax Peace Conference, John Anson noticed her name published as a supporter 'in a personal capacity' in an advertisement for another conference, 'Citizens of Tomorrow', to be held in Leeds on 26 May 1956. Other supporters included Boyd Orr and Bertrand Russell. On 27 April John Anson wrote to Joan:

> I have made enquiries into the bona fides of the organisation and find that the Young Communist League is really the sponsoring body, and I am asked to advise you that it would be inadvisable for members of the Labour Party to be associated with it . . . So far as I can find out, Mr Harry Newton, who is the secretary of the Communist organisation known as the Yorkshire Youth Assembly, is the self appointed conference secretary.

Joan was beginning to have enough of Anson and was more confident it would be the responsibility not of him but of the constituency Party to expel her. Fortified by this realisation and inspired by G. D. H. Cole's article in the *Daily Worker* she decided compromise was not for her. On 10 May 1956 she replied:

> Dear Mr Anson
>
> Thank you for your letter of 27 April about my support for the Conference

'Citizens of Tomorrow'. I did not know that the sponsoring body was the Young Communist League. I seem to remember that one of the sponsors was Len Hutton. In any case I cannot see any possible harm in my supporting a conference on an important issue, even if Young Communists are the sponsoring body. Surely at thirty-four I am old enough to make my own political decisions. I am in any case strongly opposed to all bans and proscriptions which are placed on members of the Labour Party, I think it is time we grew up, and started fighting the real enemy the Tories. As G. D. H. Cole has just said, 'Socialists and Communists have much in common and it is ridiculous to say that they cannot work together', particularly in view of the changed Soviet Leaders.
Yours Sincerely
Joan Maynard

The following week she drafted her own article for the *Daily Worker* which it published on 2 June 1956 under the heading 'Don't Make the Tories Laugh':

It's time we Socialists and Communists got together to talk things over . . . I have been a member of the Labour Party for 10 years, and I have always been very depressed to find so much time devoted by members of my Party to attacking the Communists . . . How the Tories, the political spearhead of capitalism, must laugh to see the working class movement split in this tragic way . . . There is a difference between the many people who call themselves Labour and people who are Socialists. The former believe that capitalism can be reformed, they are in favour of the Welfare State, but they do not basically want to change society. It logically follows that these people cannot believe that the responsibility for building the new society rests on the working people . . . As Socialists we need always to encourage working people, give them confidence because they suffer from an appalling inferiority complex. We need to get over to them that they are the real power in the world . . . When Social Democrats and Labour Leaders say the Communists have taken away or destroyed democracy in Russia and Eastern Europe they talk nonsense. These people have never known political democracy as we know it, therefore Communists cannot have taken it away from them. These people in fact have

> much more democracy, both economic and social, under Communism than they ever had under the despots that ruled them previously . . . Our fundamental interests are the same. It is because I feel this so strongly that I want to see an immediate end to bans and proscriptions in the Labour movement . . . All my experience has taught me that Conservatives only believe in democracy so long as it suits the purpose of their class. Once attack the real citadel of their power, the control of the economy of the country, then they will show you how much they believe in democracy – they will fight with no holds barred... Their belief in democracy is a myth. We in the Labour Party should be busy exposing them, not fighting the Communists.

The following day she received a letter from Richard Donaldson:

> Dear Miss Maynard
> I wish to express my appreciation of the really excellent article which appeared under your name in the *Daily Worker* yesterday. It is very courageous of you to come out in this manner, but I can assure you that whatever adverse criticism you may provoke by this forthright statement, you may rest secure in the knowledge that the vast majority of the rank and file of the Labour Party and the Trades Union Movement share your views and had it not been for our bankrupt policy and discredited leadership we should have moved along the path indicated by you, in your article, long ago. . . . I have retained my membership of the York Labour Party only because I have been confident that this mass working class movement must sooner or later wake up to the fact that a process of disintegration is taking place within its ranks which has been speeded up by bans and proscriptions and a policy which is scarcely distinguishable from that of the Tory Party . . . You will probably have to face the music for your temerity and the inquisitors of Smith Square may bear down on you, but I hope and trust that if the worst comes to the worst that you will stand your ground and go into the wilderness rather than recant your "heresy" of truth.

Another letter further encouraged her. She was pleased and relieved in equal measure to be congratulated on her article by Frank Smithson; it was he who had chaired the Halifax Peace Conference she had failed to attend.

Frank Smithson had refused to resign from the York Peace Group he had helped to establish in 1952; for this he had been expelled from the Labour Party. He wrote to Joan (11 June 1956):

> Dear Comrade,
> Just a note to congratulate you on and thank you for your recent article in the *Daily Worker*. I am sorry you were not able to come to our Peace Conference at Halifax on April 14th. It was not as well attended as I had hoped but it was enthusiastic and invigorating. We are told we live in the "Free World" and yet you are not at liberty to come to the conference and Davidson asked me in introducing him not to mention that he is on the staff of the *Daily Herald*. 'Free World'?!!!

Acknowledging his letter Joan explained again why she had not attended the Halifiax Conference. His reply reassured her (9 July 1956):

> I am satisfied that you made the right decision in regard to the Halifax Conference. It would have been a tragedy if you had been expelled from the Party – and I feel that whatsoever sacrifice of principle you made or feel that you have made was justified by your service and loyalty to the rank and file members of the Thirsk Labour Party who like all in similar constituencies are grossly neglected by regional and national officials. Yes Thirsk division needs you and I sincerely hope you may have health and vigour to serve them for a long time. If I may say so my case and that of my dear sweetheart was rather different from yours. I had no office of any kind in the Party and from my close friendship with some of its Socialist members I am able to exert some influence still.

He enclosed for Joan a carbon copy of the letter he'd sent – to no avail – to James Griffiths MP, Deputy Leader of the Labour Party:

> I am aged eighty-three, my late wife and I worked for Socialism and World Peace for close on 60 years in the LRC [Labour Representation Committee] and ILP (my wife also in the Women's Labour League), the Cooperative Peace Movement and in various Peace organisations which seemed to us to be

> worthy of our support . . . In 1935 I was Parliamentary Labour Candidate for the Barkston Ash Division – reducing the Tory majority by 6,000. . . Eventually my wife and I committed an unforgivable crime – we joined the York Peace Group – composed of men and women of different shades of political opinion – some members of the Labour Party, some Quakers, a Methodist minister, and a vicar of the Church of England, and I was eventually elected chairman. We decided to send a delegate to the People's Congress for Peace held in Vienna in Dec 1952. The Yorkshire Regional Organiser, Anson, wrote to me insisting that if we wished to retain our membership of the Labour Party we must sever our connection with the York Peace Group as the Congress had been banned, or to use his words, proscribed by the NEC. It was a terrible shock to us both – we had been ostracised in the pioneer days from opponents of the Movement but this was something entirely new and startling and after very serious thought we decided we could not allow the NEC to deprive us of our liberty of thought and action and must therefore calmly take our stand for liberty and suffer the penalty. We felt that if 60 years of faithful service had not revealed our sincerity we had hopelessly failed . . . My only object in writing to you is to let you see what pain and suffering these forty or more proscriptions cause and what far-reaching effects they have on the Labour movement.

Joan felt wretched. Here she was, working for the Party responsible for dismissing two lifetimes' commitment to Socialism. Where was Labour's commitment to Socialism? She considered its policy of social reform was degenerating into a policy of expediency. Post-war consensus and revisionist attempts to promote egalitarianism within capitalism were progressing apace:

> Whilst public or parliamentary rhetoric gave the impression of fundamental differences and disagreements, the reality was that both of the main political parties shared a commitment to making the existing system function more effectively and fairly. The question was over means, not ends. (Dorey 1995, p. 60 discussing David Bell's *End of Ideology*, 1960)

On 3 February 1957 Joan's mother Effie Maynard died. Friends of Joan in and outside the Party and the Union were extremely concerned how she would cope with living alone for the first time in her life. Within four years her home life had changed from the comfortable family intimacy of shared routines in the post office and smallholding, to living by herself in the rather dismal Lansbury House. She never forgot that first night alone, longing for the comforting chimes of St Oswald – across the road from her bedroom – to continue throughout the night.

Looking back on this time Joan was thankful her many interests and commitments took her out of the house. As well as her job, she was a magistrate, county and rural district councillor, district secretary in the NUAW, secretary to the Northallerton and District Trades Council and branch secretary of the WEA. Much of her effort continued to focus on raising money for the Party through collecting members' contributions, organising events and arranging for the sale of lottery 'draw' tickets. On occasion the Thirsk and Malton Party was 'broke' and Joan offered to forgo her own pay. She had even offered to forgo it when she took time off to care for her dying mother – an offer the Party refused to accept. Her commitments served the interests of others but she didn't take care of herself. Friends were alarmed; she was working too hard and barely eating or resting. They would invite her to their homes on the pretext of talking over an issue when the main purpose was to provide her with a wholesome meal. In the early 1950s she had been an active member of the Thirsk film club, but now she made little time for it. Even the prodigious reading of her youth had been displaced by her work. But she always made time to walk in her beloved countryside of North Yorkshire.

*

Having increased its vote in the 1955 General Election, Thirsk and Malton Labour Party was determined to select a good candidate for the next election. Although, in April 1957, they had again won the membership shield in the Northern Region for the greatest percentage increase in members, Head Office ruled they would not be granted financial aid. The priority was to improve election chances nationally by concentrating on the marginal constituencies. Once more Thirsk and Malton Labour Party felt ignored and in May 1957 passed a resolution 'deploring the attitude of Head Office and the region on the matter of financial aid to rural constituencies'.

Although being 'written off' by Head Office (which at the same time grasped their members' contributions) was infuriating, Thirsk and Malton Party members were incensed at its refusal to endorse the candidate they wanted to fight the next General Election – Joan Maynard. In December 1957 she was nominated as prospective Parliamentary candidate by the Thirsk and Malton Party but four months later they learned the NEC was asking the division to seek further nominations. It was undesirable to have only one person for selection and particularly so when that one person was the paid part-time agent.

The following June the division was again asked for a nomination and again the nominee was Joan. Once more the NEC considered the validity of her nomination. In October the NEC confirmed Joan's nomination to be invalid because she was part-time agent for Thirsk and Malton and it had disqualified her under the same rule that applied to full-time agents. Thirsk and Malton pointed out there was no rule disqualifying part-time agents; they were convinced of the validity of her nomination. Some members of the local Thirsk Party felt so strongly that if they were not allowed to choose their own candidate, they should not contest the election. Joan dissuaded them, emphasising it was always policy that should prevail and not personalities. Nevertheless the NEC decision was always to rankle with her; she would have loved to contest the division as a Socialist.

Given the close personal relationship between the regional and national officers of the Party through John Anson and national agent Len Williams, it is not surprising Joan's nomination was not endorsed. Her speech on land nationalisation at the 1958 Labour Party Conference would add to the Labour leadership's consternation.[12]

In January 1959 the Thirsk and Malton Executive Committee met at Lansbury House to consider other possible Parliamentary candidates. They approached Jeremy Bray, Morris Sutherland and Thirsk local Party chair John Ellis. John Ellis had to be persuaded to allow his name to go forward; he had been a firm supporter of Joan's nomination. At the selection conference in York on 25 January Jeremy Bray was chosen.

Instead of the years of preparation the local Labour Party had intended for its Parliamentary candidate, Joan as agent had barely nine months to introduce Jeremy Bray to the electorate in one of the most widespread constituencies in the country. It was a short hard campaign in which Bray impressed the Party and Joan with his enthusiasm and commitment. He travelled tirelessly throughout the huge division, frequently speaking at more than one public meeting in an evening and sometimes getting lost between villages if Joan was not accompanying him.

Though physically 'shattered' Joan was delighted that in the General Election Thirsk and Malton raised its vote by nearly a thousand – against the national swing. As well as having a good candidate she considered the campaign organisation to be an improvement on the previous election, with greater attention being paid to operational detail as well as to policy.

During the three weeks prior to the election Jeremy Bray had made Joan's salary up to £10 a week and after the election the Party agreed to continue to pay her this sum, (in addition to the ten shillings a week they paid for the use of her front room as an office).

Replying to a warmly appreciative letter from Joan after the election Bray wrote:

> Right from the beginning I felt that much my toughest test in Thirsk and Malton was whether I would win your respect, and if I have begun to do so I should feel I haven't failed. It has been an immense help both before and during the campaign, to be able to discuss everything freely with you – policies, tactics and personalities – I have relied very heavily on your judgement and I don't think it has led me astray. I do hope, wherever we find ourselves in the future, that there will be times when we can talk over the beloved cause in the country, in Thirsk and Malton, and indeed the world.

Whilst Thirsk and Malton had increased its percentage of the vote in the three General Elections of the 1950s, nationally the margin of Labour's defeat increased each time. Gaitskell's immediate response following the 1959 defeat, was to demand at the Labour Party Annual Conference the abandonment of Clause 4 of the Party's constitution with its commitment to 'the common ownership of the means of production, distribution and exchange'.

This attempt was bitterly opposed by Joan and members of Thirsk and Malton Labour Party Executive. Indeed, they thought one of the reasons why the Labour Party had come 'unstuck' at the election was precisely because it had been apologetic about nationalisation and had failed to propose real Socialist economic and social policies. In June 1960 the Thirsk local Party agreed a resolution for the Labour Party Annual Conference that Conference reaffirm its wholehearted support for Clause 4.

Gaitskell was forced to back down over Clause 4 but was determined to win the next battle – against calls for unilateral nuclear disarmament. Joan attended the Labour Party Conference in Scarborough in 1960, where the resolution for Britain to unilaterally renounce its nuclear weapons was passed in the face of the stiffest opposition from Party leaders. Gaitskell, refusing to accept the decision of Conference, made his memorable vow to 'fight and fight and fight again'.

As a committed supporter of the Campaign for Nuclear Disarmament (CND) and as a believer in the primacy of Conference in policy making, Joan was aghast at Gaitskell's refusal to accept the democratic decision of Conference. She distributed copies of the leaflet *Appeal for Unity in Support of Conference Decisions* and arranged a meeting of the Thirsk and Malton Executive Committee at Lansbury House to discuss the 'serious position of the Party'. The Executive agreed to protest to Head Office about the use by Gaitskell and his supporters of the Party platform and funds to oppose Party policy. It wrote to the region demanding that conferences and meetings be organised to publicise official Party policy, as agreed at Scarborough, and it resolved to write to members of the NEC – Tom Driberg, Barbara Castle, Dick Crossman and Ian Mikardo – requesting them to produce a leaflet setting out Party policy as agreed at Scarborough.[13]

Disunity in the Labour Party nationally was reflected in Thirsk and Malton Division. A resolution was passed by the Kirbymoorside Party:

> Having read in the *Yorkshire Evening Press* that resolutions have been passed at Thirsk and Malton Executive Committee leading to a protest against Party platforms and Party money being made available to Mr Gaitskell and his supporters, Kirbymoorside Party wish to dissociate themselves from such resolutions. We feel that in the past Labour Party money and platforms have

> frequently been used against official policies and see no good reason why the present situation should be treated as an exceptional circumstance.

Joan had been introduced to Hugh Gaitskell by Jack Brocklebank at an NUAW district dinner in Northallerton in September 1958. Seizing the opportunity, she asked him for financial assistance from the Party nationally. Disdainfully, Gaitskell told her it was necessary to be realistic because Thirsk and Malton Division was a Tory stronghold. Joan was outraged: 'What a good thing the early Socialists weren't operating on that basis or you'd never have been Chancellor of the Exchequer, would you, because if they'd only done the realistic things we'd never have got anywhere, would we?'

SIX

Cutting blue grass in local government

In April 1958 Joan defended her seat for the Thirsk Division of North Riding County Council. The focus of her election address, 'Let's give them a fair chance' was educational provision in Thirsk and, in particular, the need to secure funding for the second half of the new school at Thirsk to which 'all children in the area, 11 and over will be admitted'. For Joan, education was the most important service the county council provided. She was committed to comprehensive schooling and opposed to schools in rural areas having a 'rural bias'. Although supportive of agricultural education for school leavers seeking employment in agriculture (she was a member of the Agricultural Board for Further Education) she was intensely critical of agriculture being the curriculum focus of rural county secondary modern schools. Among the school governors were landowners and farmers whose own children attended private schools. Joan recalled

> They were always trying to angle the education into some kind of vocational studies in order to encourage the young people to go into agriculture; they needed more labour then. But it used to really annoy me. I said, now that's got nothing to do with education; education is about helping each individual to express their potential to the full, we don't want to go channelling people into the prevailing industry in the area. They used to try it on, I can tell you. The powers that be really did lose out when they lost the all-age village school. It

> meant that our children found in the bigger secondary schools a wider world with new horizons, and other jobs than agriculture.

In May 1953 Joan had written to the local paper's 'Thirsk Post Bag' responding to remarks made by Sir Thomas Dugdale (MP for Richmond and Minister for Agriculture and Fisheries) when he opened the new county secondary school at Market Weighton. 'I am perturbed,' she wrote, 'as I have been perturbed before, with the reference to an agricultural bias in the new modern schools in the countryside. I object most strongly to any kind of bias in education; in fact, the word bias makes nonsense of the word education. Bias is more akin to propaganda than to education.'

In her election addresses Joan always located local issues within the context of national politics. 'Some people protest that national politics have no place in local elections. That is a mistaken and short sighted view . . . your best protection against the vicious policies of the Tory Government is a Labour County Council.' She then went on to explain the implications for local education of the Tories' move to a 'block grants' funding system.

Joan's opponent in the 1958 county council election was the Lord of the Manor, Peter Bell. Bell's address declared that whilst he was a Conservative he did not believe in standing under a party label:

> I believe that councillors are elected to do their best for the district they represent and for the people who have elected them, and this can only be done if councillors are free to vote as they think best and not according to party dictates. I will not believe that Thirsk, Sowerby, and Carlton Miniott are predominantly Socialist and I believe that more people will vote against the Labour Candidate than for her, and I ask you to prove this for me by returning me to the North Riding County Council as your representative for the next 3 years . . . vote for me and show that you do not wish to be represented by a Labour Councillor on the County Council.

Joan wrote to the electorate, rebutting Bell's 'personal attack on me and my politics' and concluded: 'I have the courage of my convictions, and stand honestly as a Labour Candidate, I claim to be more representative of the majority of people in Thirsk County Division than Mr Bell – most of you work for your living as I do'.

In subsequent private correspondence between the two candidates Bell rejected Joan's invitation for the two of them to jointly address public meetings: 'I am no politician and I cannot agree that politics enter into the contest between us.'

The Lord of the Manor won the election (Bell 939 votes, Joan 881, a majority of 58 votes). The local paper reported:

> It had been widely expected by students of local politics that the Lord of the Manor would deprive Miss Joan Maynard of the seat which she had held for 3 years since beating the Rev. J. C. Dupuis . . . At the declaration Miss Maynard said she hoped Major Bell wanted to do the job as much as she. She and her supporters were not the victors that night but they were certainly not the vanquished. They would be back.

And back they most certainly were. Three years later, against all expectation, Joan defeated the squire by a majority of fourteen votes. Her supporters were ecstatic; they sang *The Red Flag* at the declaration at Thirsk Town Hall and bore Joan aloft round the town. Celebrations continued throughout the night with a party in Lansbury House. Joan remembered a tremendous feeling of high morale amongst Labour supporters the following day as joyfully they declared 'we won yesterday'. It was the 'we' Joan appreciated. 'It was just as much their victory as it was mine, because I could never have won without their help and support. It was an important political lesson – working together with your own people, makes for victory.'

The victory was a remarkable achievement. Joan remembered her next-door neighbour saying, 'She'll never beat him. Nobody'll ever beat the squire, like. But we did.' Years later Joan told the Labour leader Michael Foot her views about contesting elections:

> I said you win them by sticking to your principles and making clear where you stand, and then the people will support you. And he said, we're not talking about safe seats like Sheffield Brightside, you know, Joan. And I said, I'm not talking about Brightside. I'm talking about rural, feudal North Yorkshire,

that's what I'm talking about! Anyway that's what we did here. People used to say round here, she's a bloody Communist, you know and daubed graffiti on the house. Others used to say, well, I don't care; I shall vote for Joan because I think she's the best councillor. And I used to say, well if you're right about that, don't you think it's because I'm a Socialist? I really wanted them to vote for me because I'm a Socialist.

If people didn't vote for Joan because of her Socialism it would be wholly unremarkable given the pervasive conservatism. Lionel Twiss, a teacher who moved to Thirsk in the early 1960s, remembers: 'This was a very conservative town with a large and a small "c". When I came here there were only sixteen copies of the *Guardian*. You could not just buy it, I was questioned as to why I wanted it. It was kept under the counter and I collected it.'

Joan said she 'really loved' her local government work. Councils maintained considerable control over policy and budgets. 'I wouldn't enjoy it today, the national government has so much control, it's awful, I couldn't bear it. It's anti-democratic, councils are having to carry out Government policy. The danger with the old authorities was their parochialism and the danger of the new their remoteness.'

The oligarchy of the old councils went unchallenged for years:

Often there were no elections; certain people carved the area up for themselves and would be returned unopposed. This was particularly the case with the county council. They could tolerate you being a district councillor, but they did feel that the county was very much their prerogative.[1]

Some forty years after opposing each other on county and rural district councils Joan and Colonel Peter Consett met one evening in Brawith Hall and reflected on the elections.

With a chuckle Colonel Consett recalled the early 1950s:

This fellow Hill-Walker was the first to stand as a Conservative... You see, we'd arranged, Hill-Walker and I, that if anybody else put up, one of us would stand down. I mean, we weren't thinking about politics at all. We were just friends. And so I rang him up and said, I hear Miss Maynard is standing as a

> Labour candidate. Do you want to toss or cut through cards? Oh is she! he said, well, then I'm standing as a Conservative. Oh, I said, right. So I stood as an Independent. Just like that. So then it was a three-cornered fight, and I'm proud to say that I got more than both of them!

The Conservative and Independent seats on the county council were stacked with farmers, landowners and the retired military establishment. An exception was Conservative member Peter Jaconelli, a 'self-made' businessman who recalled 'retired generals and colonels and brigadiers. They'd think they were born to rule. I didn't fit in with them because I was from the bottom drawer'.

Peter Jaconelli remembered Joan as a formidable figure on the county council. 'The meetings were like Parliament – very formal and commencing with prayers. Joan would commence her statements authoritatively with "it seems to me, Mr Chairman . . ." and then demolish anybody in a debate. She always knew the facts.' Joan observed ruefully: 'You could beat them with argument, but you couldn't beat them with hands; you didn't have enough hands to put up.'

Jaconelli described how the Conservatives would meet together with the Independents as the 'Black Hand'. 'This Black Hand seemed to pick us all up and meet before the council meeting. Then you got into the council chamber and battled it out. If the Black Hand got a hold of you, you had to vote that way.'

Joan battled on in local government into the early 1970s, never losing her enthusiasm. On the rural district council she clashed with the chairman, Colonel Peter Consett, concerning the timing of council meetings. It was obvious to Joan and a minority of the council that it was anti-democratic to hold the RDC meetings on Monday afternoons because it was impossible for most working people to participate. Councillor Ron Williams, an Independent and teacher at Thirsk School, had been forbidden by school governors (some of whom were themselves Thirsk councillors) from taking time off on Mondays to attend council meetings. For Joan it was 'scandalous that a public body like the school governors should take this attitude. If you follow it through to its logical conclusion then we would have a council of either retired or self-employed people – which is just about what we have got!'[2]

One of the school governors, also a councillor, defended afternoon meetings arguing a teacher was paid a salary to teach children and could not therefore be spared on Monday afternoons. For other councillors it was a matter of personal convenience. 'People come from long distances to the meetings in work time. I do not think it fair that they should have to come in the evening and give up all their leisure time to the Council.'[3]

Joan and Williams organised a petition throughout every village in the district in support of evening meetings. They presented it to the council:

> Well, really it was to Colonel Consett, because he was the chairman. It was totally ignored. When Colonel Consett spoke I think they all thought they were under starter's orders! Never mind that the survey of 3,000 people in fifteen villages in the Thirsk area indicated over 80% in favour of evening meetings.
>
> The Chairman of the Council, Councillor Peter Consett concluded that whether councillors met in the afternoon or evening was nothing to do with the electors, 'It is a matter for the councillors themselves to decide . . . This question of the time of meetings is considered every year and a democratic vote taken among councillors at the annual meeting.'

He described the campaign which Councillor Maynard and Councillor Williams had mounted as 'dishonest and deceitful', an allegation that Councillor Maynard strongly denied.[4]

Councillor Consett's remarks were greeted with loud cries of 'here, here.' Joan stressed how those who had conducted the survey had gone out of their way to be fair. She was refused permission to submit a copy of the survey to the council on the grounds that it was not an official document.

According to Dr Brenda Thiede (Independent councillor), a supporter of evening meetings:

> The farmers had the meetings on market day when they came into market. They had the meeting as a sort of social event and went home for the milking. There was no way they were going to come back and have a meeting in the evening. They were not going to turn out at night. A lot of them were getting on and at that age once you've done your milking and gone in the house you

> don't go out again. A lot of them had been on the council traditionally father and son for a long time and they had a narrow idea of what would benefit the community.

Throughout her time in local government Joan was to struggle for openness and transparency. The issue might seem petty but for Joan there would be a principle at stake. In May 1959, for example, Thirsk District Council agreed to pay a guinea out of ratepayers' money towards a retirement gift for an official. The local paper reported how councillors refused a suggestion that each should contribute a shilling; the money, it was agreed, could come from the rates. 'Miss Joan Maynard protested. Good for her . . . But it is a sad reflection on the quality of other councillors that she was the only person who had the guts to speak out on this important matter of principle… it's not the guinea that counts. As Miss Maynard said, it's the principle.'[5]

Doubtless such critical reporting contributed to the press being forbidden to report on committee meetings of Thirsk Council. Joan argued for the press to be allowed at rural district council committees rather than be restricted to meetings of the full council, where committee decisions were proposed for ratification. 'The aim', said Joan, 'is to extend democracy by keeping the public informed of what their representatives are doing and how public money is spent. Those are most desirable aims.'[6] Although only four members of the 27 present voted in support of Joan's motion to admit the press, only three of those opposing attempted to provide a reason. Councillor Harry Toothill referred to the danger of actions of slander and Councillor Gerald Turton was afraid that if people's characters were discussed in the open it would 'set people talking'. Despite the paucity of such views, hands, not argument, prevailed.

Joan reflected:

> I have sat for years with councillors who have only opened their mouths to have the window closed. Others look to see how others are voting before they put their hand up, others haven't read the papers before coming to the meeting, and so one could go on. You couldn't win, because it wasn't about logic, but you could show to the people outside the bloody racket that was going on. That's what we did. We used it as a platform and of course that's

> what won us votes at the election because people could see what it was all about.

Joan's fearlessness as a councillor was legendary. No big name among the farming and military elite could intimidate her. Neither was she unduly respectful of paid council officials; referring to a decision of the county surveyor she insisted: 'We are representatives of the people and we are entitled to put our views forward, it is our point of view that matters, not his.' She raised awkward questions about the pecuniary interests of fellow councillors and caused uproar when she accused some Thirsk councillors of collusion when house improvement grants were being allocated:

> North Riding farmers, members of Thirsk Rural Council, winced when Councillor Miss Joan Maynard tackled them with having winked at one another in the Council Chamber by way of expressing their satisfaction at having 'got another £100 for a friend of theirs'. Miss Maynard made the allegation against the conduct of some of her fellow members on Monday, after she had failed to find a seconder for her proposal that a committee recommendation that house improvement grants should be increased from £250 to £400 should be referred back to the Finance Committee.[7]

Unable to prevent the allocation of improvement grants for private housing, Joan proposed an equivalent amount be paid from the general rate fund to the housing revenue account for council houses. This would help keep down council house rents.

In response to criticism about 'further subsidising council house tenants' Joan turned to the farmer members of the council, warning how they might in turn cease to benefit from subsidies – 'the axe might fall on you'.[8] Commenting on her remarks, the leader article in the *Thirsk, Bedale and Northallerton Times* was scathing. 'There can scarcely be comparison today between state support for a vital industry and providing roofs for some people at the expense of others who may be no better off.'

Joan responded to the newspaper:

> You say there can scarcely be comparison between giving state support to a vital industry like agriculture and providing roofs for some people at the expense of others who may be no better off . . . £260 million a year in subsidy is at the moment going into the Private industry of farming, and these same people vote against a 3d rate or subsidy for Public Property which would bring in approximately £900 a year. You say this rate would be at the expense of others who may be no better off than Council Tenants, but you say nothing of the 3d rate, which we are all paying to give improvement grants to private property owners to improve private property not public property. Yet this is certainly being paid at the expense of people less well off than those receiving it.[9]

When Thirsk Council sought to increase council house rents Joan shocked members by establishing a council house tenants' association. The Labour Party produced and distributed a leaflet with a tear-off slip for tenants to complete.

> The Labour Party has asked me to get this leaflet out so that you may understand what is happening and how much politics do matter in local government. The Labour people voted for a proposal that would have kept the rents down a little, and all the so-called Independents voted against it. It is amazing how all these Independents think like Tories when it comes to an issue of this kind. We hope that you will bear these things in mind when the local elections come round again.[10]

On 31 May 1963 the *Northern Echo* reported:

> The call for a rent strike in Thirsk had been well supported, the Rural Council Tenants' Association reported yesterday . . . Councillor Miss Joan Maynard said many tenants had never been asked to take such 'militant action' before. As this is the first time, we consider it has been a very strong protest. A total of 172 tenants have paid their increases over to us instead of the Council, and we have paid it into a special bank account. We are sure that many more would have paid but for unfounded fear of possible consequences including eviction.

Joan's concerns over the increased rent were exemplified by Louise Wilson, married to a farm worker, who gave the council a copy of her weekly budget based on her husband's pay of £9.10s. a week. 'After rent, milk, meat, wash payment, groceries, papers and insurance, she has £1.18s. for coal and electricity, bread and vegetables. "I can't remember when I last had a new coat and we can never afford a holiday," she said'.[11]

When the concept of differential rents was proposed by the council Joan protested to the editor of the local paper:

> Differential rents: I object to them because they entail a means test. We do not intend to go back to the 1930s, we intend to go forward to the 1970s. A rent differential, and the means test that goes with it, makes it a crime to be poor, by putting a stigma on those who pay the lower rent . . . the following do not have to face a means test to get public money: farmers, who get subsidy; parsons of the Church who recently got a 50% reduction in rates from the Government; property owners who get grants to improve their property. Why should council tenants have to be singled out for this obnoxious treatment . . . If Councillor Peter Consett is really worried about the tough time ratepayers are having to make ends meet, he can move at our next Council meeting that we do not give any more improvement grants. This will save the ratepayers a 2d rate. I will second the proposal. (14 May 1963)

From her earliest weeks on the council at Thirsk Joan had emphasised her commitment to housing. In July 1952 she had expressed concern about the lack of new houses planned for villages in the Thirsk district and how the proposed new homes were to be concentrated on Thirsk itself and Sowerby. She was unimpressed by the argument from the clerk that experience proved building four houses in a village took as long as building twenty or thirty houses in Thirsk or Sowerby. What about the living conditions of farm workers and their families? Why shouldn't there be quality public housing provision in the remote areas?

The attitude of some councillors towards council tenants appalled Joan. In February 1954 the council resolved that the furniture of prospective council tenants should be examined prior to taking up tenancy. Within two months Joan had organised a petition of 130 people, some of whom were prospective tenants. She told the council there were two issues involved, one being a practical problem about health and hygiene and the other a much deeper issue, the liberty of the subject:

> It was not merely the question of whether people were clean or dirty, it was an infringement of their liberty. Even the police are not allowed into a house without a warrant. Yet this council gives authority for its inspectors to enter private homes to inspect the personal belongings of prospective tenants, just because of a paltry £200 or £300 incurred by the Council through unsatisfactory tenants. How much is freedom worth, if the Council will sell it for so small a sum?[12]

Councillor S. F. McCann pointed out that if everyone's furniture was inspected, there was no stigma on any individual. As for there being an interference with liberty, if anyone wanted liberty today, they would have to do as the Pilgrim Fathers did: find some uninhabited [sic] land, and settle there.[13]

Joan's attempt to rescind the resolution to inspect tenants' furniture was defeated by a large majority and her proposal that health visitors and a welfare officer be appointed to support needy families was rejected.

For Joan housing was the essential element of social provision, in particular housing for the elderly. It was due largely to Joan's tireless efforts as secretary to the Thirsk and District Old People's Welfare Committee that an old people's home was opened in Thirsk. In July 1961 she wrote persuasively to the Minister of Health informing him there were no county homes for old people south of Northallerton to York, an area whose population was 53,000. This was the only part of the Riding without provision. 'Our old people are having to wait up to 2 years to get into a County home, and then it is miles away from relatives and friends. Our small hospitals at Thirsk and Easingwold are usually full of old people, though these are supposed to be for acute cases.'

Joan received enthusiastic support from E Gordon Williams, the York-based consultant geriatric physician. 'I fully support your efforts to induce the North Riding to provide some Welfare Accommodation on this side of the County. We find the North Riding quite the worst of the four local authorities with whom we deal on this matter of Welfare Accommodation.'[14]

Joan received backing from Robin Turton MP who in turn obtained a supportive note about a loan sanction from the Minister, Enoch Powell. When she was re-elected to the county council in 1961 Joan was in a position to campaign successfully for the building of an old people's home (and to deal with the mountains of related correspondence concerning sites, access and suitability).

The old people's home in Thirsk is called Cherry Garth, a charming name. Sounding resigned rather than bitter, Joan reflected years later:

> They made sure I never got any credit for this home; they never had an official opening for it because they would have had to ask me. Normally it would have been called after the county councillor for the area but they called it Cherry Garth. But of course it will get lost in history, won't it?, anyway, the main thing is we got the home. It's a lovely home looking right across to the Hambleton Hills.

Keenly conscious of the limitations of her own schooling Joan was committed to improving the education system. She felt rural children had always suffered from educational disadvantage and regarded many village schools as poor places with inadequate premises and equipment. At the conference marking the fiftieth anniversary of the WEA in 1953 Joan had spoken of five and six year old children sitting on benches without backs, their feet not touching the floor. 'The ministry say they are providing places, but if the minister considers a backless bench is a school place, I don't'.[15] She worried that small rural schools did not attract the more able teachers and, indeed, that many of the teachers were older and set in their ways, lacking breadth of vision and new ideas. She also recognised the challenge of teaching children of different ages in the same class. In some village primary schools in the county none of the children had progressed to grammar school.

On the county council Joan was a member of the Education Committee and supported the policy of building new primary schools based in the larger villages and bussing children from the smaller villages. Although this meant the closing of the small one-teacher schools Joan supported the policy, considering it educationally sound. Unhappy about bussing five-year-olds she proposed that every village should have a nursery school for children aged four to six.

As a Socialist Joan advocated comprehensive schooling for eleven year olds and the abolition of fee-paying 'public' schools. Years later it mildly amused her to read political portraits referring to her attending Ampleforth College (the most prestigious boys' Catholic public school in the country); how wrong could you get? For Joan:

> The public schools, so called, should be abolished; they help to perpetuate the class system with a vengeance. They are used to train a privileged class. So long as some rich people can opt out of the state system of education it will remain poor that much longer, for if the rich had to send their children to our state schools, they would quickly do something about improving them.

In a speech to an NUAW branch dinner in March 1966 Joan attacked the head of Ripon Grammar School, Robert Atkinson, for criticising comprehensive education during his school speech day the previous week. She invoked the academic successes of the comprehensive school in Thirsk:

> We do not wish to destroy the grammar school, but to incorporate what is good in it into the comprehensive system. If it is so good, then let us share it among the maximum number of children, not reserve it for the minority... I believe (the parents') real objection is on social grounds, not educational, though they use the educational argument. Many of us are sick of educational privilege. We want to see all children get an equal opportunity.[16]

For the previous fifteen years Joan had been attacking the selection process for eleven-year-olds. She had raised questions about the eleven plus exam. What about children who were 'late developers'? Why were children in private schools allowed to be set homework whereas children in state junior schools were not? What about the disproportionate number of children admitted to state grammar schools who had previously attended private junior schools?

She was acutely aware of the poverty of some children in the area. Lionel Twiss, who taught at Thirsk School, referred to the 'hidden poverty' of many rural children, particularly children of farm workers who lived in tied cottages. From his experience of working in other regions he observed:

> These children were probably the poorest children that you would get anywhere of people who were actually in work. In rural areas it's hidden. For starters there were far fewer of them. I remember one group of children who were going to lose their house because the farmer and the farm worker had fallen out, and they lived in his tied cottage. Where were they were going to go and what was going to happen to them? A few of us in school managed to get some clothing together; they really had no clothing, never mind much food and that really shocked me. I came from a Lancashire mill town in the 1950s where there was little in the way of food and clothing, but here it was hidden poverty for these children, because they were not, if you like, en masse. They were isolated.

Joan respected the director of education of the North Riding, F. Barraclough, 'a damned good fighter for education'. In response to her good wishes on his retirement in 1965 he wrote: 'Thank you very much for your extremely kind letter and good wishes. I have enjoyed working with you and if we didn't always agree on points, we did on the main principle i.e. more for education and much more still to do. I have always genuinely admired not only your courage but your assiduous work for your constituents.'

Joan was an active governor of the Thirsk Bilateral School and with the support of the Thirsk and Malton Labour Party had campaigned for funds for the second part of the school to be built. Several teachers in the original grammar school were incensed that their school was to be incorporated with the secondary modern to form a bilateral (comprehensive) school. In a 'round robin' to school governors, they angrily objected to an advertisement for the new headteacher referring to the bilateral rather than the grammar school:

> The standards set in a grammar school are recognised throughout the country, whereas each modern school sets its own standard and in a large bilateral school with a small 'grammar' stream, this general loosening of standards cannot but have a deleterious effect upon the work of the 'grammar' stream . . .

> Academically the modern stream is likely to suffer as the best teachers would probably be fully occupied in directing the 'grammar' stream. Socially the modern stream would benefit little, as the offices of responsibility among pupils are likely to be filled mainly by 'grammar' stream pupils.[17]

Joan worked for many other issues of concern to people in Thirsk District such as road safety and acquiring Thirsk market place from the squire to transform it from a muddy lorry park into the delightful cobbled square it is today. Joan was widely respected as a councillor who would listen to people and get things done. Thirsk jeweller Charlie Pattison said: 'She is one of the few politicians that I could say I would put my hand in the fire for her honesty. There are very few of those.'

One of the last local government issues she fought was the location of the headquarters of the new Hambleton District Council. Thirsk and Northallerton were the chief contenders:

> But Councillor Joan Maynard, who is heading the fight for Thirsk, said today (8 August 1973) . . . We do intend to make a fight of it. We have always had the mentality that we were prepared to take second place to Northallerton, but this is no longer true . . . If we got the headquarters at Thirsk it would provide many clerical jobs, of which there is a great shortage in the town, and this would also help to push up the level of wages in the district. We feel we have equal rights (with Northallerton) and we are prepared to fight for them.[18]

It appeared at first that Thirsk would succeed, with Joan and her long-time political adversary Peter Consett joining forces. But on 10 September 1973 the Policy and Resources Committee of the interim body for the new Hambleton District Council agreed that in the short term the offices would be located in Northallerton. After several months of committee battling the full district council met on 17 July 1974. An amendment, proposed by Councillor J. R. Bumby and seconded by Councillor V. J. Maynard, that the word 'Thirsk' be substituted for the word 'Northallerton' in the last line of the resolution, was lost on the casting vote of the chairman – a Northallerton-elected councillor. Thirsk had lost out to Northallerton by a single vote.[19]

Joan was elected to the new Hambleton District Council in 1973. The following year, when she was elected to Parliament, she stood down from the council. Unlike MPs who remained in local government she knew too well the time and commitment required to do it justice.[20]

Lionel Twiss said of Joan's return to local government as a parish councillor after she retired from Parliament:

> I think it is a mark of her greatness, having gone from the Parish Council to the Rural District Council to the County Council to be a Member of Parliament that when she retires from being an MP she goes back to the Parish Council. It was a marker, saying I'm back in my community and this is the way I know I can serve people.

SEVEN

The Union

Throughout the 1950s Joan had been developing her formidable qualities – energy, commitment, fearlessness, an ability to acquire and learn skills that would advance her aims – and she was becoming a familiar figure on the national stage as well as in North Yorkshire. Cycling around the dark lanes she could with full justification sing Blake's great poem:

> I will not cease from mental strife,
> Nor shall my sword sleep in my hand.

It must also be acknowledged that a factor in her effectiveness was ingredient 'x'. Joan was tall, black-haired and handsome. She took after Matt. Many people commented on the impact of her physical presence. Frank Allaun remembered her as a very attractive young woman and Tam Dalyell recalled her at the Scarborough conference in 1958: 'As was her wont… a striking jet-black haired Yorkshire lass (no gender balance then) strode to the platform, and with no inhibitions whatsoever harangued us all on the urgent need to nationalise the land – every arable acre of it. This was the perennial delegate from Thirsk and Malton Constituency, Joan Maynard.'[1]

Helen Dunman, the celebrated photographer, said of her:

> The interesting thing about Joan of course was that she was surrounded by men, and it was puzzling to the wives of the men, that sex didn't come into it

> at all. One never thought of Joan stealing one's husband. I was overwhelmed by how beautiful she was; one of the most attractive women I have ever seen; lively, and always a comradely feeling with everyone around. In this very sexy world we live in now, it's a huge aspect of people. But with Joan it never cropped up; it was always politics, great discussion and arguments.

She didn't consciously deploy her sexuality, yet on the conference platforms, in a man's world, there stood behind Joan, in imagination, the historic incendiary women who declared for freedom and justice – Delacroix's Liberty, Rosa Luxemburg, la Apassionara. It was a heady cocktail, though not to everyone's taste. Dalyell noted the look of 'pained impatience' on the face of Gaitskell at the Scarborough conference as Joan took the stand.

She can hardly have been unaware of the impact she made, yet just claims, plainly spoken, were her weapons. However, as she found in local government, you may cleave the enemy from skull to crotch with the sabre of sound argument, and they will smilingly reconstitute themselves without a scar when you don't get the votes – 'when the hands don't go up'.

In the NUAW, the major obstacles were also grounded in accepted practices, but because the general objective was ostensibly shared by all – improvement of the farm workers' lot – the arguments about 'what' and 'how' were more difficult and subtle. The Executive generally took the line that excessive demands would meet with failure and break the negotiating machinery that brought gradual amelioration. In any case the composition of the Agricultural Wages Board ensured that radical demands would never be agreed to. In which case, what strategy could be adopted to further a radical demand? Here it was frequently Joan's comrades who, while agreeing with her objective, took a pragmatic approach to strategy. For Joan the way to a just objective was a straight road. Her temperament, her belief in the ultimate sound judgment of working people, her experience in winning people to the Labour Party, supported her belief. The pragmatists were cautious about the possibilities of organising successful workplace action. Joan recalled Jack Brocklebank's tempering advice, 'Now Joan, don't get too far ahead of the troops, like.'

Alarming news reached the NUAW leadership in July 1958 when Joan, as delegate to the Yorkshire County Committee of the Union, was elected to the influential position of county secretary. Only the previous year the organiser for Dorset, Arthur Jordan, had invited her to lecture on Labour's pension plans to a Union weekend school in Weymouth. She had spoken on this subject at the Labour Party 1957 Annual Conference, excoriating Labour's pension proposals.[2]

Under the NUAW letterhead Jordan had typed: 'I must stress that in order to satisfy the Executive Committee of the NUAW the material must be presented objectively although this does not by any means infer that full and frank discussion should not be encouraged.'

The letter was accompanied by another from his home address, written by hand:

> Dear Joan,
> In case you wonder what the other letter on the headed notepaper is all about I will explain.
>
> 1. Head Office phoned to officially warn me that you are in 'bad odour' at HO. [Head Office]. You have challenged and defeated the President at the York conference.[3]
>
> 2. It is being questioned as to your suitability as a Labour agent since you oppose Conference policy.
>
> I have expressed ignorance of your activities other than your competence to do the lectures required. Head Office asked me to write giving an assurance that you have been clearly briefed as to the 'objectivity' of your lectures. Why do the right wing of the Union and Transport House want to get at you? It is because you are a true socialist and you fight for socialism. Furthermore, you are capable of leading other people behind your ideas, of rallying support for a socialist policy and against the treachery of the right wing. (November 1957)

Although Arthur Jordan used the terms right and left in relation to the NUAW leadership Wilf Page found them unsatisfactory:

> The right, I believe, were quite as sincere as us on the left to get things done. But they didn't have the political theory to get going on it, to give the push. Joan had the push, but she'd got hers from a very emotional standpoint. That's where she got her push from. But they hadn't got that, they were just elected.

They were not right wing, but they were people who'd been working on farms and they liked the leadership of the union. They'd got to a more comfortable number, and weren't going to rock the boat if they could avoid it.

They had to be careful about what they said, because they didn't want to go back to the farm. All the time they were getting their expenses for going to London. Some of them used to do nothing else but committee work; used to go to London to find out if there was any more work they could do and get expenses for it. It's a fact! The left were wanting immediate solutions to a lot of immediate problems which were really not attainable. But you've got to fight for them. They might not be attainable today but you fight them for tomorrow. Whereas the right wing were very much 'well leave it, don't bother about it. It's going to cause problems if you start fighting on this issue; leave it.' They were actually defending the very things we wanted to do away with, the injustices. The Executive was a very conservative force. The countryside is a very conservative force. They represented, really, the countryside. We didn't really represent the countryside, we were in advance – if I may use that term- of the people in the countryside. We got elected because we were saying things that the countryside wanted to be said, but wouldn't think of saying it themselves, or doing anything about it themselves. You really need to have people around you who are prepared to act, whereas they say, 'oh I'll leave it to you Joan, or I'll leave it to you Wilf, you know what you're doing.' There's no doubt those of us on the left drove the Union, made it far more active than it would have been if it had been left to what we called the right wingers. The right wingers didn't want action outside the board room; mind we had good battles *in* the board room.

Bert Hazell, President of the Union (1966–1978) was critical of the Left. He had experienced hardship as a young man and worked his way through the union ranks becoming organiser for Yorkshire and NUAW sponsored Member of Parliament for North Norfolk. When Bert was eight his father, a Norfolk farm worker, volunteered to fight in the First World War. He had barely said farewell to his family when the farmer gave them notice to quit the tied cottage within seven days. As a young man Bert worked as a horseman, beginning work at 6.30 every morning with one holiday a year – Good Friday. In his view:

> When I listen to the left wing of the Labour Party, they haven't a clue what conditions were like. Progress made slowly, steadily and surely throughout years. Sacrifices made by farm workers everywhere. People from the left were not as appreciative of our efforts as those who had lived through the early times. In my opinion the people who fought and won through were the so-called right-wingers of the Executive Committee. They had ups and downs, they knew the Union when it was virtually forced out of existence in the early 1920s but they carried on. The left, with its disquieting propaganda, would never have stood the test, would not have survived in fact. The left, I know, like to put forward they are responsible for building up the organisation. Not true. The left never made the progress they hoped for or contrived to establish, they were always beaten. You have to have those who think, talk extravagantly but at the end of the day, it is the people who do the job who really count.

Suffering was not confined to the right wing. Wilf Page recalled his family's destitution and how he had to share a bed with his grandfather. He awoke one morning to find the old man dead beside him and, to save money, Wilf and his father buried him themselves.

Joan attributed the conservatism of the Union leadership to their reluctance to return to the privation and hardship of farm work:

> They didn't want to conduct the battle, you see, because if they conducted the battle it was going to be hard, and I suppose they get into positions which divorce them from the rank-and-file members of the Union, who had a very poor kind of living really, and they get more aligned with the sort of people they are dealing with every day.

Referring to one Executive Committee member:

> This man eventually got on to the Executive, he was terrible. He came from a bitterly poor background, and I think those people are often the worst when they get into positions because they remember what it was like down there. You see, the Benns of this world don't behave like that because they've never been down there. I find the people who have started from the worst situations

> are the worst people when they get into these positions. They are pretty ruthless in hanging on to their positions because they don't want to go down there again, they know what it is like.

Joan recalled another Union activist, an active lay member who got on to the Executive Committee:

> He became much less progressive as years went by. I was very amazed at that because I used to think a lot about him. People get on the Execs and then that opens possibilities for other positions and possibilities, expenses paid, dinners, trips abroad. I realised that. When I got on the executive of the Union I began to represent the Union at industrial tribunals. In those days they paid something like £18 a day. I mean £18!! I only earned £21 a week, so £18 a day was a tremendous amount to me. I remember thinking I can see how when people get on to certain things you don't want to lose it. And that begins to change people.

Joan's allies on the left were rather proud of their performances at the Union's national Biennial Conferences. With careful planning they frequently defeated the platform. They were not of course without their critics.

Executive member Dennis Hodsdon would observe how Joan and her allies operated at conferences:

> Joan had sycophants; they were round her, at her skirts almost. If Joan said yes, then they all said yes; if Joan said no they said no. There was no discussion among them. At the very beginning, when Joan started to become prominent when she first became the Yorkshire Committee secretary it was very hard to know who was leading who, whether it was Joan leading Jack Brocklebank, the organiser for the area, or Jack Brocklebank leading Joan. But in the end it was very clear Brocklebank was following Joan. It was the beginning of this period in the Labour Movement when it changed from the concept of 'the minority have rights' to 'the minority *are* right'. At conference time you could see it; it was organised that the people round them in their particular areas were all of one mind when it came to the conference. There

> was no discussion; . . . I'm not suggesting that Joan was a Communist, but the tactic was absolutely classic, the tactics of disruption. The activists were always well informed and they knew how to exploit issues.

John Hose remembers how Joan had 'never taken kindly' to him since their first encounter at the Union Biennial Conference in 1956. Delegates had been staying at the Wellington Hotel and at 2.00 a.m. John Hose returned with four other county secretaries carrying crates of beer, the hotel bar having run dry. Joan's frosty words were – he should spend less time on beer and more on Union business. He recalled: 'I was a forestry worker first, and while the business of the day needed to be argued, I was not prepared to sit up in smoky rooms half the night plotting. I thought you argued your case on the floor of the conference, not plotting and scheming outside.'

With the conferences convening only once in two years, despite all the planning and plotting real decisions were made by the Executive Committee.

Joan said:

> We usually managed to defeat the platform, more often than not. It didn't do us much good, we were only there one week in two years, but they were there for the rest of the two years, so they ignored us when they wanted to, rather like the Labour Party. I began to realise that the real power resided in this Executive Committee, not in the lay conference. So I started to stand for the Executive. Over the years I began breathing down the neck of the bloke Robinson who was on.

As Joan's support in Yorkshire grew, Jack Brocklebank began to, 'get hammer from the Executive'. The last thing they wanted was Joan Maynard to be elected on to the Executive Committee of the NUAW. Although she was worried about the pressure on Jack as a full-time employee of the Union, Joan refused to temper her behaviour. Years later she chuckled recalling how

> the Executive Committee hated to be criticised and that was why our organiser Jack was such a thorn in their flesh; either he didn't want to do anything about me or he couldn't. He was having a hell of a time because they were really

putting the pressure on him. They couldn't do anything with me because I was a lay member. They kept telling him to forbid me going to meetings. They never thought that their members could think anything out for themselves. If anything happened in the area it was the organiser who got the blame. In a way it's the same sort of paternalism you get in farming... Jack and I sometimes had deep down arguments at meetings when I'd be trying to persuade the members to oppose a point, sometimes he won, but I won quite a lot of the time. You had to be a strong personality to win against the organiser. He wouldn't have had the problem in relation to me if I hadn't been breathing down the Executive member's neck. That was the bitter end; they didn't want me on the Executive.

Joan faced tough opposition for the Executive Committee seat. Frank Robinson had been the Yorkshire member for 29 years and a member of the Yorkshire County Committee for 26 years. In 1959 Joan polled 2,971 votes against his 7,150; over the next six years she and her supporters campaigned hard at branch meetings and County Conferences; by 1965 the vote was Robinson 6,551 to Joan's 5,738, a majority of 813.[4]

Although she was narrowing the gap, some of her friends worried about her strategy; Charlie Leathwood wrote (15 April 1965):

As far as I can tell your support in the West Riding is as great, if not greater than in previous years . . . If there are any who have changed horses, and they could only be the smaller branches in the main, it is because of your swipes at the establishment in public at such places as County Conferences. The conservative type like to see a united platform and feel that criticism of the Union personalities or policies should be voiced in the committees, and that on no account should there be differences of opinion voiced from the same platform. I may be wrong, but I would not be at all surprised if it is this type of conservative-minded branch secretary in all branches which are your chief stumbling block.

Elections for the Executive Committee were conducted through the branches, not on the floor of the Biennial Conference.[5] Joan always maintained that voting through branches rather than the floor of the conference appeared more democratic, but wasn't:

> I've been to a lot of branch meetings and you've got the ballot paper in front of you and members say, well, I don't know any of these, Joan, do you know any of them? It happens all over the country, so you can't be everywhere, or one of my friends. Who has the power? It's the organiser (appointed by the Executive). He knows all the candidates and so quite innocently members turn to the organiser, 'Jack, do you know any of these people?' Of course the E[xecutive] C[ommittee] were instructing Jack to stop me going to branch meetings, which he couldn't do in any case. Because I was getting close to the Executive member they wanted him to go round saying don't vote for her, vote for Robinson. He wasn't prepared to do that, so that's what nearly got him the sack. But once I was elected vice-president of the Union that took the heat off the Executive member and all the pressure on Jack just faded away.

Naturally, Joan didn't trim her Socialist sails to get elected – not all Union members supported Labour. In June 1959 she wrote to the *Land Worker*:

> Socialism may seem alien to farm workers because of their peasant background and their attachment to the land. All the world over people who work on the land are noted for their conservative point of view...The job of our Union is to obtain the best possible conditions for our members under the present capitalist system, but it should also work to remove that system at the earliest possible moment and replace it with a socialist society.

She received a robust correction in the following month's issue of the *Land Worker* – only this time not from the right. 'The English peasantry has a revolutionary tradition second to none – the 1381 peasant revolts . . . the 1450 uprising . . . the 1549 agrarian revolution . . . we have a great tradition. May we prove worthy of it! (David Nagington, Market Drayton, Shropshire)

*

In 1960 Joan visited East Germany as part of a Union delegation invited by East German farm workers. They went to first to Berlin – seeing the bunker where Hitler committed suicide, and then on to state and cooperative farms, which had mass tractor and implement service centres. Union membership was 100% and pay determined by output. A welder at the service centre did not earn as much as a farm worker – this was wrong, Joan thought, because the farm workers' output depended on machinery being in working order. Large estates had been taken over by the state and good flats were rented by workers for twelve shillings a week. Union contributions were higher than the NUAW but benefits included union holiday resorts for workers and their families at very reduced rates. Joan enjoyed every moment of the visit, except the sea crossings when she was as sick as a dog.

The following year the *Land Worker* referred to the excellent union organisation in Dorset. The county organiser, Arthur Jordan, was a member of the Communist Party, and a Union ally of Joan. Five years previously the *Land Worker* had carried a long article he'd written about effective organisation. Since arriving in Dorset he had inspired and increased the membership and encouraged progressive members like Les Shears and Ted Sales. Dorset farm worker John Fry disapproved of Arthur Jordan addressing him as comrade: 'I thought, brother, fair enough, but he would call me comrade. But he really believed in what he was doing – that he could help his fellow man.'

Jack Dunman, also a Communist Party member and Union activist, had warned Arthur Jordan against saying he was representing the Union when making political speeches or attending political events. But in December 1962 Jordan was summoned to a meeting of the Union Executive Committee in London and given notice to quit.

Dennis Hodsdon, who became assistant general secretary of the NUAW, remembers the period: 'There was a very real fight in the Trade Union Movement to prevent the Communists and hard left taking absolute control. The Electrical Trade Union was controlled by the Communist Party. In America it was gunfights not tactics. You have to see all this in the context of the atmosphere of that time. The majority of the membership did not want that'.[6]

Nevertheless, the Dorset County Committee was outraged at Arthur Jordan's sacking and insisted on meeting the general secretary Harold Collison to get it overturned. In a letter to Joan, Les Shears, County Committee chairman, described the meeting in Dorchester. Eight of the ten Dorset County Committee members had managed to make it through the blizzard that January night. Les had struggled on foot along three miles of country road. In his words:

> Collison went on to attack Arthur for what he called his Communist jargon and his furtherance of Communist aims by telling us the petty things Arthur had written in our monthly bulletin and an article he wrote for the WFTU [World Federation of Trade Unions] about the problems of British farm workers. Things that were small but nevertheless true. Bro[ther] Jordan must not do these things as a Union organiser of the NUAW. In fact Collison admitted that a ring had been put round him some years ago, over which he was not allowed to step. But according to Collison he had from time to time overstepped this ring by his news items in the bulletin, by an article he once wrote in the *Daily Worker*, and now this article in this journal. Honestly, Joan, it was as much as I could do to keep quiet.

He explained to Joan how the Executive Committee justified its decision; if they allowed Arthur Jordan to continue it would show a weakness on their part:

> Then came our turn and Ted [Sales] started off. We had agreed not to argue heatedly, Joan, as we were out to get something more. We wanted to get a delegation to go before the E[xecutive] C[ommittee] and demand Arthur's reinstatement and we reasoned that if we really went to town on Collison we would never get this request. But oh how difficult it was to control oneself. Each member had a go and all spoke up for Arthur. At one stage I nearly went off the rails and told Collison that what Arthur said and wrote was the truth anyway and was it the truth that was hurting him. At this he began to get red in the face and threw up his hands and said, there you are, what's the use of arguing with you.

A deputation of the Dorset Committee travelled to London but the Executive Committee was adamant; Arthur Jordan had been dismissed.

Joan had admired Arthur Jordan and felt the Executive Committee had been trying for years to be rid of him, fearing he would be elected general secretary when the vacancy arose. 'They really were a load of bastards. I never forgot that. What they were doing was against the interests of the members, that's what I couldn't stand; this man was crushed, a wonderful representative of the members. They chopped off our head when they chopped off Arthur; he was a great inspiration to us all.'

When anyone had the temerity to suggest to Joan that Arthur Jordan shouldn't have written the article; she would respond 'Now look, it wouldn't have mattered what happened, sooner or later they were going to get him. They were drawing the circle; that's what they were doing.'

She was worried Arthur Jordan's dismissal would lead to others. On 17 January 1963 Jack Boddy, organiser for West Norfolk, wrote to Joan saying that if successful Jordan's dismissal would be only the first of similar moves to intimidate the more progressive elements of the organisation. He felt under threat himself with both his County Executive Committee member and the vice-president, who lived right on his doorstep, gunning for him; he was living on the edge of a volcano. 'I don't think the powers that be have yet recovered from the effect of discovering me in your company planning the bloody revolution when we held our conference in Harrogate in 1960!'

Joan tried to persuade Arthur Jordan to demand a recall of the Biennial Conference to overturn the Executive Committee's decision – membership of the Communist Party was not a breach of Union rules. He was unwilling, fearing the publicity would prevent him ever getting another job. So adamant and persistent was Joan that Ted Sales and Les Shears had to insist she got off Jordan's back. Joan could be something of a bully with her comrades – even at a 300-mile distance.

Her exacting demands could exasperate her friends. She would petulantly chastise them for ending their letters 'yours sincerely' instead of 'yours fraternally', and would accuse them to their face or in harsh letters of being too fearful to make a necessary stand. Her critisism could provoke furiously indignant responses from her friends.

Fears that Arthur Jordan's dismissal would give the leadership confidence to 'pick off' other radicals were almost realised. Jack Brocklebank attended a meeting of the Yorkshire County Committee in April 1965 where discussion was dominated by resolutions from branches across the county deploring the Rent Bill, which was before Parliament. The York District resolution concluded: 'We wish to place unanimously on record our complete lack of confidence in the N[ational] E[executive] C[ommittee] of the Union and of the General Secretary.' Though the resolution was defeated by the County Committee seven votes to four Joan criticised the Union leadership for selling out to the Labour Government, and Jack Brocklebank reported he'd expressed strong reservations about the legislation to the general secretary. When the Executive Committee got to hear about the County Committee's discussion Jack was accused of speaking contrary to Union policy. The following month, on the eve of the Annual Union Staff Conference in Weston-super-Mare, Somerset, he was summoned to a meeting with the Executive.

Unlike Arthur Jordan, isolated in Dorset, Jack Brocklebank was in the company of fellow organisers; their left-wing vice-chair Jack Boddy accompanied him into the meeting:

> Jack [Brocklebank] was told in no uncertain terms that unless he withdrew his comments then he was going to get the sack. There was half an hour's discussion with the Executive, they were furious. We were in effect dismissed from the meeting and as we walked towards the door the then general secretary said: 'Jack', and pointed to Jack Brocklebank, 'say nothing of what has been said in here.' So as soon as we were outside the door I said, Jack, you keep quiet, that comment was directed at you. It wasn't directed at me. So of course Jack kept quiet as he was told to do and I reported to my colleagues precisely what had happened. And without any discussion really, I said, right, that's it, we're going home, that's the end of the conference.[7]

On 25 June Jack Boddy was able to report to Joan: 'We had quite a successful day on Wednesday insofar as we persuaded the Executive Committee to tear up the agreement which Jack had been pressurised into signing. But despite protestations of goodwill I am still certain that relationships are at an all-time low.'

Joan was convinced the attack on Jack Brocklebank was because she had almost caught up with Frank Robinson in the recent election for a seat on the National Executive Committee. Worse, she was rocking the boat whilst tense negotiations about the tied cottage were taking place between the

Executive Committee and the Labour Government. Tom Gascoyne, Jack Brocklebank and comrades in Norfolk and Dorset devised an alternative strategy for getting Joan on to the Executive Committee: she should stand for the vice-presidency of the Union.

The position of vice-president was first proposed at the 1958 Biennial Conference on the Isle of Wight. For the first time in thirty years illness had prevented President Edwin Gooch from attending. Amidst heated factional exchanges over who should deputise for him the conference threatened to collapse. To prevent the Executive Committee selecting one of their own number to deputise for the president, Joan and her friends argued for a new post of vice-president to be elected by conference delegates.

The post was agreed by the 1960 Biennial Conference and Albert Hilton was elected. Joan challenged him unsuccessfully at the 1964 Biennial. On 2 August 1964 Edwin Gooch died, having been president for 34 years, and the Executive Committee agreed Hilton would serve as acting president until the next Biennial in Weston-super-mare, Somerset. By the 1966 Biennial Conference Hilton, a former MP, had been elevated to the peerage, where he was appointed 'Lord in Waiting'. Mindful of the continued existence of the tied cottage and farm workers' desperately low wages, Joan and her friends would tauntingly chorus, 'What's he waiting for?'

Optimism infused the 1966 Biennial Conference in Weston-super-mare. The Union was celebrating its diamond jubilee and just two months previously Labour had won the General Election with a 98 seat majority, its best since 1945.

Tony Benn, the Post-Master General, spoke to the 155 delegates on the eve of the conference (1 May), substituting for George Brown, Secretary of State for Economic Affairs, who was unable to attend. Joan suspected he couldn't face the farm workers after failing to fully implement the tied cottage pledge he had made to them three years before.

Benn proposed that as an experiment in certain rural areas, post office vans might be converted to minibuses designed for the dual purpose of delivering mail and carrying passengers. He told delegates his department was looking into the possibility of postmen linking with social and welfare services for people living in the most remote rural areas. Joan listened to his ideas with interest but she would much rather have laid into George Brown over the tied cottage.

Hilton had decided not to stand for the presidency because of other responsibilities as a peer of the realm. Bert Hazell, now a Norfolk MP, was elected president. Joan's carefully planned nomination for the vice presidency was vigorously contested by Ted Calver and Andrew Baynham. Calver was a powerful member of the Executive Committee and Baynham, unlike Joan, was employed in farm work – a strong point in his favour and emphasised by his proposer. Joan was nominated by a member of Wilf Page's Norfolk delegation and seconded by her good friend Ted Sales of Dorset.

The result was a resounding victory for Joan (Maynard 48 votes; Calver 32; Baynham 31; Clarke 24; Hanson 20). Scrupulous organisation and lobbying, and optimism about Labour's recent General Election success doubtless contributed to her victory. Jack Brocklebank attributed it to delegates being 'swept up in a streak of idealism and romanticism'. Joan and her supporters were overjoyed – she had captured the coveted seat on the Executive Committee of the Union as well as a national platform. At the close of conference Ted Sales told delegates: 'For the first time, I believe, you have elected a delegate straight from the floor to the platform, in the form of Sister Joan Maynard our new Vice-President. I think she has found it very tough going, being stuck up there this week, instead of being down here.'[8]

Joan's victory made an indelible impression on Wilf Page:

> She suddenly got elected to the leadership, so what does she do; does she now give up this battle against the leadership as she is one? No. She came to the microphone and had a real go about the leadership although she was on the platform. It showed tremendous courage to do that, really. Once you get caught up with the leadership it's very difficult to disentangle yourself. But she knew that her members up in Thirsk wanted to get some issue over and she intended doing it, whether she had been elected vice-president or not. I'd never heard of it happening before; anybody else would say, oh well, now I'm vice-president of course I no longer have the authority to speak on behalf of the rank and file. Not Joan.

Breaking with conventions of platform solidarity Joan didn't mince her words. Criticising the recent legislation on the tied cottage she told delegates: 'I want to deal with the attitude of our Executive Committee in what I call this sordid sell-out of our membership on this issue, because I believe that for too long our Union has hidden behind the Labour Party.' Attacking the general secretary's contribution on the tied cottage debate at the previous Labour Party Annual Conference: 'This is not leadership for our people. If we go on in this way we will never get rid of the tied cottage system.' As vice-president of the Union Joan was invited to speak at County Conferences, branch meetings and rallies across the country. The subjects were principally wages and the tied cottage. Every speech was meticulously researched to ensure the force of her argument couldn't be undermined by flawed information.

On top of her Labour Party agent job and local government work, she found the commitments exhausting. 'It was interesting but hard work, often at weekends after a week's work, and there was a good deal of travelling.'

She was invited to present compensation cheques to members represented by the Union in industrial injury claims. The accident rate on farms was horrific: in the year she was elected vice- president there were 115 fatalities on farms in England and Wales. Joan would never forget presenting a cheque for £11,000 to a member who had lost both legs in a farm accident and how movingly grateful he was to the Union for the tremendous fight it had put up on his behalf.

Farm workers would tell Joan how they would be instructed to use chemicals they knew to be dangerous such as 245-T; how they would be ordered to hide faulty agricultural machinery from the health and safety inspector – it required considerable ingenuity to effect the temporary disappearance of tractors and long trailers. The men felt unable to object; they worked in close proximity to their employer and there was the ever-present fear of eviction from the tied cottage.

Joan loved meeting with older members of the Union in the different counties and hearing their experiences. 'The farm workers are such characters, they are such lovely people who have been exploited so much.' They were 'the salt of the earth'. At County Conferences and branch and district dinners she presented long-service Union badges to members and branch secretaries. After one presentation she warmly praised the recipient's service and Socialism; one of his sons hesitated. 'Well, the trouble is, Dad only ever sees one side of the question.' 'Aye,' said Joan with feeling, 'that's what I like about him.'

*

Joan gave and got a hard time on the Union Executive Committee.

From 1966 the fourteen-strong Executive Committee of the Union met monthly at its new head offices in Headland House, Gray's Inn Road, London. The boardroom was a dark intimidating place with sound-proofed walls. For Joan the meetings were an ordeal. To begin with she joined the others the night before at the Northumberland Hotel, King's Cross. Their cold reception soon decided her to travel from York to London on the sleeper arriving at 7.00 a.m. The Executive met on Thursdays and would continue till lunchtime the following day so Joan could not escape the hostilities of the Northumberland completely. It was such a relief to return home to North Yorkshire to the comfort and commiseration of Jack Brocklebank:

> It was very bad. Nobody talked to you very much and you could feel the atmosphere as soon as you walked into the boardroom. The meetings were rough as well. I was usually in a minority of one. There was one man, Stan Hall from Lincolnshire, he did support me occasionally, but that was all. And then, eventually, we got a lovely old friend of mine from Hampshire, Ted Parry, he was a gem of a Socialist. I can see Ted now walking into the boardroom, coming forward to shake hands and give me a kiss and say, it's lovely to see you, Joan. And I thought, my God, nobody's ever said that in here before, like. And then we got Wilf on and of course that was another ally and eventually we got Jack on – he had resigned as an organiser and I persuaded him to stand for the Executive. I didn't find it easy to persuade him, but I managed it. He only just did it, mind, so that was marvellous. Then there was Ted, Wilf and Jack. We were still in a minority.
>
> It was very unpleasant. Of course they were always passing censure on me for some thing I'd said or done. One of the interesting things they had they

> called a secret minute book. I must say it's never been found. I don't know whether it really ever existed, I suspect it did. They used to record all the occasions they had a go at me or Jack or whoever it was on the left, whether it was an official or a lay member. I've been a member of a number of organisations, but I've never been in one where they've had a secret minute book! [laughs] . . . They hated the sight of me; they were feeding all sorts of lies to the national press about me, people like Woodrow Wyatt. I was also standing for the National Executive of the Labour Party quite a few years before I got on. Of course that brought the national press in, and so they'd start about July, not just against me but against any Socialist who was standing, all sorts of lies about you. It could be quite damaging with the members. I remember one ghastly bloke had a story about me at one Union conference that I'd claimed money I wasn't entitled to. That was just one of all sorts of terrible lies they put about to try to damn you in the eyes of the membership, they'd stop at nothing.

Whereas Bert Hazell politely described Joan as 'very vocal' on the Executive Committee, Wilf Page was more blunt:

> She used to argue like a ruddy tank and upset everybody in the room, especially if it was an attack on the leadership. She'd be howled down and they'd shout at her, well that's a load of rubbish, we don't want that sort of thing. In fact they thought she was a Communist, underground Communist. They used to say, why don't you go to bloody Russia. Joan used to say things to the press, quite rightly, but she used to say things about the leadership and attack the leadership in the press. They'd read it and be up in arms and criticise her for it. She was doing right, sometimes by the wrong tactics. She had made up her own mind and thought this had to be done and went on regardless. She hadn't thought how she'd win some allies. She'd get one or two allies at times, but they'd disappear when she got too sharp.

Dennis Hodsdon certainly observed the sharp side of Joan at conferences. 'I'm not saying the generous warm-hearted side of her didn't exist, but I never saw that side of Joan Maynard. I saw her as cold and calculating; you knew before the issue arose what her reaction would be.'

When Wilf Page was elected to the Executive Committee in 1970 he went into the boardroom and saw Joan's eyes her light up: 'At last there was somebody in there prepared to second some proposal that she had moved. It was a marvellous experience to see her like that. She said to me afterwards, it was wonderful to see you come into the room, at last I've got a friend. It's a terrible situation having thirteen people in there all waiting to get at you.'

*

A fundamental issue of dissent between Joan and the Union leadership was the means of securing decent wages for farm workers. According to the National Board for Prices and Incomes in 1969 farm workers were 'by a fair margin the lowest paid body of workers of significant size in the country'.

An eighteenth-century, paternalistic, centralised system operating behind closed doors, was how Joan and progressive members of the Union regarded the Agricultural Wages Board (AWB). The AWB has remained the mechanism for determining the national minimum wage for farm workers and comprises eight Union representatives, eight farmers' representatives from the National Farmers' Union (NFU) and five independents appointed by the Ministry of Agriculture (which also appoints the chair). The leader of the Agricultural Trade Group within the Transport and General Workers' Union (TGWU), Barry Leathwood, described the wage bargaining as, 'unlike other negotiations; because they are tripartite, it really means that each side of industry has to get the support of the majority of the independent members in order to get their view across. So what happens effectively is we don't negotiate with the NFU, we negotiate with the independent members and that's sometimes difficult'.

For years Joan had listened to Jack Brocklebank reporting the AWB annual wage settlement to disappointed and angry members in North Yorkshire. Even in the 1950s when farming was booming they had received miserable awards of a few shillings. Jack would fulminate about the AWB employer and independent members

> taking us to be a straw sucking lot of clod hoppers. The old story of plenty of fresh air, plenty of sunshine in the summer and autumn, and a lovely job

> working among the snow in the winter seemed fun to these people. Like snow scenes depicted on Christmas cards, they did not know the realities of the workers' lot.[9]

Joan's perception of the independent members mirrored her view of independent local government councillors. Speaking to the October 1967 Conference of North East Yorkshire union branches, she denounced their attitude in recent wage negotiations as, 'how little can we get away with?' She argued that future appointments to the AWB should be equal numbers of trade union and employers' representatives from other industries, a view supported by her political friends.

Joan and her friends were also critical of their own Union representatives on the AWB. According to Wilf Page:

> The right wing, generally speaking, were the people who were having to do the negotiating and they weren't prepared to stick their neck out any further than they had to, and then they'd go through the ritual of having wage negotiations, but they were quite happy to accept the results. It was always 'there's another year yet'. I remember one general secretary saying we'll go back and back and back until we do get it. Well, he knew perfectly well that his superannuation would be along within that time.[10]

In a year when the negotiations resulted in no increase, Joan led the attack on the Executive to get them back to the AWB. 'My God, they were furious. They hated my guts really so they were determined to get rid of me if they could.'

The left wanted the Union negotiators to press for a high stated figure; the negotiators preferred to negotiate for a substantial rise. As Dennis Hodsdon pointed out, with the high stated figure, 'if you don't get it you've failed; Joan was always for a high stated figure'. For Bert Hazell some of the stated figures proposed by the left were 'nonsensical'.

Joan thought securing the future for farm workers depended on conducting a battle on two fronts: one, get rid of the tied cottage; two, increase the wages of farm workers. Neither objective would be achieved without a fight. 'We will never win a decent wage for farm workers by simply putting a good case to the Board.'

She was convinced the only way to win decent wages was through industrial action; no amount of talking would bring improvement, neither would the farm workers' productivity record; arguing with farmers about farm workers' productivity was a waste of time. Her views were echoed by many farm workers, 'When it came to the Board it was the farmers saying we can't afford to pay any more. We've got to live as well at the farm workers, and it's been a bad year. There's a saying in the country, you never see a satisfied farmer or a dead donkey.'[11]

At the 1969 Trades Union Congress, when farm workers' minimum wage was £12. 8s. for a 44-hour-week, Joan told delegates:

> If it were a question of productivity, and on Monday the Prime Minister told us that the real basic reason for getting a wage increase was increasing productivity, then the farm workers' record is second to none. For farm workers have increased production by some 6% a year in recent years, which is over double the rate which has been applicable in industry.

She went on to attack Barbara Castle's White Paper *In Place of Strife* and concluded to thunderous applause. 'I say to the Prime Minister: it is not productivity that gets you an increase in wages – it is organised might in the kind of society we live in.' Calling for a special conference on low pay she proposed it be called 'In Place of Poverty'. In November 1969 the Union organised a huge rally in London in support of a minimum wage of £16 for a 40 hour week. Three thousand farm workers marched past Parliament to Trafalgar Square.

President Bert Hazell warned that farm workers were taking the most radical of steps – by quitting the land for higher paid jobs in industry. Other speakers doubted farm workers would follow the example of the dustmen, firemen, miners and other low-paid workers by striking in support of their demand. Joan exhorted the demonstrators to be in the vanguard of the low pay revolt, not in the rear; if productivity was the key to high wages they'd be at the top of the table.

When the AWB met on 9 January 1970 to confirm its decision (£13.3s. for a 43-hour week) a bus full of Yorkshire farm workers, supported by Joan, headed to London in an unofficial protest to confront AWB members. To their disgust Board chairman A. L. Armitage refused to meet them. The *Land Worker* reported frustration leading to scuffles with the security guards. The farming correspondent of the *Yorkshire Times* (16 January 1970) wrote:

> It is now clear that the time-honoured sensible and just methods for solving farming differences are now in danger of being thrown overboard . . . Agriculture would have been well advised to have kept clear of this outrageous spate of militancy. It is not uplifting to read that a Union of Yorkshire farm workers thought fit to take a 'decomposing chicken' to London for presentation to the chairman of the Agricultural Wages Board.

Poor Frank Robinson, recuperating from a heart attack sustained the previous March, 'nearly shot through the roof when he read about the smelly chicken incident. He thought it was totally disgraceful and did more harm than good.'[12]

Joan was at pains to point out the Board chairman had not been given a decomposing chicken: it was a chicken skeleton with a message attached, 'We have had the bones for too long, you can have them for a change. We want some meat.'

The 1970s had opened for the National Union of Agricultural and Allied Workers (NUAAW) with a new general secretary, Reg Bottini, elected in December 1969 to succeed Lord Collison. Bottini had been head of the Wages Department and had narrowly defeated Dennis Hodsdon, the assistant general secretary, thanks to the campaigning of Joan and her friends. They had seen Hodsdon as the brains behind the dismissal of Arthur Jordan and were out to get him; in Joan's eyes Jordan was 'the best organiser we ever had'. In the election for the general secretary she voted for the candidate least likely to win, Edgar Pill. Whilst determined to block Dennis Hodsdon, whose formidable abilities she recognised, she couldn't bear to vote for Reg Bottini. She couldn't stand him and the feeling was mutual.

Jack Brocklebank's position had changed significantly by 1970. He had resigned as union organiser because his recent appointment as deputy chairman of the newly established Northern Pennines Rural Development

Board was a salaried post. Frank Robinson had retired as Executive Committee member on health grounds and Joan had directed all her persuasive powers towards Jack to stand for the Executive Committee. He was very reluctant, but she finally succeeded.

Reg Bottini and Joan held opposing views about achieving wage increases for farm workers. He considered it utterly impracticable for farm workers, distributed among several thousand employers, to down tools and take industrial action such as picketing docks to prevent food imports. For selective strike action on farms to be in any way effective, it would need to take place on the large employing units, yet the larger holdings paid the best wages. 'I say these things not for defeatist reasons but because in the long run we should get nowhere unless we can maintain our reputation as a credible organisation.'[13] Joan saw Bottini's approach as reinforcing passivity, 'Our people need encouragement. Members would do nothing if they were told nothing could be achieved.'

She considered an all-out strike to be unrealistic; hardly surprising given that 'in England and Wales, of the 116,000 holdings employing regular full-time workers over 90% employed fewer than five people.'[14] Joan could not support Bert Hazell's conclusion that pay and working conditions had improved substantially over many years through discussion and negotiation and that his was the most effective approach. Her strategy was for farm workers, through the Union, to take selective strike action. The areas chosen should be where the Union was strongest, in Yorkshire, Lincolnshire, Norfolk and Essex, and a particular product would be targeted. The pea harvest would be especially vulnerable as cut peas had to be in the processing factory within ninety minutes; another target might be sugar beet. A one-day token strike throughout the country would send 'an electric shock to the farmers'; another option could be a ban on overtime, especially at seedtime and harvest. Without the use of industrial muscle she felt farm workers would be forever condemned to low wages. Such action would require 'ground work with our people' by setting up action committees in every county. She called for a coordinated response from related workers – from production to distribution. 'We will get damn all from farmers unless we are prepared to give 'em a belt up the bracket.'

Writing in the *Socialist Worker* (29 August 1970) she acknowledged the difficulties:

> The farm workers feel a special loyalty to the land. Even the most loyal trade unionist would see his loyalty stretched in some circumstances, say, a demonstration fixed for a weekend in September which fell on a fine Saturday following a couple of weeks of rain. You can only farm with the weather; you can't farm against it.

Recognising farm workers' sense of responsibility for the welfare of the animals in their care, 'no one is suggesting that we don't milk the cows - that would be cruel and a non-starter for our people.[15]

John Hose was scathing about her calls for strike action; it was an easy option for Joan to call for a strike since she herself was not employed in the industry. He couldn't envisage, say, tanker drivers putting their own jobs on the line in support of farm workers' pay disputes; like Bottini and Hazell he was all for negotiation. 'It's easier to get people out than to get them back. You've got to sit down and talk and negotiate. It's dead easy to sound militant and make speeches.' His reading of the history of farm workers' strike action in the 1920s had taught him 'you eventually have to sit down and negotiate'.

A long-standing point of dispute between Joan and Jack Brocklebank was the concept of a wages structure whereby the more skilled farm workers would earn higher wages. Jack was a founder member of the British Socialist Agriculture Society (founded in 1947), which favoured increased pay for more highly skilled farm workers. Joan's position developed from early discussions with Tom Gascoyne, who would always insist the Union should concern itself with 'getting the basic rate right, before thinking about super-structures. One does not start building a house until one gets the foundation right.' However, Jack Brocklebank and the Union Executive saw a wages structure as an avenue of progress for farm workers, a means of rewarding their skills. Minutes of the Northallerton Branch record:

> Joan said this structure was coming from top level, but it was us who worked the machines and manned the industry, and we could still oppose a wages

> structure if we did not want one. We were not forced to have it as we were into having to accept the 47 hour week having failed to get a shorter week. On these points a lively discussion began.[16]

Believing wages structures to be divisive, Joan had spoken against them at Biennial Conferences during the 1950s and 1960s; there should be no plus rates until the basic rate was commensurate with other industries. When the introduction of plus rates appeared inevitable, she would argue that the job should be graded, not the individual worker.

Although Joan failed to win over the membership on the wages structure issue, she did eventually succeed with Jack Brocklebank, possibly because by 1971 he was no longer a paid official of the Union. In January of that year the *Land Worker* reported:

> Both Vice-President Joan Maynard and E[xecutive] C[ommittee] Member Jack Brocklebank attacked present proposals for a farm wages structure at the North and East Yorkshire Conference. Joan objected to proficiency tests, especially for older workers, Jack said that this was the biggest departure in the agricultural wages field since 1924. The Union could afford to wait another two years to get the structure right before it was introduced. More work could be done in improving the minimum rate. Stan Hayward (Head Office) had put some positive points in favour of the structure. He estimated that after November 1 1971, on the basis of the 10% premium on over-time alone farm workers could benefit by more than £2 million a year from the January adjustment. He said that inevitably some would benefit more than others. No one will be worse off (a point disputed by Jack). Above all a wages structure combined with the Training Board's schemes would at least offer reasonable career prospects for the new entrant. There were some heated exchanges between Jack and the Editor (Stan Hayward) evidently enjoyed by the 180 or so delegates present.

Members were attracted by the idea of a wages structure, seeing it as a means of progression and betterment. It came into effect in 1972.[17] But in Joan's opinion, 'you just split the cake up differently and the people on the basic will suffer'.

The month preceding the 1972 Biennial Conference Joan's unbridled attack on the Union leadership was published in the bulletin of the Institute for Workers' Control:

> Our leaders have recently been going the round of ministers in London in relation to the freeze appealing for justice for farm workers, or a measure of justice. 'Please lift the freeze on farm workers, it is unjust to freeze the wages of such low paid, highly skilled workers with a tremendous production record'. Where have we ever got by going round with a begging bowl? Nowhere! We have steadily over the years been losing the wages battle. A successful selective strike would do more good than years of talking.[18]

Her public attacks outraged the leadership. They were also very worried about the Union's finances. A way forward suggested itself.

In his statement to members (the *Land Worker* January 1972) the general secretary Reg Bottini drew attention to the Union's increasing financial difficulties:

> We have come through a year of unprecedented inflation in which the cost of all the services upon which the Union relies has risen sharply. One has only to bear in mind the extent to which postal and telephone charges, printing and stationery costs, fares and petrol and insurance etc. have increased to recognise the burden falling upon our Union, dependent as we are on long distance travel and communication . . . In the circumstances and taking into account future likely increases in costs, the E[xecutive] C[ommittee] will be asking the Biennial Conference for an increase in Union contributions. That increase will be vital for the future of the Union.

In the *Land Worker* the following month he hammered the message home, 'we must balance the books'.

Joan was opposed to raising members' Union contributions; she advocated getting rid of paid recruitment officers. The general secretary would produce figures pointing to the efficiency of recruitment officers in increasing Union membership and covering their own costs, but Joan was not persuaded. She was committed to the voluntary principle and to Union officers and the leadership inspiring farm workers to join:

> The Union was getting into financial difficulties and the Executive decided, I thought wrongly, to appoint paid people, to recruit in the Union, whereas my view was that if we, the Executive, did our job properly it would enthuse the lay people who had always done the recruitment in the past. And of course recruitment officers would be very expensive, you'd have to recruit a tremendous number of members to pay for their salaries. They could only recruit in the evenings and weekends, they couldn't recruit in the day. So here was this campaign, which I was leading, to say we shouldn't have these people, we should make them redundant because they were bringing us to ruin. And I was succeeding in this.
>
> They saw that as an opportunity which – typical of me, like – I was concentrating on what I was doing. I didn't see the danger which might be coming to myself. They said, right, if we need to cut back we'll cut back on the vice-presidency.

The axe fell at the 1972 Biennial Conference in Weymouth.[19]

In moving the motion to abolish the post of vice-president Andrew Baynham, a delegate from Worcestershire, was at pains to point out that it was not a 'personal issue' and, indeed, that efforts should be made to get Joan into Parliament to represent the Union. Since Bert Hazell's defeat in the 1970 General Election the Union had no representation in the Commons.

Supporters of the motion emphasised the need to cut costs at the top of the organisation; members shouldn't be approached again to increase Union contributions. John Hose, who had crossed swords with Joan about recruitment officers, spoke in support of the motion – it had originated from his county of Nottinghamshire.

Though angry and worried, Ted Sales calmly kept to the figures and reminded delegates how, as a lay member of the Executive, Joan cost the Union next to nothing. Beyond expenses, she was not paid for her many speaking engagements and commitments. Also supporting Joan was a delegate from Buckinghamshire: 'We have a lady vice-president and a lot of you are against that because you feel a lady's place is in the home washing the dishes. That is one of the troubles.'

Demands for a card vote were rejected and after a show of hands the motion was carried by 50 to 37 votes, though not everyone had voted. Following an ignominious debate about whether Joan could now remain on the platform or, indeed, at the conference, it was agreed she should, though John Hose advised against 'bending the rules' to let her stay; several delegates then claimed there had been a miscount and the motion had in fact been lost. Wilf Page and Jack Dunman demanded another vote. President Bert Hazell refused. For Joan, 'it was the worst blow I ever had, because the Union meant more to me than anything else; it was the saddest moment in my career. In my life'.

Wilf Page's verdict on the whole business was:

> As vice-president she went to different county conferences to speak on behalf of the Union. She'd get her expenses to get there, probably overnight accommodation and some subsistence. If the national officer went, he got his travel allowance, he'd get his wages for the Saturday – he'd get double time for working on a Saturday and probably treble time for working on a Sunday; it was a terrific bill plus subsistence and so on. So she was really saving money, but they used that as the excuse, they couldn't find another excuse and we were at that stage very worried about finances. They didn't want her as vice-president, she was having far more influence than they wanted her to have.

Wilf Page's fears had been realised; some years previously he had written to Joan: 'Whilst I admire your courage, we must always remember that courage is not enough. We must at all time consider tactics and always try to avoid uniting our opponents . . . It would be a disaster to give the right wing the opportunity to remove you from office.'

John Hose has refuted the notion that abolishing the post of vice-president was a means to remove Joan's power base; like other Executive Committee members he insisted the move was purely financial. He said he was 'never a political animal', but in future years he and Joan would be opponents for the post of president of the Union and John Hose would be the victor by eight votes.[20]

After the conference, Joan consulted delegates round the country (driven in his car by the ever loyal Bert Waind). She secured forty-five signatures from delegates confirming they had voted for her; yet as she ruefully observed, 'it wasn't possible to see everyone, they were all over the flipping country'. Perhaps Joan was naïve; some of her friends have commented how two-faced delegates could be, giving their support to her in person but voting against her.

Friends advised her to consult solicitors about the legality of the conference decision. The solicitors advised she had a strong case to ask for a recall of the Biennial Conference as Rule 14 stated: 'In cases of dispute the President shall order a further vote.' After much anxiety and fraught correspondence with friends, she decided against it. She could not afford to bring the case, and recalling the conference would greatly deplete Union funds, which would be used against her.

On 16 January 1973 Joan wrote to her solicitors, Gaster & Co: 'I have been consulting with my various comrades throughout the country about the Vice-Presidency. They are scattered and they have taken so long to make up their minds. I now write today that I have decided to drop the matter following refusal of legal aid.'

A few months previously, at the 1972 Labour Party Annual Conference, Joan was elected to the National Executive of the Labour Party, but she was unable to share the jubilation of her friends and comrades. Demoralised and suffering from shingles she wrote to Ted Sales on Christmas Eve 1972: 'Winning the seat on the Labour Party National Executive Committee has been some compensation, but nothing can really compensate for what happened at the Biennial and I'm afraid my heart aches on that account.'

EIGHT

Into the national arena

'A Pearl Harbour Election' was the press portrayal of NEC election results at the Labour Party 1972 Annual Conference in Blackpool. Nominated in previous years for the five-member Women's Section of the NEC, Joan had been runner-up in 1971. Now she had ousted the popular moderate and former Minister Baroness White. It was a remarkable achievement. Unlike the Trade Union Section of the NEC, with its high-ranking union officials, almost invariably those elected to the Women's and Constituency Sections were current or former MPs. Some ten years later when David Blunkett was elected to the Constituency Section, 'it was the first time for 35 years since the departure of Harold Laski that one of these places had been taken by someone who had never been an MP' (McSmith 1983, p. 158). Joan's success was of similar magnitude.

She was now a well-known figure in the Labour movement:

> My base was my own Union and the Thirsk and Malton constituency. As vice-president I had led the Union delegation at the TUC and was also speaking at the TUC. That's how the two big unions got to realise what my politics were. I was usually the delegate from Thirsk and Malton so I was often speaking at Labour Party conferences as well. These were the two platforms I had which were crucial; that was how I got known publicly, nationally.

Remembering the outcome of the 1972 NEC election, Joan said:

> it was quite nerve-wracking really, particularly if you were on the left because it was always a bit of a struggle. If you were an established right-winger you could be confident because there were so many votes particularly in the trade unions. If you were standing in the Constituency Section you needed to be on the left because the constituencies voted left at that time.

Being voted on to the Women's Section was something of a lottery. Also as Dennis Skinner has pointed out, 'it's a bit of a misnomer, because it was mainly the male trade union leaders who carried the block votes in their pockets'.

Recalling later NEC elections, Joan described how Joyce Gould, head of the Organising Department:

> would come round and discreetly tell you if you'd lost so you knew before they announced it publicly. And Dennis Skinner was always on tenterhooks about my position. I used to say, now look, Dennis, I've done my best, I've done what I thought was right and that's it, I can't do any more. He used to say to me, has Joyce Gould had a word with you, knowing that was the kiss of death.

Joan polled 2,974,000 votes, just 105,000 more than Eirene White – a narrow margin:

> I think you needed around 3 million to get you on so you needed the two big unions which I had at the time because they were moving to the left, the TGWU and the Engineering Union. You had to pick up every single small left-wing union as well and then the maximum vote in the Constituency Section. What eventually put me on was NUPE switching from somebody else to me. I think they had about 600,000 and that did the trick.

This time she had the backing of her own Union, 'My Union were quite glad to unload me on the Labour Party NEC, anything to get me out of their hair, so they got to be quite good, they used to just plump for me, they didn't vote for anybody else and that just saved the day really.'

Conference delegates in Blackpool attributed Joan's success to her blistering speech on the Monday afternoon. To loud applause she moved a resolution on land nationalisation demanding Labour's next manifesto include a pledge to bring all land under public ownership. The resolution was overwhelmingly carried on a show of hands.

Seeing her NEC success as a clear indication of a leftward shift by the unions, Joan told the *Morning Star* of Saturday 7 October 1972:

> This year some major progressive unions, like the TGWU and the AUEW, [Amalgamated Union of Engineering Workers], continued to vote for me, but what is new, they also refused to vote for some of the sitting right wingers as well... My vote went up by over 100,000 and one of the interesting things is that people I never met before came up to me to say that they would be supporting me. As far as being on the NEC along with so many right-wingers is concerned, I know I will enjoy being an NEC member inasmuch as I will be able to argue for progressive policies. These include fighting against any kind of incomes policy under capitalism, pressing for equal pay and opportunity for women, and putting the farm workers' point of view, in particular an end to the tied cottage system. I will continue to work for the party to adopt Socialist policies as quickly as possible. I have never believed in consensus politics. We must refuse to continue with the so-called mixed economy which enables the private enterprise to milk the public sector...Working people must take land into public ownership, along the lines of the successful resolution I moved at the party conference in Blackpool earlier this week...The Labour Party must take over the banks and end the subsidies of multinational companies in Britain; the 300 largest corporations should be nationalised right away. It is important for our Trade Union Movement to cooperate with those in other countries to curb the power of multinationals. Incomes policy under capitalism does not help the low paid...I'm not very happy about the Labour Party and the TUC planning an incomes policy. It is a bad mistake for the TUC to be discussing the same thing now with the Tory Government and the CBI [Confederation of British Industry]. Tories want to clamp down on wages to help ease Britain into the Common Market. I think there should be closer relations between the Labour Party and the unions. In my area (Thirsk and Malton) my Union plays a big part in the Constituency Party of which I am agent. In the trades councils we are striving for closer cooperation between the branches of different unions in order to strengthen the fight on such things as

> the cut in school milk and the Tory rent-raising Act. In the coming week we are holding two rent protest meetings. A combination of Labour-controlled councils, tenants and the Trade Union Movement can smash the Housing Finance Act. This will not be done by talking at Westminster, but by a combination of Socialists working in parliament and workers in action outside, in the factories, on the farms, or wherever they are. We have had too many leaders in the Labour movement who show a lack of confidence in the working people, and yet confidence in the people is the touchstone of a genuine Socialist. We've got to find a way of making the Parliamentary Labour Party respond to the decisions of the Party conference. This is one of the major problems we on the Left have to solve, and I shall pursue this policy on the NEC. We must see that conference policies are carried out...Unions can play a bigger part in the constituency selection committees for local and parliamentary candidates. Those constituencies with MPs who consistently vote against conference decisions on major issues should select different candidates. A major issue is the Common Market. I think it is very important that the Party has now decided to consult the people over remaining in the Market.

Letters and telegrams of congratulation greeted Joan's arrival home:

> It came as a wonderful surprise to me although your sterling record of struggle for the underdog and socialism more than qualifies you for this position. Your courage and integrity will amply fortify you for further struggles ahead. It will give me and my progressive colleagues added strength in the knowledge that one of our comrades occupies a seat of influence and will be readily accessible when assistance is required.
> Richard Donaldson
> Secretary of the York & District Trades Council 6 October 1972.

The leftward shift of Labour's NEC was mirrored by a shift to the right of the Parliamentary Party. Joan shuddered remembering the Parliamentary Labour Party (PLP)'s November Shadow Cabinet elections – Shirley Williams and Reg Prentice topped the poll.[1] Within a decade Shirley Williams, as a member of the 'Gang of Four', would form the breakaway Social Democratic Party, and Reg Prentice, deselected by his Newham

Constituency Party, would join the Tories. 'We can see from this disposition of the various forces all the ingredients were there for a struggle of unilateralist and Clause 4 proportions.' (Hatfield 1978, p. 192)

Joan of course was up to the struggle. Audrey Wise remembered their conversation during the Blackpool conference; Audrey had recently been selected as Labour's Parliamentary Candidate for Coventry South West:

> We had this little jokey conversation, except it was oh so serious in a way. It was a pact that I would keep an eye on her on the NEC and she should keep an eye on me in Parliament, to make sure we both stayed on the straight and narrow. Because so many lose, or leave behind, or throw away the principles they had before they got whatever office it is, and Joan and I were both determined not to do that. We made this little pact, I keep an eye on you and you keep an eye on me. In the event I don't think either of us found it necessary.

Joan's election to the NEC prompted the question, 'well, why don't you stand for Parliament?' She was reluctant, preferring to concentrate on fighting Bert Hazell for the Union presidency in 1974. But she was becoming increasingly concerned about the extent of her responsibilities; she was a nationally known figure in her Union and active member of the Labour Party NEC; locally she was a parish and rural district councillor, contesting county council elections, sitting as a magistrate and working as Labour Party agent across one of the largest constituencies in the country. She thought:

> I'm going to end up doing nothing properly, I'll have to make a decision about what I'm going to do. Am I going to continue here locally or am I going to move more into the national arena. I thought I may have made the maximum contribution I can here – I'd been agent for 21 years – so I decided I would have a go.

It would be a challenge of epic proportions. If elected she would join the tiny band of working-class women who had left school at fourteen and made it to Westminster. Friends in the Union were encouraging; since Bert Hazell had lost his Norfolk seat in 1970 there was no NUAAW sponsored Member of

Parliament. The farm workers' interests needed a champion in Westminster. There was a job to be done – getting rid of the tied cottage system.

She tried for the Chester-le-Street nomination but it went to Giles Radice, head of the Research Department at the General and Municipal Workers' Union. As she recalled:

> I never had a look in there really because of the GMB [General and Municipal Boilermakers Union] . . . Andrew Cunningham was tremendously powerful in the north-east: he was chairman of everything almost, including the police committee and God knows what, and a councillor, but he was also very prominent in the GMB union, so they packed the meeting with GMB people and got the seat for Giles Radice, who was very right-wing. At that time Cunningham was on the NEC and I was on it; I must have got to a meeting a bit early because when I got into the boardroom the only person who had arrived was this Cunningham fellow. So he says, you didn't succeed then at Chester-le-Street. I said, well no, you saw to that didn't you? I thought I might as well let him know I knew.

This was not sour grapes on Joan's part. A letter about Andrew Cunningham to the Labour Party's national agent was copied to the NEC Liaison Committee of the PLP:

> This party boss was allowed to spread his power by nominating allies for key positions in Local Government and public life, was allowed to hold chairmanships such as the Durham County Council, Northern Regional Council, Police Authority, Regional Secretaryship of the General and Municipal Workers Union, thereby controlling the selection of Parliamentary candidates, and one must not forget his membership of the National Executive of the Labour Party till 1973. Mr Justice Waller at his trial commented on what to me was, and is, the most disturbing aspect of his involvement in this sordid case. 'You exercised your power ruthlessly.'[2]

Another unsuccessful attempt was made at Newcastle East. Joan's reluctance to move to the constituency, if elected, was held against her and she was up against a popular local candidate. Friends of Joan wrote to her afterwards:

> Please don't think that you let us down in anyway here. The only ones to let themselves down were the Newcastle East GMC [General Management Committee] . . . The main factor which destroyed your chances was the lack of union delegates at the meeting. I am confident that you will find a constituency with a Socialist majority on its GMC, and then you will be selected. On Socialist grounds your speech could not be faulted and your knowledge of Socialist policy, experience of practical Socialism and heartfelt belief in everything you said shone through like a beacon. My only possible advice to you in the future is never stop saying what you believe; and soon you will find a constituency with enough sense to realise when it has the chance to choose a real Socialist.

Joan was approached informally by Lincoln[3] but declined on the advice of friends, 'They said, I don't think I'd get involved in it Joan; it will be nasty.' She didn't, of course, know a far dirtier fight awaited her.

By early autumn 1974 everyone was expecting Wilson to call another election. It seemed Joan's last opportunity to win a nomination would be High Peak, a constituency bordering Sheffield. The agent was keen for her to contest the seat believing she would stand a good chance. 'The constituency had a mixture of smallish industry and agriculture of course, sort of sheep and dairy farming – a good tie-up with my interests and he also liked my politics.' But it was a marginal seat, Joan thought Labour had only held it once. The vacancy arose because the Labour candidate, Peter Jackson, had stood down at the last moment.

Because High Peak appeared the last chance for aspirant Labour MPs, it attracted an uncommonly large field. One of the hopefuls was the journalist Chris Mullin. Although he did not appeal to the selectors – not least because he got completely lost in the remote countryside around Snake Pass going to the second of the evening's selection meetings – he certainly appealed to Joan. 'It was Chris I took a fancy to. I thought now there's a good chap.'

Chris Mullin retains vivid memories of his first encounter with Joan. Whilst driving his Citroën 2CV up the M1 in bucketing rain, the wind blew the soft roof off the car:

> I really arrived in no condition to make much of an impression . . . I met this lovely woman Joan, who would have then been in her mid-fifties. She was

> already a member of the National Executive so to that extent I knew of her. We chatted away and got on very well, finding ourselves agreeing about all sorts of things while we were waiting for our turn to go in. I assumed she'd get it because she was already a well-known and popular figure.

Joan failed to secure the nomination and she was very despondent. She had originally planned to spend a relaxing week with her niece Anne Hepburn and family in Hertfordshire; instead of the rest she badly needed, she had found herself 'galloping up and down the M1 from Anne's to High Peak and feeling it was all a complete waste of effort'. The TUC was about to commence its conference in Brighton and she was exhausted.

As Chris Mullin oberved, had Joan got the High Peak nomination, 'we probably wouldn't have heard much more about her. The irony is that had she been selected for High Peak it would have remained Tory by a wide margin and she would never have got into Parliament because I think she was 53 or 54 years old and it, frankly, was probably her last chance'.

Arriving in Brighton for the TUC Conference Joan was told by a member of her Union delegation that Richard Caborn, an AUEW delegate, had a message for her. Unsure where Caborn was staying that night she sought him out the following morning. She was stunned when he asked if she would be interested in standing for Sheffield Brightside. She couldn't imagine anyone *not* being interested; the only thing she knew about Brightside was its reputation as one of Labour's safest seats with an unassailable 20,000 majority. But why, she wanted to know, wouldn't a local person be standing? Caborn explained they would be getting rid of their sitting MP Eddie Griffiths and had decided nobody in the area should stand, to prevent him claiming the real reason they wanted rid of him was to secure the seat for a local person. Ever practical, Joan pointed out they hadn't yet got rid of Griffiths; Caborn assured her it would happen the following Friday night. Joan was to keep in touch with Jock Sturrock, who would move that she be on the selection shortlist.

Eddie Griffiths had been elected MP for Sheffield Brightside in the by-election of 1968 occasioned by the sudden death of Richard (Dick) Winterbottom. He had worked as an industrial chemist at the Shotton steel works on the coke ovens before being appointed as a worker–director of the nationalised British Steel Corporation. The link with steel and sponsorship from the Iron and Steel Trades Confederation had attracted many at the Brightside selection conference.

Dick Winterbottom, and his wife Lillian, had moved from Oldham to live in Brightside, where they were held in great affection and respect. Winterbottom had fought tenaciously and selflessly for jobs in the steel industry and was always available and willing to discuss constituents' problems. Eddie Griffiths, who lived across the Pennines in north Wales, promised the selectors he would move to Sheffield within six months. He won the selection by 26 votes to 25 but failed to honour his promise.

Complaints about Eddie Griffiths mounted – he was inaccessible, he rarely spoke in Parliament, he didn't consult with his local Party, he criticised extra-Parliamentary action against Conservative policies and he was right-wing. The Brightside Party decided to remove him, but it was going to be tough as the old rules applied for the deselection of MPs. About a year before the deselection, Jock Sturrock offered to play devil's advocate to the Brightside Management Committee: 'Let me be Griffiths for five minutes and I'll answer your case. So I did this and they realised that everything they could put up to him, he could give an answer. I said, I should leave him because he is going to really put his foot in it and sure enough, it was only two or three months later he went to Ipswich.' By today's political standards Eddie Griffiths's date in Ipswich in April 1974 would be entirely unremarkable, but for Griffiths it proved to be his nemesis.

He was a lay preacher and had gone to Ipswich to preach in the United Reformed Church where the minister was a family friend. Sheffield United was playing Ipswich on the Saturday and the Conservative MP Ernie Money invited Eddie Griffiths to make a weekend of it. Dressed in dinner jackets Griffiths and Money went to a Junior Chamber of Trade dinner. Reports of the weekend were relayed to Brightside – Eddie Griffiths was consorting with the enemy.

The Brightside Management Committee met in June and warned that his behaviour was unacceptable. The following month the Executive voted 19–1 for him to step down and this decision was confirmed a week later by the Management Committee.

Eddie Griffiths portrayed himself as victim of an extremists' coup. Patrick Seyd quotes his complaint to the Sheffield press. 'The Brightside

Party's thinking seems to be that unless you have a cloth cap, a muffler and a boiler-suit, you are not fit to be a Labour MP.' (Seyd 1987, p. 60)

Brightside Party activists Bill and Joan Eddison described the process and pressures of trying to deselect him; there were no precedents in Sheffield to guide them:

> Everything within the party structure was to stop you deselecting. It was such a massive struggle to actually unseat him because we were fighting the National Executive, we were fighting the Regional Executive. The Executive in the region never let us alone as they were coming down every week; they were calling us to meetings, you didn't have any life of you own. We'd had over a year long trying to remove him. (Joan Eddison)
>
> But we did have a good secretary at that time, Clive Betts. He went into every little detail so that he knew we were bang on the right course all the way through. (Bill Eddison)
>
> He'd just come up from Cambridge University. We'd got into this mess which was never ending and we said, we don't know what we are going to do. And he just took it in hand. He was only young; really enthusiastic about Labour and he saw to everything. I honestly believe that without Clive Betts we wouldn't have gone ahead with it because nobody could have been so structured about it all. He knew every move that they would make next and he knew the rule book; it was absolutely unbelievable, because he kept saying to us, 'now then, you'll receive another paper from me.' We'd no means of typing, everything that came through was handwritten. I don't know how he did it; there was no area that Clive Betts missed. He would say, so-and-so will say something about so-and-so, and if we respond to that we'll be absolutely slaughtered. (Joan Eddison)

Ensuring the procedures were correct was crucial; any irregularity could be used by the NEC's Organisation Committee to uphold an appeal by Eddie Griffiths.

The delegate from Sheffield Brightside, Peter Price, told the 1974 Labour Party Annual Conference:

> It is not an experience I would like to recommend to any of you here. It is a very lengthy drawn-out procedure, one which leaves the Management

> Committee to come under extreme fire and stress from the press and people. Dirt is thrown around, people are accused, you cannot walk down the streets without people accusing you of being Marxists, International Socialists; everything is thrown at you . . . [Yet] I put it to you that it is the duty of your constituencies, the duty they have to the electorate, to put up a man in whom they have full confidence. There is nothing worse than a local party putting up a man who has lost their confidence. (Panitch and Leys 1997, p. 141)

By September 1974 members of the Brightside Management Committee were desperate to be rid of Griffiths; it was clear another General Election was imminent. Griffiths was 45 years old and if they didn't do it now he might hang on for a further twenty to thirty years. The General Management Committee vote, confirming a formal resolution for him to step down at the next general election, was an overwhelming 40–10.

The press continued to support Eddie Griffiths, provoking Lillian Mosley to write:

> At last, thanks to Mr Martin Flannery, a voice of protest has been raised against the biased support of Mr Eddie Griffiths, by the media, especially the 'Star' . . . the dismissal of Mr Griffiths was conducted in a democratic manner under the unbiased surveillance of the Regional Organiser Mr Sims. The conduct of the Chairman, Coun[cillor] Roger Barton and the secretary Mr Clive Betts is to be commended for the dignity and restraint in which the meetings were conducted.

In the *Morning Telegraph* (28 August 1974) Jonathan Foster concluded: 'Some political scientists see events such as those in Sheffield as proof of the numbering of the days for MPs who regard constituency parties as faithful shadows of whatever political stance they care to adopt.'

Neither Bill nor Joan Eddison had heard of Joan in September 1974:

> Richard Caborn had been to a conference with the AUEU Union. He said I saw this smashing woman, absolutely great. We were all saying, who is she? We were all talking in the kitchen of the Labour Hall and he said I think we ought to go for her. He talked about Joan and what she had been like, and how she'd put herself across at this speech . . . One or two people didn't really want Joan

> because she was a woman. They'd never heard her speak or talked to her about anything so they didn't know anything other than she was a woman. There were one or two men in the party who definitely didn't want to have her because she was a woman.

There had never been a woman MP in Sheffield: only four women Parliamentary candidates had ever been selected in the city's history. Brightside didn't have a Women's Section, believing, like Joan, gender to be subsumed by class. However, Joan was the second woman politician to be approached by Richard Caborn.

Audrey Wise recalled:

> They were wanting to get rid of their Member of Parliament and they asked me if I was interested in being put forward. I represented a very marginal seat, Coventry South West. It was early September and Richard Caborn asked if I would like to change constituencies. I said, no I didn't think I could do that, because I would be letting down the constituency I represented – I mean, everybody knew there was going to be another election. I said I couldn't, because if I was the sort of person who would ditch my constituency because of a better offer, I wouldn't really be the sort of person they should have. So I said no. I said, the person you want to contact is Joan Maynard and I know exactly where she'll be at the moment, she'll be at the TUC. I always feel a sort of proprietary interest in the fact that she became the MP for Sheffield Brightside.[4]

According to Joan:

> The real person behind approaching me was Richard Caborn's father, George Caborn, who was the district secretary of the AUEU in that area and a member of the Communist Party, and that's how he knew me, did George, and through my work on the NEC. George was a much better Socialist than Richard will ever be. I'm sure his Dad would turn in his grave if he knew the positions that Richard takes up nowadays.

Joan didn't know Sheffield, having only ever passed through on the train.

On the evening of the Brightside selection conference, 18 September 1974, Richard Caborn met her at Sheffield station:

> He said, I'll give you a quick run round the city in the car, but won't take you to the meeting, I'll take you back to the station and you can get a taxi. He didn't want to be seen to be doing too much influencing, you see. So I took this taxi from the station and gave the address of Firth Park Labour Hall. I could see it was in a working-class area and if it wasn't the right place they wouldn't have any more taxis, so I said, hang on a minute till I make sure I've got the right place.

Women waiting outside the hall assured her she had.

There had been over 200 applications to the Brightside selectors. Three of those shortlisted for the selection conference were local councillors but Joan had been assured they posed no threat. Peter Jackson was the front-runner. He had been MP for High Peak from 1966 to 1970, and had become well known in Brightside, Labour's fifth safest seat. He enjoyed considerable support among Sheffield city councillors.

Joan recalled:

> There were certain people, I found out subsequently, who were quite keen supporters of his, quite understandably, in the constituency. They'd often gone from Brightside and canvassed for him because he would need the help, they wouldn't need any help in Brightside. High Peak was a pretty rural constituency – they said it was like canvassing on the North Face of the Eiger.

The Monday prior to the selection conference Jock Sturrock attended a Group Meeting of South Yorkshire County Council. Sitting next to him was Alderman Mrs Sheard. 'I understand you are having a selection conference next weekend. Well, I honestly and truly hope, Mr Sturrock, you will pick someone who remembers where they come from, not some people who are apparently trying to make their case in Brightside.' Jock Sturrock assumed she was referring to Peter Jackson. She responded: 'Well, I didn't mention the name but you might find it interesting if you went and found the *New*

Statesman' for the period when he was in office.' Jock Sturrock was amazed 'She was a really intellectual personality, a wonderful, quiet woman. I considered her a right snooty person, a Charlotte Brontë type'.

Until that evening Joan's supporters had nothing on Peter Jackson.

Together with Bett Sturrock and their son, who had worked part-time in the library, Jock Sturrock ploughed through back copies of the *New Statesman* at the central library in Sheffield. Sturrock liked the bit in the article where it said 'Mr Peter Jackson, who is of the Left but not on the Left'. At work the next morning Jock Sturrock showed photocopies to George Caborn, whose response was, 'this is beautiful, it's absolutely gorgeous'. Peter Jackson's supporters in Sheffield were horrified.

Firth Park Labour Hall was small. Apart from a kitchen at one end and an office, there were no adjoining rooms for the candidates to await their turn so they sat in vehicles outside. Fortunately it was a fine evening.

As always, Joan was well prepared. Audrey Wise had helped write her CV for the selection and Joan was confident her politics

> fitted those of Brightside like a glove. Nothing was dug up to throw at me at the selection because at that time the constituency very much shared my politics – very, very much. One of the questions I've never forgotten was from a lovely comrade who asked, did I think incomes policies were helpful to workers in relation to getting better wages? I said I certainly did *not* think they were. I thought they were just the opposite. I realised the significance. It's the sort of question as a Socialist I would have asked, I'd have wanted to know where they stood.

She was asked if she would be willing to live in the constituency. She would – she had learned from her Newcastle East experience and knew Eddie Griffiths's refusal to move for so long had been held against him. Brightside remembered the ever-open door of their much-loved veteran MP Dick Winterbottom. 'They thought it was more important than I did. I think it was a psychological thing really, because living in the constituency doesn't make you a better MP. I suppose that psychologically people feel you're closer to them and their problems and environment; you can understand that approach.'

Jock Sturrock refrained from questioning any of the candidates until it was Peter Jackson's turn to speak:

> I brag about it because I've never had an opportunity like it in my life. I had the papers all ready, and his last words in his statement were, if anyone wishes to question my stewardship as a Member of Parliament . . . I let a couple of questions through and then I put my hand up. Mr Jackson, that statement you made about the stewardship of your membership as an MP, did you really mean that we could question that? Oh yes sir, certainly sir. So I said, well can you explain this, and I started reading the article. He stuttered and muttered and somebody else got up and asked a question, then somebody else got up and said, now about this matter with the Liberals, and about five got up and they all went for him.

The AUEW certainly had it all worked out. Peter Jackson's credibility had to be destroyed to prevent a split vote – when Eddie Griffiths had been selected in 1968 it was by a majority of just one vote. After the meeting some expressed deep misgivings about Peter Jackson's harsh treatment: 'Why did they have to destroy him like that?'

Joan got the nomination with a resounding overall majority on the first ballot and Firth Park Labour Hall rang to the singing of 'The Red Flag'. The result was: Joan Maynard 38 votes; Peter Jackson 8; Peter Horton 5; David Blunkett 2; and Roy Thwaites 2.

Joan was almost overwhelmed. The chance to contest a seat like Brightside with its 20,000 majority was rarely enjoyed by people on the left, especially women; the chance would be even more rare if, like Joan, they'd never previously contested a General Election. After the selection Joan went to Jock and Bett Sturrock's house to phone Jack Brocklebank and her brother Rowie. 'Jock Sturrock wasn't a man who talked a lot – until he got to know you pretty well. I remember he wasn't saying much, he was just going round dishing out these drinks in his house.' Jock had a lot on his mind; that very day Harold Wilson had called the General Election for 10 October – less than a month to get Joan known by the Brightside electorate.

The next week Richard Caborn, union convenor at the factory where Jock Sturrock worked, negotiated with management to get him three weeks' leave of absence to take over from Roger Barton as Joan's agent, a position he would occupy for the next thirteen years.

The Sheffield media declared war on Joan the day after the selection conference. One paper carried a photograph of her taken some eight years previously by a local newspaper in the front room of Lansbury House. Under the headline 'Lenin looks down on the new Labour Candidate for Brightside' Joan was pictured standing before her picture of Lenin. She recalled:

> I had stood innocently where they asked me on the mat in front of the mantlepiece and they'd included my picture of Lenin as well as me in the photograph. They tried all the way through the election to smear me with that tack. And of course the Communist Party, which was quite powerful in Sheffield at that time, in a way made it worse because they didn't put anybody up. They'd always stood for that seat you see. Because I was standing they decided not to put anybody up; they'd fought every election since the war. I was so close to them you couldn't tell any difference really, so that didn't help. The local people were worried, which I could understand. I was worried myself. There seemed to be a new scare story every day. So the menfolk were always trying to calm down the womenfolk, who were getting more and more agitated, like. It was a very tough time, they were worried that this campaign against my politics would prove a disaster.

The choice of Joan as Brightside's candidate confirmed Eddie Griffiths's decision to stand as Independent Labour. He was convinced large numbers of 'moderate' supporters would flock to his support. Joan and her campaign team had not anticipated this; she couldn't believe he was entitled to use the term Independent Labour.

Though the election was a four-cornered contest, with the Liberals and Conservatives putting up candidates, in reality it was a fight between Joan and Eddie Griffiths. It was a dirty fight. Joan's campaign team tried to play down the issue of Griffiths's sacking to protect her from, 'the political mud which flew from both sides during the campaign to out him. But it is clear that both Mr Griffiths and the Conservative candidate will make this the centre of their campaign'.[5] Joan said: 'We were lucky we had a 20,000 majority to share between us if it had been a 2,000 majority I'd have lost.'

Polly Maynard
(née Richardson), Joan's
'Grandma Maynard',
c. 1934.

Matt and Effie Maynard
(Joan's parents) at Post Office
Farm, Thornton-le-Street,
1951.

Edric Maynard,
c. 1946

School photograph of Ampleforth Church of England School, c. 1933. Joan is standing on the far left in the second row of girls. Her elder brother Edric is in the first row of standing boys to the left of the lamp post.

A VOTE FOR JOAN MAYNARD IS A VOTE FOR PROGRESS.

North Riding County Council Election.

Electoral Division of Thirsk.

VOTE BETWEEN

8 a.m. - 9 p.m.

ON TUESDAY, 5th April, 1955,

FOR

JOAN MAYNARD, J.P.

YOUR LABOUR CANDIDATE.

It takes only a few minutes to vote. Where possible a car will call.

If you need a car please ring Thirsk 2355.

IF YOU LIVE IN :

THIRSK vote at the Church of England School, The Green.

SOWERBY vote at the Church of England School, Sowerby.

CARLTON MINIOTT vote at Carlton Miniott School.

Joan Maynard, Labour Party candidate, North Riding County Council, 1955.

Above: Jack Brocklebank, NUAW organiser and Chairman of Thirsk and Malton Divisional Labour Party.

Left: Jack Bowen at the NUAW Biennial Conference at Great Yarmouth, 1956.

Below: Dorset NUAW County Committee deputation to Downing Street against the tied cottage. From left to right: Jess Waterman (EC member), Les Shears (County Chairman), Jess Lovell (District Committee member)

Clockwise from top left: Joan with agent Jock Sturrock; with Dennis Skinner at the House of Commons; with (left to right) Richard Caborn, Fenner Brockway, Bob Cryer and Martin Flannery; and with Sheffield councillor David Blunkett

Joan with a TUC delegation to North Vietnam, September 1970. On her left is Clive Jenkins.

Joan addressing a public meeting on Northern Ireland organised jointly by the Troops Out Movement and the British Peace Committee, November 1974.

Joan speaking at an Anti-Informer Delegation meeting, February 1984.

Joan meeting relatives of the Birmingham Six at the House of Commons, June 1984.

Joan at the Burston Rally. *Clockwise from top*: addressing the rally in front of the banner reading 'Burston Strike School – The Longest Strike in History' (1985); applauding Tony Benn (1986); with Rodney Bickerstaffe (1988); with Bill Morris and Peter Medhurst (1995).

Joan with Frank Hooley and Martin Flannery leading an Anti-Racism demonstration in Sheffield, December 1977.

Joan with Jo Richardson MP and Margaret Beckett MP outside HM Prison Holloway. Joan was a member of the Howard League for Penal Reform.

Eddie Griffiths portrayed himself as a staunch member of the Labour Party who supported 'sensible policies' in Labour's election manifesto. His fight was with the local Labour Party, which had betrayed him: 'My battle is with the local constituency party not the Government. I want to save Labour from the kind of political vandals we have in Brightside.'[6]

He claimed eighteen Labour MPs had sent him messages of support, and Labour councillors in Sheffield had raised money for his campaign funds. When challenged by the chair of the Brightside Party, Councillor Roger Barton, he refused to name anyone.

The Eddisons recalled: 'People were split on the estates. They said, we're not going to vote for her, she's a Communist. They put it out that she was a Communist. We'd say, just come and hear her, hear what she's like, listen to her and you'll know. She was so sincere, she never talked patronisingly to anybody.'

True to character, Joan fought on issues, not personalities; she couldn't base her campaign on local issues because she didn't know the area. Instead, she focused on the state of the economy arguing that nationalisation was the key to controlling prices, wages and inflation. She emphasised her desire to get Britain out of the Common Market, 'I hope the people of Brightside will give a resounding NO to the Common Market'.

Her election address included a warm endorsement from MPs in Sheffield and the surrounding areas:

> Dear Joan
>
> Congratulations on being elected as the official Labour Party candidate for Brightside. We are certain you will become Sheffield's first woman MP and be a welcome addition to our ranks. Your long experience and reputation as a 'BONNY FIGHTER' for the underdog will be invaluable in Brightside and we look forward to a long and happy relationship. Signed Peter Hardy, Brian O'Malley, Eric Varley, Dennis Skinner, Tom Swain, Joe Ashton, Frank Hooley, Martin Flannery, Dick Kelly, Fred Mulley, Pat Duffy.

Joan was very encouraged by the support from Labour MPs: 'The right-wingers in the area, even Merlyn Rees, came to speak for me, not a single one opted out. Merlyn Rees's body guards were a bit disconcerting.'

Eddie Griffiths accused Brightside Labour Party of 'importing speakers whose politics they despised, to support Miss Maynard. Mr Pat Duffy, Labour candidate at Sheffield Attercliffe and Mr Fred Mulley, Transport Minister and candidate at Park would not normally be allowed within five miles of Brightside,' he said. 'They are politically respectable and moderate voices in the Labour Party – the Brightside Party probably hates them more than it hates me.'

Joan was delighted with the support from the 'ordinary people – all the wonderful helpers. A lot of miners came to help me, and all the Skinner boys, and a lot of money was donated to the constituency. Messages of support were pinned to the walls of the Labour Hall'. Farm workers and other members of Thirsk and Malton Labour Party came down to Brightside to canvass for Joan during weekends; one stayed for two weeks. The contrast between the two constituencies could hardly have been greater. The industrial working-class Brightside had been Labour since 1935 and most of the 60,000 council houses on the north side of Sheffield fell within its boundaries. Rural Thirsk and Malton constituency was a bastion of Tory domination. After the election the farm workers were invited to see what work was like in a factory; the shop stewards committee at Firth Brown organised the visit and lunch in the canteen. The verdict of the farm workers was 'I couldn't work in there – all that noise and dirt and being cramped in'.

On the eve of the General Election Joan's campaign team offered silent thanks for a letter published in Sheffield's *Star* newspaper (9 October 1974). R.P. O'Brien, of Topcliffe Road, Thirsk, a former resident of Sheffield, had moved to Thirsk three years previously. 'I am appalled to hear of any attempt to represent Miss Joan Maynard to the voters of Brightside as an extremist and generally dangerous woman.' He referred to Joan topping the poll for years in local elections,

> standing openly and honestly for Labour in one of the most conservative of areas… they vote for her because they trust her to speak her mind, to work for everyone regardless of views or natures and to be absolutely incorruptible. Not bad qualities in a prospective MP these days. People also respect her for a lifetime's work for Labour and the unions in an area where it took, and still sometimes takes, real courage to speak and act for Labour. If being open,

> honest, trustworthy and brave, and if hating injustice and being in basic agreement with Keir Hardie, Lansbury and Bevan are what people mean by being extremist, they should say so and let the voters of Brightside make a fair choice.

Concerned that electors would be confused – Eddie Griffiths was styled as 'Independent' Labour and Joan as 'Official' and Griffiths's name came first – Joan's campaign team had her name printed on tickets to distribute at every polling station throughout election day. Next to Joan's name was a cross.

Polling day proved eventful for Joan's agent, Jock Sturrock. In the morning Eddie Griffiths made an official complaint that Joan's team was issuing bogus election cards. Around 11.00 a.m. an election officer, accompanied by four police officers, came to see Jock Sturrock in the Labour Hall. 'I said, that's not an election card, there's no other candidates on it. He said, I know that and you know that, but it's my official job to come and tell you he has complained. I said, well bloody good luck to him. He said, alright, and went.'

In the afternoon a canvasser rushed into the Labour Hall complaining that Jock Sturrock wasn't answering the phone they had installed for the day:

> I said it's not ringing. He said, well, I've been trying to ring you. I picked up the phone and couldn't get through. I said, go down to the phone box, ring the engineers and tell them there's a problem on this line and can they do something about it. In a couple of minutes the phone rings – engineers. I said, I'm in the middle of a bloody election and I haven't got a phone! He came back in five minutes and says, you've been what we call in a technical term 'hung up'. Somebody who knew what they were doing had remembered that in the outskirts of Sheffield there were some old telephone boxes with coins and buttons; there were only a few of them left. Someone had gone to one of these phones, dialled our number, put in their threepence, pressed button A, got through and just left the phone. So nobody else could get through. The engineer said, it's alright, we've traced it; leave it to me. I'll guarantee you, mate, nobody'll do that to you the rest of the day, I'll have a man sit and watch this number. It was only because it was a Labour candidate.

Around 7.00 p.m. a coach arrived with miners sent across by Arthur Scargill – Joan had given firm backing to the miners' strike. Jock Sturrock remembers: 'They were big lads – "come to help you out, mate" – so we gave them jobs.' A message came in from Sowerby Green School that Griffiths's people were threatening Joan's people who were distributing the tickets with the cross next to her name. Two miners were sent round:

> There were two young people with Joan's tickets and the miners said, alright, let us have these, you two go and stand over there. Then this car drew up with Griffiths stickers on it and two louts got out and came swaggering over. These two miners walked up to them clutching the tickets and kept walking nearer and nearer. These two jumped back in their car and were off. Good South Yorkshire diplomatic technique.

Joan Eddison described the night of the count in Sheffield Town Hall:

> Joan was so cool and calm about everything. I walked into this room where the count was taking place and I couldn't believe it because there was this pile of votes for Eddie Griffiths and a pile for Joan. To me they were nearly level. I went back down the corridor and Joan was sat in this chair further down the corridor and I just started crying. I said to Joan, oh we're going to lose it; we're losing. Because he had told so many lies and a lot of muck stirring. And she just laughed at me, Joan. She was so calm, she said, we're not, we're winning. I said, how can we be winning if he's got all these votes. She said, I'm used to this, I'm telling you now that we're winning. So I found some of the others who were upset and said, we're winning! Joan says we're winning! We went out into the street, all of a sudden we heard this really big shout, I don't know who it was, but it were absolutely unbelievable the shout, 'We've won! We've won!' You couldn't believe it unless you were there. We were so used to winning heavily, we never bothered to take any notice. We'd never been as near as that. We just danced on the tables, I'm not kidding. Mind you, we'd had a few which you weren't supposed to, drinking whisky in the town hall toilets. But Joan, I've never known anybody like it. Whether she were calm inside I don't know, but she was dead calm. Oh, don't get worried about it, she said, Oh I don't want you to get worried like that.[7]

Rowie was in Brightside's Firth Park Labour Hall when the result came through. He thought the hall was going to erupt; well, it did. Like Joan, Jock Sturrock was confident she would win the seat; nevertheless, when he reached the Labour Hall, the tough Glaswegian couldn't speak. A young lad asked: 'What's the matter with you, Jock, look at everybody celebrating and you're just stood there saying nothing. I looked at him and said, I fear opening my mouth I may burst into tears.'

Joan would always remember: 'The Brightside people said to me that night, now you won't forget the farm workers, will you, when you get down here. I think it was a wonderful thing coming from an absolutely industrial constituency. There was no fear that I would, like. There was that feeling in me that they were both workers and that was the thread or bond. I thought I must try hard and not neglect the workers in Sheffield, there was no question in my mind that I wouldn't remember the farm workers.'

Messages of congratulation poured into the Labour Hall. Audrey Wise sent a brief 'Congrats, but could you ring about your meeting in Coventry. It's important'. Joan laughed. 'That's typically Audrey, never mind all this messing about!'

Friends from Sheriff Hutton, York wrote (13 October 1974): 'Hearty congratulations on your splendid win. How proud your father would have been today to know of your untiring work for the cause he had at heart (perhaps he does). You will now come to new problems and responsibilities, but you will be more than equal to them.'

Joan treasured Jack Bowen's message: 'You'll excuse me using Union paper but I would have had to write if it had been nought but a paper pound. Don't forget you can get drunk on success. I'm sure I can trust our Joan not to do that.'

After the election, farm workers from North Yorkshire joined all Joan's other supporters at a party in Brightside's Labour Hall. A huge red banner was held aloft and they sang 'The Red Flag' till they were hoarse; it was as if they had taken a Tory stronghold.

NINE

Not our place – the House of Commons

'Politically, remember it's not our place, it is not geared for our benefit. All its traditions are alien to working class people. It could be made our place, it could be made to work for us, but so far we have never had a Parliamentary Labour Party, as a majority, prepared to make the House of Commons work more democratically and in the interests of working class people.'[1]

In Joan's view the operation of Parliamentary processes led inexorably to a dilution of Socialist policy:

> My experience is that whatever goes into the Queen's Speech is less good than what is in the manifesto. Then what is in the Queen's Speech has to be translated into legislation, so that means that civil servants get their hands on it, and they are not Socialists! By the time the legislation, the Bills, arrive on the floor of the House of Commons it may well look even less like the manifesto. What I'm saying is, all the way through the system, their system waters it down, it works for them not for our people. Political power resides in the Commons, but real power, economic powers, still reside in the hands of those who own land, money and what's left of the commanding heights of our industry. When a Labour Government is in power the economic power outside Parliament exerts control, and has always done so.

She saw Parliament as a hot-house of privilege divorced from the realities of life.

> You could soon get delusions of grandeur, in fact some members do! I feel it is very important to keep a sense of the right kind of humility, and to always appreciate that when you are a Labour MP you are very privileged to have been chosen by workers as their standard bearer. I often used to think when I saw MPs strutting around in the Commons that the important thing to remember is the working people. Not only are most decisions taken behind Parliament's back, I would say quite a few are taken behind the Cabinet's back, via a small group of people.

*

Joan agreed with Ann Taylor's assessment of becoming a MP 'no one tells you anything until you get it wrong'. Although Joan knew her way around the public areas of the House of Commons through numerous meetings of NEC committees over the previous two years, she still found it a bewildering place when she took her seat, 'I'd been to lots of county council meetings and lots of political meetings and on the National Executive of the Union and the National Executive of the Labour Party, but I'd never been to a place where things were so different.' Although in 1974 there was no induction for newly elected MPs, Joan was able to rely on friends who were members, 'so they – as far as they could – and as far as they could remember what they should tell people, helped me a lot'. Audrey Wise secured Joan a desk and a telephone. She enquired whether Joan had been to the post office – there were two in the House, one in the central lobby for the general public and one in the members' lobby. 'I said to her, well no, why would I go to the post office? She said, I think there'll be some mail. And when I got there, there was a tremendous amount of letters stacked up for me.'

Several doors were marked Members Only; friends said: 'Now be careful about that, Joan, because a lot of those are men's toilets.'

The whip system was unknown to Joan:

> There was this question being asked, have you got the whip? And I said, no, I haven't had the whip. But of course I had had it, but I didn't realise what it was. There was nothing at the top of it which said, this is the whip. You just get this thing which gives you the next week's business and underneath the

> lines – if it's one thick black line it's a one line whip, two if it's two, and three if it's a three-liner. One means you can please yourself, two means you can pair, three means it's an instruction to be present. So of course when they explained it to me I said, oh, I've had one of those.

Dennis Skinner explained to Joan how it wasn't like working in a pit or factory, 'you don't clock on and clock off'. Joan singled out Dennis Skinner as the best example of championing the workers' case on the floor of the House. The only issue on which they disagreed was the matter of pairing 'Dennis didn't agree with pairing, you see. Well I did. I thought you could usually do more good outside the House than you could do in there. So I did have a pair and I did pair. But Dennis never pairs, you see. He calls it organised truancy'. Joan's pair, Ivan Lawrence (Conservative MP for Burton), obviously had an appreciation of her warmth and good humour; he would send her mischievously lascivious notes; underneath a hand-drawn plump red heart he wrote, 'Would you care to pair. After 10pm every night this week?'

Joan remembered: 'Tony Benn advised me "Knowing your politics, Joan, I think you should sit below the bench. You see, if you sit immediately behind the front bench that means you are a firm supporter of either the Government or the Opposition, depending". And Tony said, "the other thing I would advise you is to always try to sit in the same place so that the Speaker knows where to look". So that's what I tried to do, of course.'

Parliament was not televised in the 1970s and so it came as a complete surprise to Joan, after losing the 1979 General Election, that the parties moved to the other side of the chamber. 'I thought that was a funny feeling when you've got used to sitting in one place; you've got your mind orientated that way and suddenly you were shoved over to the other side. Of course, we had plenty of experience of sitting on the other side, unfortunately.'

*

During the week, Joan lodged with Mollie Prendergast in a flat in St John's Wood. This 'temporary arrangement' was to continue throughout Joan's thirteen years as an MP. Joan had known Mollie Prendergast since the 1950s and had been a frequent visitor with friends when in London on Union business and CND rallies. It was a great relief for Joan to arrive at Mollie's, have tea and wash her feet after the Aldermaston marches before the long coach journey home to North Yorkshire.

As a young woman in the 1920s Mollie Prendergast came to London from the Lake District to be a domestic servant for the Rothschilds. 'It was like being in the cloisters; you went out one half day a week and every other Sunday half day. It's a terrible thing to say, but the war was a liberator really. We did things we thought we'd never be able to do. We were given the opportunities of doing things.' Mollie joined the St John Ambulance Brigade and on free evenings attended classes in English and typing. After the war she took a clerical job with an insurance company and later she was appointed to similar work with the civil service. She had also married and become a member of the Communist Party. Inspired by the Trafalgar Square meetings addressed by Haldane and Russell, she attended classes in political economy run by the Communist Party. The theoretical ideas chimed with her own experience and family history – her father's father owned no land and had no vote, neither of course did any of the women, but her mother's father had two votes because of the two pieces of land he owned.

Mollie Prendergast's niece Audrey ran a pub in South Kilvington, near Thirsk, where Joan had been elected to the rural district council in 1952. Whilst canvassing during local elections Joan had called into the pub and was amazed to see in the kitchen a pile of *Daily Workers*. Audrey explained how her aunt in London, Mollie Prendergast, would forward them to her – 'she's always trying to make me as left as she can'. On Mollie's next visit to South Kilvington Audrey took her to a meeting Joan had organised at Lansbury House; to Mollie's astonishment she recognised the speaker – Bert Ramelson, Communist Party district organizer 'It was a bit of a dangerous thing to do. It's a wonder she wasn't thrown out.'

When Joan was elected to Parliament she immediately telephoned Mollie; she needed somewhere to stay in London and she needed a secretary. Mollie, recently widowed after the death of her second husband, had retired from the civil service in 1968 aged sixty and was committed to campaigning in the pensioners' and tenants' movements, but she agreed to help Joan out. She asked whether her being a Communist would be a problem and Joan reassured her. 'She said I needn't worry about it. I never got mixed up with her politics. I was more left, I didn't want to embarrass Joan at all. I was a Communist and I didn't want to embarrass Joan because the Labour Party is quite sensitive about that sort of thing. So I didn't get involved in the House.'

Mollie wasn't intimidated working in the House of Commons; through her recent experience in campaigning, she was used to meeting MPs and preparing lobbies. But she remembered the House of Commons being 'a terrible place to work'. There were very few offices for the MPs:

> There used to be a place down in the Archives, I used to call them, and there were little places almost like broom cupboards and we could go in there and Joan would dictate, or we could sit outside in a sort of big corridor and she would dictate. That's what we had to do. I used to bring it home and type it because there was just nowhere to have a typewriter.

Every morning Joan and Mollie collected the mail from the post office. Joan was assiduous, replying informatively and politely even to the many insulting letters. But on one occasion:

> There was a man who was always writing scathing letters – negative – never anything positive and very rude. One morning Joan wasn't feeling very well and she really tore a strip; she was quite entitled to because I was getting fed up with him too! I could see she was very annoyed, and it wasn't Joan. So anyway off she went. The next day she said, you know Mollie, I was a bit worried about that letter to the man, I was a bit too rude really. I said, well don't worry, you didn't send it. I'd done it as I knew she would when she had been all right. But he didn't deserve it, you know.

Mollie's flat was a haven for Joan:

> Joan wasn't a town girl, she didn't like London. I think really she was frightened of it. She must have got the wrong idea about it. I once managed one morning to get her to go to the National Gallery, which is on the way to the

> House. It was an exhibition of Turner, who she liked very much. She hadn't a lot of time, she had to go to the House in the morning, because there was nearly always a meeting of some kind, and she'd be there till late at night, sometimes the early hours of the morning. Sometimes she'd go up to Sheffield on a Thursday evening, the latest would be Friday morning. She had to go to Sheffield to her surgery and for her meetings.

Most nights Joan would be met at the underground station by Mollie and her little dog. Joan and Mollie slept in adjoining rooms, 'we'd be listening to the radio and used to shout at each other through the door. When somebody like a politician was speaking we'd both roar out at the same time and call them what we thought about them. It was really very funny'.

After two-and-a-half years Mollie persuaded Joan that she now needed to concentrate on her own political activity with the tenants' and pensioners' movements. Joan approached Olive Cartwright, whom she knew through Bernard Cartwright, a member of the farm workers' Union in North Yorkshire. Reluctantly Olive was unable to accept; it would mean giving up her pensionable job in Yorkshire; at the time there was no pension scheme for MPs' secretaries.

Joan appointed another secretary, but their working relationship proved unsatisfactory and Joan was relieved when she handed in her notice after a year. The experience determined her to choose as her secretary Marian Neville, a highly organised and trusted friend.[2] Joan and Marian worked as a team throughout the rest of Joan's time as an MP; 'Brightside had two MPs after Marian began working for me'. Joan relied very much on Marian's research abilities and those of her husband Richard. But she considered British MPs to be generally badly served compared with American politicians. She'd learned during visits to her sister Elsie how members of the House of Representatives each had several members of staff; 'mind, you've got to be fair and say they were representing little over a quarter of a million people whereas we were representing thousands. But even proportionally we had nothing like them. Unless you've got that kind of back-up you can't possibly keep tabs on the Executive. When you think of all the civil servants *they've* got!'

In Sheffield, Joan was equally well supported by her agent Jock Sturrock.

Immediately after her election he organised a Sunday morning meeting with all the Brightside councillors to brief Joan about local issues. He was a councillor of many years' experience and his strategy was that constituency concerns raised with Joan should, as much as possible, be addressed by local councillors. Issues would be dealt with more quickly, and because Jock would forward them to the councillor who was coming up next for election it raised their profile. He took on many of the cases himself, calling on his extensive range of long-established contacts. He was a firm believer in personal contact and arranged for Joan to meet all the key local authority people. You could get things done more effectively when you were on first-name terms, when you could just pick up the phone.

Jock Sturrock always accompanied Joan to her twice-monthly Saturday surgeries in Brightside. He felt protective towards her, but was also concerned about her being taken in:

> She's a very soft touch for the sob story. An instance was when a bloke came in one day and told us a real story about compensation that was due to him from the local authority; some business that he had had to pack up. How he was in dire straits because he had been waiting all this time for this compensation and could she do anything about it. Fair enough, but the case he was putting was so heartrending. When he walked out she said, oh my goodness! I said, Joan, why don't you open your eyes, didn't you look at that bloke? You were sat there, he had a sports jacket, flannels and brown brogues, a Van Heusen shirt and a nice silk tie. I says, to start with, the clothes he was wearing were about three weeks' my wages. I says, and didn't you look at his hands? He had a gold bloody Rolex, two gold rings on this one hand with a bloody diamond. I says he's more stuff on his hands than I've got in the whole of my capital. That's why I used to sit in with her because sometimes she'd have got herself tied up in right knots with some of them. Joan's tough on principles but if somebody comes to her with a sad tale, you'd have to watch her; the heart sometimes takes over. It's a good thing for the heart to take over from the head, but it's better for them to work together.

If Joan was unable to get to Brightside because of an NEC or Union commitment elsewhere in the country, Jock Sturrock would take the surgery. He had an arrangement with Marian Neville that he would make rough notes, write a report, add his own comments to it and then

> bung it straight off to Marian and she did most of the work when it got down there – cases to be handled, DHSS [Department of Health and Social Security] this or that ministry, she would take it from there. Marian and I used to get on great together. Many a time we've run into problems during the week and Joan's been away somewhere, I'd ring Marian, 'oh, leave it to me', so she worked on it from that end. We really had it buttoned down. It was always that personal approach, because I've always considered that very important with public figures, people working with the public. Nowadays you get bloody letters.

It worked a treat – constituents would say: 'that Joan Maynard, she can't half get things done, can't she?'

Whilst the world of steel and heavy engineering was, to begin with, foreign territory for Joan, the concerns of her constituents were all too familiar. Her long years in local government had prepared her – health, education, jobs, money worries, housing, saving a local sub-post office. Only immigration issues were completely new. No problem was too small – the vegetarian resident in the old people's home who was expected to eat meat, or the pensioner seeking a cash refund for a few telephone stamps. Joan took up the case of a steel worker in her constituency whose wife and four children in Pakistan were trying to join him and having to wait two years before even being granted an interview with the British Embassy in Islamabad; to Joan this was 'a scandal'. A constituent wrote to her: 'I shall never fear again to ask my MP for help if I feel I have a just cause. Before, I would have just accepted the decision made to me.'

On health issues she championed the cause of brick workers seeking compensation for pneumoconiosis. She accused Middlewood hospital of tranquillising mentally ill patients because there were insufficient nurses to care for them. A case that remained fresh in her mind, and infuriated her in the remembering, was of a low-income woman suffering from rheumatoid arthritis and using a wheelchair, whose husband and daughter had scrimped to give her the holiday of a lifetime. She returned from the short holiday in

Spain to discover that the DHSS had stopped her invalidity benefit. Joan soon saw to that.

As sponsored MP for the NUAAW, Joan took up members' individual issues as well as the collective problems of the tied cottage, low wages and dangerous conditions. She understood, for example, the impact on the family's standard of living when the local authority withdrew the children's school bus allowance from the farm worker.

The combined efforts of Jock Sturrock and Marian Neville over the years meant Joan was not subject to constant demands from constituents and Union members. Asked how she combined her work as an MP with all her NEC and Union commitments she responded:

> Partly, and I was about to say unfortunately, the demand for my help from people in the constituency wasn't terribly high. Now I put it down to the fact it was a very working-class constituency and workers aren't good, unfortunately, at making demands from what they think are their elders and betters. If you are representing, say, Cambridge or Oxford they'd never be off your doorstep, would they?

George Matthews, for a time a member of Brightside's General Management Committee, recalls walking through the constituency with Joan:

> I think she had a way of possibly disarming people; she had a lovely approachable nature. People didn't tend to make judgements that she was a woman, possibly that she'd never been to Sheffield before. Her lovely rapport with people was reciprocated. We were in the heart of Brightside, a huge shopping area with a variety of different kinds of property, private and public, and people would know her and acknowledged her, it was, hello Joan, are you alright love?

As a Sheffield MP the first thing Joan needed to learn about was steel. Within a week of being selected she had attended a mass meeting of 4,000 workers at British Steel's River Don works. She was determined to meet with workers at steel and engineering works across the city:

> The main way I found out about steel was to meet the men in the factories and in the unions and talk to them, because my view, as a Socialist, is that they are the people who run the industry every day. They know more about it than anybody else. I talked to the people who worked in the industry, either directly or by meeting them in a canteen over lunch or at a trade union meeting.

Where managements would not allow her in to speak inside the factory (claiming 'political neutrality') shop stewards organised factory-gate meetings. After more than fifty years living in rural North Yorkshire, visiting the Sheffield factories was

> a bit of a traumatic shock because some parts of the steel factories are quite frightening where the furnaces are running. There's white heat melting the steel, and to see steel running in a liquid form, it's an amazing experience, it's quite scary. You had to be all geared up for it with helmets and things, it was a different world altogether. It brought home to me how much better the steel workers were organised, some of course were engineers as well. They would take me round the factories and explain to me the processes. I realised that steel workers were much better organised and much more articulate than the farm workers. All they really needed was for me to arrange for them to see Ministers in London. They could put the case, they were perfectly capable and competent. I remember walking along with them to the Department of Industry and saying, there's all these offices round here, they're like us in the House of Commons pushing paper and talking. I said, workers like yourselves and coal miners and farm workers – the productive workers – are carrying all these other people. But they knew all that, I needn't have explained it. They were very sophisticated politically, particularly the engineering union, more than the steel union. Of course I ran fairly quickly into the run-down of the steel industry in the country. They said it was related to overcapacity and that we had to run ours down and that other countries in the E[uropean] C[ommunity] were having to run down their industries. Where actually ours was run down more than some of the others. I felt that the decisions about our steel industry and investment in it and how big it should be were being taken in Brussels. As we were having discussions in the House, the decisions were being taken in Brussels about how much money was being invested in the

> British steel industry; it wasn't being taken in London. Unfortunately the unions weren't able to stop the destruction of the steel industry, I think first of all because the steel union was a non-militant union and the problem about the engineering union, because it mainly represented craft workers, skilled workers, it had an elitist approach and rather looked down on general union people. Of course, employers are very clever at exploiting these sorts of nuances. The old thing – an injury to one is an injury to all – if we could have stopped them in relation to the steel industry, then that would have strengthened the miners' struggle when their turn came, because everybody was picked off in turn eventually.

The Sheffield newspapers gradually ceased giving Joan a hard time, acknowledging she was speaking up for Sheffield and the steel workers in the face of the industry's decimation. In industrial disputes Joan was always full-square behind the strikers. George Matthews said:

> The trade union movement was at the heart of her life; she realised the importance of people organising to protect themselves. If your comrades are in trouble you support them. Like in Lloyds and places like that, they support each other, don't they, the capitalist class; they'll not see one another go down. Joan supported working people whatever the issues were.

On entering Parliament, Joan immediately put down her name to make her maiden speech. Despite the years of public speaking, she was very nervous as she prepared to deliver her first speech in Parliament on 6 November 1974. She had been alerted to the convention that maiden speeches should include positive reference to the MP's predecessor but, 'I'd never met him; I'd passed him and said hello to him twice probably, that was all, and as I couldn't find anybody who had a good word for him in the Commons, I decided not to refer to him at all. I decided that if I couldn't say anything good, I'd better say nothing at all'.

She made clear at the outset that she represented the interests of two constituencies, Brightside and the farm workers; the interests of each were reflected in her speech – the taxing of widows' pensions and the scandal of the agricultural tied cottage.

Two months after entering Parliament, Joan collapsed and was rushed to Westminster Hospital. Although the problem was her liver, the main cause was exhaustion. At first Rowie didn't know she had been taken to hospital 'you can't even be ill, privately. As soon as an MP is ill it's blasted all over the front pages. Because Rowie wasn't a political animal he'd missed all that publicity'.[3]

Bob and Ann Cryer visited Joan in hospital. Attached to drips and monitors she appeared to be in a very serious condition. Apprehensive, and concerned to say nothing to excite her, they tentatively began to make small talk. Joan wasn't having that, so the three of them discussed the political issues of the day and laughed at Bob's irreverent jokes.

Joan received affectionate good wishes from all sides of the House:

> I do hope you will get some rest in the recess. Believe me, I've been in politics long enough to know no-one misses you when you're dead! SO BE GOOD.
> Love
> Gwyneth (The Dreaded Dunwoody)

After being cared for by her niece Anne, Joan returned home to North Yorkshire where she was looked after by Olive and Bernard Cartwright. Before her collapse she had invited the Cartwrights to stay in Lansbury House whilst the council modernised their house – the council had brought in caravans to accommodate tenants, which Joan thought would be terrible in the depths of winter.

Because of her weakened liver Joan stopped drinking alcohol and was even more careful about what she ate.

Her collapse might have been predicted. She had felt extremely tired even before the Brightside selection and she had fought a ferocious election campaign in an unknown city. In London she was trying to master the arcane ways of the House of Commons; she was a member of the NEC and its sub-committees and study groups, county secretary of her Union and, at weekends, committed to either surgeries and activities in Sheffield or being company for Rowie in North Yorkshire.[4]

Through her illness Joan determined to focus her energies. In an article advising new Labour MPs she wrote: 'Being an MP is hard work if you do the job properly, and if you are not good at saying "no" you can run yourself into the ground. So the best thing is to decide to specialise in not more than two or three subjects. Realise you cannot do everything, not if you want to do it well.'

TEN

True friend of Ireland

Joan treasured a leather purse inscribed 'Joan Maynard True Friend of Ireland'. It was hand crafted, and made with the support of his commanding officer by a young Republican prisoner, Tommy Eccles, in Portlaoise Prison. The purse was presented to Joan at a party held in the Jubilee Room at the House of Commons on 26 October 1987 to, 'thank her for all the good work she has done for Ireland'. As well as an appreciation of Joan, the event aimed to inspire a 'new generation of MPs' to work for Ireland.[1]

The celebration was one of several held across the country as a tribute to Joan's commitment. In Scotland she was guest of honour at the Connolly Association Easter Commemoration *ceilidh* as 'an expression of thanks from the Irish in Glasgow'.

In the *Irish Post* Frank Dolan's valediction portrayed Joan as 'a noble lady who stood with Ireland through thick and thin since she entered the Commons in October 1974. She deserves a deep vote of gratitude from all who care about the cause of Ireland'.[2]

Also retiring from the Commons were senior figures from both sides of the House who had been steeped in the politics of Northern Ireland. Four of them had served as Northern Ireland Secretary, Roy Mason, Jim Prior, Francis Pym and Sir Humphrey Atkins. Mason had described Joan's approach to Northern Ireland as 'disastrous' and Don Concannon, the then longest-serving Minister in the Northern Ireland Office, thought her 'politically naïve in the extreme'.

Joan's passion for justice in Ireland was aroused during her first visit to Northern Ireland in 1970, the year after Wilson had deployed troops in the province. She went as a member of a three-woman delegation of the National Assembly of Women comprising members of the Labour Party and the Communist Party. The purpose of the visit was for delegates to see for themselves the effects of the Troubles on women and children.

Joan was ill prepared for the visit; she knew little about Irish history and politics and had not anticipated the overwhelming atmosphere of intimidation and fear:

> We flew to Belfast, the three of us. I'll never forget it as long as I live; I won't. When we arrived at Belfast airport there were British soldiers everywhere with guns. In the streets British tanks were rolling up and down and British troops were dodging from doorway to doorway with guns at the ready. I thought, this only happens in fascist countries. The women told us how the RUC [Royal Ulster Constabulary] would come to the house in the early hours of the morning and bang on the door and drag people out of bed and take them off. I would say, well, why don't you complain to your MP? They told me, it's no good complaining to the MP because they do this under the Special Provisions Act. I found out that there were laws in Northern Ireland that don't apply over here and that under those laws – they were draconian – you could do damn well anything. That really shook me. I began to learn how the nationalist population were treated differently from the Unionists and Protestants in relation to homes and jobs. This was a tremendous eye-opener to me… It really shook me… I suppose it's because I could never bear injustice – and I saw the terrible injustice of what was going on – that I became committed to the Irish cause. We have such an appalling history in Ireland and because most people don't know about it they've got a very wrong understanding of the situation, or no understanding at all, which is nearer the truth. I can understand why people in 'high places' don't want to read about Ireland and its history, but not the ordinary people. So here was this terrible injustice. Although I don't obviously like violence – and I certainly don't like killing people, my feeling was that if you really create a situation – and that's another thing that infuriates me when they talk about democracy; there isn't any democracy in Northern Ireland, that's the real truth. It's a gerrymandered state that's only been kept in existence by undemocratic

> laws, and, my God, there's plenty of them – Diplock courts, Emergency Provision Act, Special Provisions Act, all these different things, internment without trial. I think there must be something very wrong with a state that can only be maintained by repressive laws. I got into a lot of hot water over my views about Ireland because to me it was such an obvious issue really; I couldn't see how any Socialist could miss it, but most people kept their heads down. I got death threat letters. It was very frightening.

She discussed her fears with Sheffield MP Martin Flannery and London MP Jeremy Corbyn. 'Jeremy was probably one of the very best MPs – he was wonderful on Ireland, and Benn of course. Skinner would follow our lead on Ireland.'

What Joan had felt and heard on this visit was confirmed by the information she sought from the Northern Ireland Civil Rights Association (NICRA). NICRA had been established three years previously to campaign against the discrimination experienced by the Catholic minority in relation to the Special Powers Act, housing, employment, voting rights and gerrymandered electoral boundaries. The Northern Ireland Parliament, with its inbuilt Protestant majority, determined social and economic policy and NICRA's approach in mounting extra-parliamentary opposition to these policies resonated with Joan.

Subsequent visits to the north and south of Ireland with the British Peace Committee and Labour Party NEC study groups confirmed her view that Northern Ireland was created by the British Government in 1921 to 'divide and rule as we've done in so many other parts of the world'. She drew parallels with the struggles of other oppressed groups in Vietnam and Africa. When criticised by friends and opponents for not condemning violence perpetrated by nationalists, she would insist: 'If one creates injustice one must expect to have trouble; oppression brings many acts of barbarity and intolerance.'

The *Morning Star* (27 April 1973) published her criticisms of the Conservative Government's White Paper:[3]

> Peace can only be secured on the basis of elementary justice and it is manifestly lacking in this document. It is no more than a trade-off between various

> political interests, offering a carrot to the so-called middle-ground politicians, while the stick is reserved, as before, for the Republican and progressive movements . . . Mr Whitelaw has bent his Machiavellian talents to maintain British power, to keep the working class divided.

She criticised the Labour leadership for failing to grasp that 'the Tory Party was named the Conservative and Unionist Party because Toryism has been historically built into Ulster, and not least to sustain Tory rule in Britain'. Turning to the trade union movement, she maintained that whilst the TUC was committed to a democratic reform programme for Northern Ireland, its General Council had 'so far failed to respond in any significant way to the situation. The essential thing is to act and work together'.

The year after Joan's first visit to Northern Ireland, the Government introduced internment without trial to combat terrorist activity (9 August 1971). Nearly all those interned were from the nationalist side. 'Sinn Fein could point to the fact that hardly any of those "interned" for suspected terrorist activities were members of loyalist (Unionist) paramilitary organisations, such as the Ulster Defence Association (UDA) and the Ulster Volunteer Force (UVF). Therefore it is no exaggeration to claim that "Internment . . . managed to unite the Catholic community against both the Unionist and British Governments".' (Dorey 1995, p. 122, quoting Connolly 1990, p. 61)

On Sunday 30 January 1972 the Derry Civil Rights Association organised an illegal anti-internment march. The British army shot dead thirteen demonstrators and fatally wounded another. Bloody Sunday was described by Simon Winchester in the *Guardian* as, 'the tragic and inevitable doomsday situation which has been universally forecast for Northern Ireland'.[4]

Three weeks later, the headquarters of the Parachute Regiment in Aldershot were bombed, killing seven people; the following month, seven people (four civilians, two RUC officers and an off-duty member of the Ulster Defence Regiment UDR) were killed in a Belfast bombing. The Conservative Government under Edward Heath suspended the Northern Ireland Parliament, restoring responsibility for security and law and order to Westminster. 'For the first time in 51 years, Northern Ireland was now ruled wholly from London.' (Elliot and Flackes 1999, p. 607) William Whitelaw was appointed Secretary of State and 'Northern Ireland was governed under a Temporary Provisions Act, and Northern Ireland legislation was brought forward by way of Orders in Council, which could not be amended on the floor of the Commons.' (*Ibid*, p. 607)

Joan's election to the National Executive of the Labour Party at the 1972 Annual Conference gave her a national platform to denounce British policy in Northern Ireland. 'This got me into a lot of hot water with the Labour Party, the unions, the Conservative Government and, of course, the press.'

Congratulating her on her election, Colin Sweet, vice-chairman of the British Peace Committee, wrote 'I am getting in first with a request to you concerning the very serious situation in Northern Ireland. We are very worried that the Labour Movement is doing so little.' (4 October 1972)

Three months later the British Peace Committee arranged for Joan to visit Belfast, where she was met by NICRA and taken to Derry on 28 January 1973. Here she talked with people who had been harassed and attacked whose cases had been taken up by NICRA. She was escorted on a walk around Derry where she met residents of the Bogside and other areas of the town before participating in the Memorial Meeting of the Civil Rights Association.

Joan was horrified at what could be done under the Special Powers Act. She spoke with people who had been imprisoned in Long Kesh; during interrogation they had been hooded and beaten. She met people who had marched on Bloody Sunday. She heard how children in their teens were snatched from their beds. She was shocked to learn that Ireland was one of the few places in the world that retained a property qualification for voting into the 1970s, thereby disenfranchising nearly a quarter of the adult population. She likened Ireland with Vietnam, saying the people of Ireland would win their struggle as the people of Vietnam had won theirs against foreign interference. In Joan's opinion, the inequalities in Northern Ireland were so glaring they could only be maintained by force. The ultimate aim must be the reunification of Ireland.

This view was in stark opposition to the bipartisan position of the Labour Party leadership; Joan accused Wilson's Labour Government of having turned a blind eye to discrimination against the Catholics in the 1960s and of having no long-term strategy.

Following Labour's election victory of February 1974, Merlyn Rees was appointed Secretary of State for Northern Ireland. Within three months the Ulster Workers' Council strike had resulted in the collapse of the power sharing executive established in January of that year, and virtually brought Northern Ireland to its knees. Direct rule from Westminster was resumed and plans announced to establish an elected Constitutional Convention to seek a political settlement.

Whilst Joan and members of the British Peace Committee were denounced by the Labour leadership for openly condemning Labour's bi-partisanship and calling for the troops to be ordered immediately to their barracks, pending withdrawal, the Cabinet was secretly discussing the implications of such an option:

> Cabinet meeting. Northern Ireland was on the agenda... It was agreed (again) under the highest secrecy, that we would begin considering the implications of a total withdrawal. Of course, if that got out, it would precipitate bloodshed but we felt we simply had to do it. Roy took that view. Jim looked very doubtful but thought it needed to be done in the event of this happening. Wednesday 10 April 1974. (Benn 1989, p. 137)

Roy Mason, Labour's Secretary of State for Defence, got into trouble for merely hinting that troop withdrawal might be on the Government's agenda. In a speech to mine workers in Newcastle-under-Lyme he 'foolishly departed from the written text to comment on the situation in Northern Ireland'. For this he was severely admonished by Merlyn Rees who left him 'in no doubt that by merely mentioning the possibility of troops withdrawals I had blundered badly, trodden with hob nail boots over his turf and made an idiot of myself' (Mason 1999, p. 125). Later he was 'ticked off' personally by Wilson.

On the fly leaf of the copy of 'Against the Tide: Diaries 1973–76' he gave to Joan, Tony Benn inscribed: 'For Joan with love for a great comrade and my teacher over the years.' In his diary entry of Thursday 6 November 1975 he observes: 'I am persuaded we should get out of Northern Ireland, but it is not the moment to say it.' In the margin of her copy his teacher corrected him with an acerbic 'Actually it was the time to say it.'

Three weeks after Joan was elected MP for Sheffield Brightside, *Labour Weekly* (1 November 1974) carried a photograph of her speaking behind a symbolic roll of barbed wire at a demonstration in London on Northern Ireland organised jointly by the Troops Out Movement and the British Peace Committee. Whilst she was speaking, scuffles broke out and nine people were charged with obstructing the police and using threatening words and behaviour. Colin Sweet thought there was deliberate provocation designed to break up the 2,000 strong demonstration; one of the organisers had seen Special Branch officers mingling in the crowd. Earlier, Joan had headed the march through London from Clerkenwell Green to Downing Street to hand in a letter to the Prime Minister, Harold Wilson. The letter called for political and military withdrawal from Northern Ireland, abrogation of the Special Provisions Act and the release of all internees.

Six weeks after the General Election, 21 people were killed when two Birmingham pubs were bombed on 21 November. The horror in the country was palpable; calls were made for the reintroduction of the death penalty. The month before, five people had been killed and seventy injured in bombings in Guildford. The Labour Government acted fast. In an all-night sitting on Thursday 28 November–Friday 29 November, the Prevention of Terrorism Bill was rushed through Parliament. The bill declared the Irish Republican Army (IRA) to be illegal and anyone suspected of membership could be detained without charge for up to seven days. Any person suspected of involvement in terrorism could be expelled from Britain to either Northern Ireland or the Republic of Ireland.

In moving the second reading of the Prevention of Terrorism (Temporary Provisions) Bill the Home Secretary, Roy Jenkins, said:

> It cannot be without reluctance that we contemplate powers of the kind that I propose in this Bill, involving as they must some encroachment, limited but real, on the liberties of individual citizens. Few things would provide a more gratifying victory for the terrorists than for this country to undermine its traditional freedoms in the very process of countering the enemies of its freedoms.

He went on to assert that innocent people would occasionally be subjected to a certain amount of 'inconvenience'.

'Inconvenience' was not Joan's view; for her, the Bill was an attack on fundamental civil liberty. She had been in Parliament less than two months and though somewhat confused by its arcane practices, on matters of principle she was absolutely clear. She determined to make a stand against her Party and the mood in the country:

> When they first put through the Prevention of Terrorism Act, you know how they say, those in favour say aye, Stan Thorne and I were the only two to shout No! We couldn't create a Division because you need two tellers, so if we'd been the tellers there would have been nobody to vote. That was the way we registered our opposition. I thought there's no way I'm going to vote for this. Apart from my feelings about Ireland, I thought it was the beginning of an infringement of our civil liberties. I could see how it could open the door.

Joan was to remain convinced that the Prevention of Terrorism Act (PTA),

> had absolutely nothing to do with preventing terrorism; there were very few people ever charged under it and even less convicted; it was really about terrorising Irish people in this country and collecting information. They could hold people for a week without ever charging them; it's scandalous.

Her assessment of the PTA was to be endorsed by Patricia Hewitt, general secretary of the National Council for Civil Liberties (NCCL):

> For the last 5 months the PTA which is to be debated and renewed by parliament this week – has been operated virtually without criticism from parliament, the judiciary or even the press . . . An analysis of the arrests, charges and convictions since its introduction suggests that, even on the most pragmatic grounds, the Act cannot be justified . . . Of 541 people who have been held for questioning, only twenty-six have been charged; four of the most serious charges have been dropped, and three of the four people concerned released after two-and-a-half months in prison . . . there is no satisfactory answer to the argument that a law which gives the executive powers

> that are exercised in secret and unchallengeable in the courts, and removes every fundamental safeguard from the suspected individual, should not remain on this country's statute books.

She urged MPs to vote against its renewal.[5]

(In 1982, against the whips, 52 Labour MPs voted against the Prevention of Terrorism Act; by 7 March 1983 the PLP voted, for the first time, against the Act.[6])

Held in the shadow of the Birmingham bombings, the 1974 Annual Conference of the Labour Party approved the NEC statement on Northern Ireland that rejected calls for immediate withdrawal.

Attacking Government proposals for a Constitutional Convention, Joan and five Labour MPs wrote to *The Times*, 13 December 1974:[7]

> We will be confronted with the intransigent demands of the Ulster Unionists. The 'solution' will be a choice between handing over power to Messrs Paisley, West and Craig, or continuing with direct rule. Either way means continued violence and repression . . . The real problem to which we have to address ourselves is not how to cling to power in Ireland, but how to relinquish it.

Joan could not rely on the support of her Constituency Labour Party for her position on Ireland; indeed, it was the sole issue on which her and Jock Sturrock's views did not 'gel'. He had grown up in Glasgow in the heart of Protestant and Catholic sectarianism, and whilst he supported republican aims in Ireland he could never support their means. Joan was criticised by many in the constituency who felt events in Northern Ireland were none of their concern. Others, through Joan, developed a commitment to Irish nationalism. Joan Eddison said: 'Ireland wasn't here, it was somewhere else; it was Joan who got us to think about Ireland. We got to be on the side of the people in Ireland when we knew they were being oppressed; we didn't know much about it so we started to read about Ireland.'

George Matthews considered Joan

> excellent on Ireland. She took criticism, certainly, within her own constituency. There were people there who felt that the Irish question should

> be left to other people rather than it becoming the discussion for the Labour Party in Britain. And of course the press, the media, used to force her on that question and try hard to embarrass her, or what they thought was exposing her. But she was firm on the Irish question. I thought she was outstanding on Ireland; other people shied away from it, to their shame. We still wrestle with it and people are still frightened to stand up.

Joan was disappointed with the lack of support from Socialist allies in Parliament and the NEC. Her friend Audrey Wise came in for criticism:

> Audrey was more thoughtful and less instinctive than me. When I was campaigning in the early days for a united Ireland and supporting republicanism, I couldn't get Audrey involved. She said to me that if she took my line nobody would take any notice of her ever again. So Audrey never got involved in the Irish question. Audrey tended, I'd say, to pick the bread-and-butter down-to-earth issues; she was articulate and could explain issues well.

(It is telling that Joan characterised Audrey Wise's commitment to feminism, as a 'bread and butter' issue.)

MPs on the Left would say, 'well, full marks for courage, Joan. But I knew they meant, not very wise probably'.

Some Socialist friends deliberately refrained from discussing Northern Ireland with her. York Fabian Hans Breitenbach said:

> Joan and I avoided discussion about Ireland. I thought she and a number of her colleagues were too sympathetic to terrorists; they did not offer support to Government attempts to combat terrorism. I think they were wrong; it stems from a lot of people on the Left who have gut reactions because it's anti-establishment and bound to be a good thing.

He conceded, 'Joan did do some good in as much as some of the repressive measures were totally out of order and not consistent with any kind of proper British justice, and they were right to oppose that.'

Joan looked beyond Parliament for support by establishing alliances with organisations working for withdrawal of British troops. As well as the British

Peace Committee, of which she became president, she worked closely with the Troops Out Movement (TOM). Her approach dovetailed with TOM strategy to establish links with the labour movement in Britain.

TOM had been formed in September 1973 in west London. The previous year, the killing in Northern Ireland of over 100 British soldiers, and wounding of a further 500, had prompted a campaign by soldiers' relatives for troops to be withdrawn. Its leader was Peggy Chaston, who initiated a national petition. Alastair Renwick, a founder of TOM, described how 'TOM keyed into this dissent'. He considered Peggy Chaston's campaign to be about bringing the troops home because they were being shot at. TOM, committed to the self-determination of Irish people, wanted them out because:

> they have no right to be there at all . . . by the middle of 1973 there occurred a downturn of work on Ireland. The radical groups who had always blown hot and cold on Ireland were concentrating on the industrial struggles which were to bring about the three day week, a miners' strike and the end of the Heath Government in early 1974.[8]

Recalling the early days of TOM Alastair Renwick said:

> We had a strong class position which Joan definitely had. We stressed the fact that it was in the interests of the working-class people of this country as well as the ordinary people in Ireland that the troops should withdraw; that the repression in Ireland was being used against the working class here. For instance, what happened to the miners – the police became a paramilitary force. The level of repression wasn't similar to what happened in Ireland, but it was quite a similar exercise and we always argued that the fact that British people were going along with the British state doing that in another country made it easier for the British state to do it back in Britain. Marx said that a nation that oppresses another will never itself be free. He said you are making your own chains if you are complicit in that oppression. We always held that position and Joan saw it very clearly.

Predictably, Joan was severely condemned by the Labour whips and the press for speaking on TOM platforms; she would simply say, 'they couldn't get anybody else'.

TOM member John Lloyd joined the Labour Party specifically to promote links between the Party and TOM; his role was Labour Party coordinator. 'Joan opened the door for us to get into Parliament and for us to meet other MPs.' Alastair Renwick said:

> Of all the MPs I ever met, Joan Maynard was the only one that I felt completely at ease with. With all the rest you felt you had to be slightly guarded on certain things, but with Joan I felt totally at ease with her. There was no side to her and there wasn't a hidden agenda. Having someone like Joan with a principled position inside the Labour Party was like a goldmine.

The TOM leadership and Joan maintained a formal relationship centred on planning events and campaigns. There were no relaxed get-togethers in the pub; the focus was on the business in hand. Joan laughingly recalled how Alastair Renwick, Liz Curtis, and particularly John Lloyd in his cloth cap, 'had a slightly conspiratorial look, I used to think. When they came to see me, these three, I used to think they looked slightly conspiratorial. They were lovely though'.

John Lloyd was keen to stress that Joan was never the 'pawn' of troops-out organisations; when the Labour Movement Delegation to Ireland sought her assistance in support of their visit to Dublin and Northern Ireland in 1976, the organisers drafted a statement to go out under her name. 'She wasn't too happy with what she read and had it changed because it didn't sound like her and it didn't really reflect her position.'[9]

Together with arranging fringe meetings at Labour Party conferences, Joan booked House of Commons rooms for discussions about Northern Ireland, several of which she chaired. Over the next decade she was to cause numerous storms with these meetings. On 14 July 1976 she invited Tomas Mac Giolla, leader of Official Sinn Fein, to speak to Labour MPs at the Commons. The Conservatives demanded he be expelled. In 1972 he had been cleared of a charge of membership of the official IRA and had twice been deported from Britain in the same year after being questioned by Special Branch policemen. Twenty years later Mac Giolla was Lord Mayor of Dublin.

On 18 July 1977 Joan provoked more criticism when she chaired a meeting at the House of Commons for three Belfast mothers to speak with MPs. Their sons had been killed by the British army. The mothers, Rosin McCooey, Annie Norney and Kathleen Stewart, were calling for a public enquiry into the deaths of their sons, Danny McCooey, Leo Norney and Brian Stewart. The women brought a letter to the Prime Minister, James Callaghan, calling for the trial of the soldiers involved in their sons' deaths and 'an immediate ban on the use of rubber and plastic bullets, the end of harassment, humiliation and degradation in the streets, the ending of torture, and all brutal and inhuman treatment'.

Nearly a decade later on 23 January 1985, an apoplectic Conservative MP, Anthony Beaumont-Dark, complained about Gerry Mac Lochlainn's presence in the House of Commons at an Irish in Britain Representation Group press conference – Joan was speaking to launch its campaign to abolish the PTA. 'I believe the House of Commons, in the shape of Mr Speaker Weatherill, should call a conference of all the Party leaders to decide a list of prohibited people who should not be allowed to enter this building.'[10]

*

By July 1975 Joan saw her predictions about the Constitutional Convention realised, with the large majority supporting the United Ulster Unionist Council. She felt there could be no effective power-sharing within the framework of Northern Ireland and called for an immediate announcement that the troops would be withdrawn on a set date six months hence. The Constitutional Convention should be wound up and replaced with a conference of all political organisations representing the communities in the North and the government of the Republic.[11]

With Labour MP Maureen Colquhoun, Joan spoke at a TOM meeting in Blackpool on 29 September 1975. She argued that initiatives such as the Sunningdale Agreement and the Convention had failed because the Unionists had always known that Britain would underwrite their position. The Irish conflict could not be ended by military means. She reiterated that a date be set for withdrawal of British troops. Maureen Colquhoun poured scorn on the previous year's Labour Party Conference debate on Ireland: 'It makes me ashamed to be a Labour MP. It was about time the Government admitted failure and asked the United Nations for a peace-keeping force in Northern Ireland.'[12]

Joan responded angrily when the Home Secretary, Roy Jenkins, refused her request to book Trafalgar Square for a demonstration. In upholding the ban on Irish political rallies, imposed in 1972 by the Conservative Government, Jenkins was denying access to a symbolic site of public debate and protest.

Together with Jo Richardson MP, Joan joined a picket outside the National Gallery at Trafalgar Square on 5 October 1975. A protest march circled the square, led by the British Peace Committee; the march included members of the Communist Party, TOM, the National Union of Students and the British Withdrawal from Northern Ireland Campaign Defence Group. It proceeded to Temple Place where Joan gave a powerful address emphasising the symbolic significance of Trafalgar Square as a place for working-class people to hold political meetings. Britain should withdraw from Ireland and allow the Irish people their most fundamental freedom – the right to self-determination. Suppressing democratic freedoms and civil liberties had been the traditional response of British Governments to the so-called Irish problem. Denying access to Trafalgar Square was an act of political censorship.

(Nine years later, Joan, together with seventeen other MPs, including Clive Soley, Labour's junior spokesman on Ireland, Tony Benn and three Liberals, called on the Conservative Environment Secretary, Patrick Jenkin, to end the ban on Irish political rallies in Trafalgar Square, denouncing it as an infringement of civil liberties.)

On 20 November 1975 Joan joined other Labour MPs and demonstrators holding 'Free Speech on Ireland' placards in a protest picket led by Jo Richardson outside the Central Criminal Court in London. Fourteen pacifists were being tried on charges of conspiring to seduce soldiers from their duty.[13] The state was obviously rattled; the last time this legislation had been invoked was during the Boer War. The MPs took a letter to the Prime Minister, asking him to pardon any of the fourteen who were convicted. The letter supported the defendants' right to express their political views and called for The Incitement to Disaffection Act to be repealed, and the conspiracy laws to be dropped; until this happened, prosecutions should not be brought.[14]

In a letter to *The Times*, 20 February 76, Joan's name headed a number of signatories asserting bipartisanship over Ireland ensured policy would continue to be dictated by the Tories and the Ulster Unionists. The alternative was for Northern Ireland to be placed within an all-Irish context. Although this would result in the Unionists being a minority in Ireland, it did not mean that they should have fewer rights than the majority; it did, however, imply that the power of the veto they had under the Constitutional Act of 1973 must be removed.

The letter emphasised the need for a clear declaration by Britain to withdraw from Ireland, politically and militarily, within a limited period of time:

> By this we do not mean a precipitate withdrawal of troops without there being steps of equal importance to end our political responsibilities in Ireland. Negotiations and actions must go side by side. There must be more democracy in Northern Ireland, a repeal of the Emergency Provisions Act and a phasing out of the role of the army... The Protestant backlash, which so often provides the last ditch argument of those who have no policy, has also to be taken seriously, instead of being used as a reason for doing nothing... In the interim period (which we propose) the importance of assistance and cooperation between Northern Ireland and Britain in overcoming the particular blight of unemployment and discrimination cannot be overestimated. It concerns all Northern Irish workers. And it concerns British workers, in that we are asked to support the compensation of fellow-workers who have suffered this particular colonial exploitation.

Later in the year it became clear the Labour Government had no intention of considering such a policy. In September, James Callaghan appointed Roy Mason to be Merlyn Rees's successor as Secretary of State for Northern Ireland. Mason was to develop Rees's 'three-pronged policy of Ulsterisation, normalisation and criminalisation'. (O'Donnell 1997, p. 28) with the aim of ending the 'war-like appearance of Ulster' by increasing the role of the RUC and reducing that of the army; by using no-jury courts instead of internment, and treating paramilitaries as common criminals by removing their special category status. The policy was one of containment and security, rather than a search for a political solution. 'I wanted the whole issue of constitutional change put on the back burner.' (Mason 1999, p. 161)

In a debate in the House of Commons (28 October 1976) Joan challenged Mason. 'Does he think that the policy pursued by the Government is succeeding in Northern Ireland?' His response was curt, 'Yes, I do and if I understand her policy aright, if we attempted to operate it that would be disastrous.'

Conservatives expressed consternation in Parliament when, in October 1975, Joan was chosen by the Labour Party NEC to be a member of its Northern Ireland Study Group. Philip Goodhart feared: 'Violence is likely to be encouraged by the appointment of a leader of the "Get British Troops Out" movement.' (Other members of the Study Group were Ian Mikardo, MP for Bethnal Green and Bow, Alex Kitson of the TGWU, Nicholas Bradley of the Young Socialists and John Chalmers, the party chairman and general secretary of the Amalgamated Society of Boilermakers, Shipwrights, Blacksmiths and Structural Workers.) The Study Group was committed to visiting Northern Ireland, meeting with a wide cross-section of political and trade union opinion, and drafting a report on its findings for the NEC. It would soon become evident that there was diversity of opinion within the group itself.

Joan recalled:

> The people who blocked us on the NEC were always the trade union people. The reason for that was most of the members of the trade unions in Northern Ireland were Protestant, because most of the people who were working were Protestant. The worst was the TGWU – the Union we are now a part of. I was on the NEC and Alex Kitson was on, who was the deputy general secretary of the TGWU, and on the left on other issues. I mean, on many issues he was very progressive, but on this issue not at all. I needed the TGWU vote to get on to the Executive, and once I was on I needed the TGWU to stay on (they counted about a million and a quarter in those days). He used to call me out of meetings and say to me they were getting reports about my views on Ireland and that if

it came to the National Executive of the Union they'd have to look into it. I eventually became sponsored by them when we merged. He asked if I would like to change my views and position on Ireland. I said, no, I would not! The inference was that if I didn't, I might get de-sponsored, that was what he was implying, because most of the Harland and Wolff people were in the TGWU and he was threatening me really. So the blocking was always coming from the trade union side on the NEC. There was always a tremendous performance to get Kitson off the sub-committee. At one time I was chairman of it, I think Kitson and his cohorts must have been late for the meeting.

By June 1978 there was growing crisis in Northern Ireland. In the spring 300 republican prisoners went 'on the blanket' in protest at the withdrawal of special category status by the Labour Government on 1 March 1976. (The Conservative Government had conceded special category status to prisoners who had committed political offences.) To the embarrassment of the Labour Government, accounts of the men's protest were relayed around the world, yet Roy Mason 'was determined not to budge. The prisoners were criminals and as far as I was concerned would always be treated as criminals'. (Mason 1999, p. 161)

To Joan, Mason's denial of the republican prisoners' political commitment was a major impediment to the search for a political solution. In an interview in the *Labour Leader* in June, she stressed the impossibility of solving the Irish question by military force. A political solution must be found. Responding to the question that withdrawal of British troops would result in a bloodbath she said 'There is already a bloodbath . . . Bloodbath was also the argument for not leaving India, Egypt, Sudan and other places. If we walked out tomorrow there might be a bloodbath but I would set a date for the withdrawal of troops and use the intervening period to try to bring about solutions.'

At the time, this view seemed 'extreme', but within two years a growing number of activists were making a similar point; Peter Hain wrote: 'I believe that we should press for the next Labour Government to set a firm date for withdrawal – no longer than 6 months from taking office – and under that target convene a target in which it will be for all the people in the whole of Ireland – North and South – to negotiate transition to self-determination.'[15]

In 1978, the PLP was still relatively subdued on the question of Ireland. Whilst this might mean the MPs supported the Government position, Joan concluded it was more probable that, 'most people in the labour movement, sadly, just think it is such a difficult issue that they hope it will go away... People are also afraid to speak out on Ireland because of the death threats and telephone calls you receive when you do . . . the basic factor is that this issue is altogether too close to us, too difficult, too much our responsibility'.

The crisis in the Maze prompted Joan to urge Roy Mason to allow an all-party delegation of MPs to visit the prison. She thought those MPs who had visited the Maze earlier in the year were, 'hand picked by the establishment of Mason and the Northern Ireland Office.'

Replying to her in the House of Commons, on Mason's behalf, Don Concannon said, 'In the present circumstances of an intensified protest over the special category issue I have concluded that there should be no further general interest visits by MPs for the time being.' Joan responded. 'If a deputation of MPs was allowed, it would help to allay disquiet in many quarters about the situation out there. This kind of answer gives the impression that we have something to hide. The situation there can be solved only by a political answer and not by force or violence from any quarter.'

Don Concannon's response was a reductive, 'what has happened in these prisons has been brought on by the inmates themselves. They are deliberately fouling and messing up one of the best prisons in Europe'.

*

The change of Government on 3 May 1979 brought no change in consensus politics related to Northern Ireland. Within a month of his appointment as Labour's Opposition spokesman on Northern Ireland, Brynmor John was warmly reassuring Margaret Thatcher that Labour would be maintaining its policy of bipartisanship.

Joan characterised bipartisanship as a 'real conspiracy' between the two parties; the concentration on security rather than political issues inflamed the violence. Whilst she felt very frustrated at the lack of political debate in Parliament on Northern Ireland, she was more frustrated with her own Party's inability to recognise, 'the grave dangers there are to the British working class from what's going on in Northern Ireland'. An example she would cite was the deployment of the Special Patrol Group (which had originated in Northern Ireland) at Grunwick and in Southall, where Blair Peach was bludgeoned to death.

Joan argued it was imperative to make clear to the Government of the Irish Republic that Britain could not expect the predominantly Protestant Northern Ireland to go into a united Ireland on the basis of the Republic's present constitution. A possible solution might be a federated Ireland, with one state or county

> having quite a lot of autonomy, which would help the Protestants, I feel, to accept the united Ireland argument. In other words I am saying that there has to be give and take on both sides. I think if we approached it along those lines with a real political will to try and help bring the various political groupings and parties together, I think we'd still have a very difficult task, but I do think it would be possible within the context of the withdrawal of British troops.

The Labour leadership resisted calls to debate Northern Ireland at the 1979 Labour Party Conference, but Jock Stallard MP, Ernie Roberts MP, Joan and a 400-name petition of constituency Labour Party activists forced Northern Ireland on to the agenda. Though the leadership conceded a mere half an hour for the debate (with Michael Foot successfully opposing calls for an end to bipartisanship and the withdrawal of British troops), for the campaigners the debate produced two successful outcomes: the formation of the Labour Committee on Ireland (LCI) and an NEC study group remitted to draft policy on Northern Ireland for the 1981 Labour Party Conference.

The principal aim of the LCI was to commit the Labour Party to ending its policy of bipartisanship and to campaign for a unified Ireland. Its first conference, in Islington, in March 1980, attracted representatives of Constituency Labour Parties from across the country and representatives from CND and the Campaign for Labour Party Democracy. In his keynote speech Jock Stallard called for mass support within the Labour Party and the trade union movement to end partition and bipartisanship. Writing in LCI's first issue of *Labour and Ireland* Joan (warmly endorsed as honorary president of LCI) emphasised 'The question of Ireland must have the top priority of the Labour Movement. Britain is responsible for the hell which now exists in that country.'[16] The LCI developed as a significant force for change within the Labour Party during the 1980s, organising fringe meetings at Labour Party Conferences, establishing groups across the country and voicing strong opposition to Government initiatives, in particular the Anglo-Irish Agreement.

In January 1980 Joan attended a meeting of Labour Party NEC members convened to establish the new Study Group on Northern Ireland – as proposed at the 1979 Party Conference. Tony Benn chaired the meeting, and in discussing the Study Group's terms of reference, proposed it should, 'set out to break the Gordian knot by aiming to bring about the unification of Ireland'.

The research secretary from Transport House, Geoff Bish, was emphatic that to include unification in the terms of reference, without considering other options (power-sharing, continuation of direct rule, etc.) would be quite premature – especially given the likely reaction in Northern Ireland. Eventually it was agreed that the purpose of the Study Group was 'to examine, after full consultation, all possible solutions to end the bloodshed in Northern Ireland'.[17]

At the meeting, Joan expressed her disappointment with Labour's conduct on Northern Ireland in the House of Commons. Only a handful of Labour Members had consistently challenged both the Labour and Tory records. She felt the current problems in Northern Ireland arose from partition in 1921, which created an artificial state with an inbuilt Protestant Unionist majority, and she reminded members how in 1921 the Labour Party had supported the unification of Ireland; the existence of the border prevented Labour politics and class solidarity.[18]

Frank Allaun MP believed a power-sharing administration outside a united Ireland should be supported. He also argued that the British Labour Party should organise in Northern Ireland to overcome sectarianism and replace the Catholic–Protestant division with a Labour–Tory division. The Northern Ireland working class should be given the opportunity to join the Labour Party and this would be the best way to unite Catholic and Protestant workers. Joan passionately opposed this view, arguing that if the British Labour Party organised in Northern Ireland, candidates would be asked to give their position on the border.

After further debate the meeting agreed 'to recommend to the NEC the establishment of a Study Group to examine, after full consultation, the possibility of adopting the ultimate objective of an independent and united Ireland as the basis of policy for the Labour Party and to report on the means by which it could be achieved peacefully'.

Frank Allaun insisted his dissent to this proposition be recorded.

Although friends and close Socialist allies on all other issues Allaun and Joan were to remain at odds on the question of the Labour Party organising in Northern Ireland, with Allaun becoming a prominent supporter of the Campaign for Labour Representation in Northern Ireland, a policy consistently opposed by Joan and the LCI.

On 25 June 1980 Tony Saunois's resolution deploring the conditions of prisoners in Northern Ireland was put to the NEC: 'The NEC is implacably opposed to the programme and methods of terrorism. Equally however we are opposed to repression and torture in the prisons of Northern Ireland.'[19]

Michael Foot's attempt, seconded by James Callaghan, to refer the minute back to the Home Policy Committee was defeated by eight votes to eleven. Callaghan wished it to be recorded that he dissociated himself from the resolution.

Prime Minister Margaret Thatcher's fury with the 'disgraceful' NEC resolution was mild compared with that of Labour's Shadow Cabinet. There the resolution was berated for conveying an impression that the Party supported the complaints of the IRA and gave comfort to terrorists.

The Irish nationalist press sprang to the defence of the NEC, and singled out Joan in particular for withstanding the subsequent 'bullying interviewer' from the BBC when she refused to climb down, and warned that the methods of repression in use in the six counties were being extended to Britain and could be used against the labour movement.[20]

Joan was heartened by the NEC resolution being carried eleven votes to eight. In the past, she said, it would have been lucky to have got two votes. Being in opposition was encouraging NEC members to adopt a more radical approach towards Northern Ireland.

In June 1980, Joan visited Northern Ireland together with the chair of the Study Group, Alex Kitson, and Tony Saunois. As a consequence of the NEC motion they asked to visit the Maze. The Conservative Government, after several changes of mind, finally turned down their request. The refusal came as no surprise to Joan.

During its visits to the North and the Republic of Ireland in July, Study Group members met with a number of organisations, though not with Sinn Fein, the Provisionals and the Irish Republican Socialist Party. Joan anticipated the views expressed by the Unionist parties and trade union delegates on issues of the constitution, the economy, emergency legislation and party organisation. What shocked her were the Labour parties in the North and South:

> We met the so-called Northern Irish Labour Party. My God, that was an eye opener. They were actually justifying our claim to be in Northern Ireland – some Socialists, this crowd. I asked them, and they didn't like it, how many Catholics are there on your committee? Of course there weren't any. The Northern Ireland Labour Party [NILP] – I'll never forget this – were justifying internment without trial. Even the British Labour Party stopped funding the NILP. If they couldn't stomach it, it must have been bad. Then we went and met the Labour Party in Southern Ireland. They've improved, I think. Conor Cruise O'Brien was one of them at the time. He was justifying our occupation of Northern Ireland. I thought, well, I've been in a few countries in my time, but I have never been in a country where people justify another country occupying part of their country, never. Anyway, when he was kicked out by the electors in Eire, didn't I rejoice? I thought, you deserve it. They were pretty poor at that time.

Labour Weekly reported in October 'In its visits to both the North and the Republic the Working Party has come under strong pressure from the trade unions and the Northern Ireland Labour Party to avoid a united-Ireland position.'

Although Joan's position was a minority in the Study Group, she felt her views had the growing support of Constituency Labour Parties. This was confirmed when the Group circulated for comment its draft document in January 1981, 'Northern Ireland: the Next Steps'. Joan was gratified that over half of the responses supported a united Ireland. The LCI expressed their 'great disappointment' at the draft document and considered it to be influenced by a strong Unionist element within the Party.

The consultation took place against the background of the hunger strikes in the Maze Prison. On 25 January Bobby Sands, leader of the Provisional IRA prisoners, made it clear that initiatives by the prison authorities to improve conditions, following the hunger strikes called off the previous month, had collapsed. On 1 March, the fifth anniversary of the Labour Government's phasing out of special category status, Bobby Sands began a hunger strike. He was to be joined by nine other republican prisoners who, with Sands, fasted until their deaths. The degree of support for Sands was evident when, in the April by-election, he was elected MP for Fermanagh and South Tyrone; support extended across the rank-and-file Labour movement in Britain, but not to the Labour leadership, who continued, up to and after Sands's death on 5 May, to support Margaret Thatcher's refusal to negotiate with the hunger strikers. Those on the right of the Labour Party considered the leadership's approach to be 'right and reasonable' (Hattersley 1997, p. 292).

At the 11 May 1981 meeting of the NEC Home Policy Committee, chaired by Tony Benn, with Michael Foot and Neil Kinnock present, Joan supported Tony Saunois's resolution condemning the Tories' position on prison conditions in Northern Ireland. She said: 'It is easy to condemn violence, but we have shut every door. Bipartisanship at Westminster builds up the IRA. World opinion is against us.' Dennis Skinner, who has acknowledged how his views on Ireland were influenced by Joan, supported her. 'We have had thirteen wasted and violent years and I am not prepared to bury my head any more.' (Benn 1992, pp. 127–128)

Forty MPs attended a meeting of the PLP on Northern Ireland the following week; Michael Foot was heavily criticised by all eighteen speakers for maintaining the politics of bipartisanship.[21]

O'Donnell (1997, p. 60) writes:

> The backbench PLP N[orthern] I[reland] Group were growing increasingly angry with Concannon and Foot. By mid May [1981] *Labour Weekly* had reported that 'The rift between the front bench leadership and MPs who want a shift away from bipartisanship only widened this week . . . A motion blaming the Government's intransigence for the death of Bobby Sands last week was signed by 29 Labour MPs (*Labour Weekly*, 15 May 1981).

The hunger strikes provoked increased and widespread violence in Northern Ireland, with 34 civilian deaths resulting from plastic bullets fired by police and the army during the protests; five soldiers were killed in a landmine explosion near Camlough, home of hunger striker Raymond McCreesh (Elliot and Flackes 1999, p. 227).

According to O'Donnell (*ibid*, p. 62) the impact of the hunger strikes on the NEC Study Group was such that, 'most members on it appear to have made quite an astonishing ideological U-turn' – as Joan observed drily, they were 'converted'. Delegates at the Labour Party Conference in Brighton demanded that the scheduled debate be extended to one-and-a-half hours. Alex Kitson vacated the chair to speak on behalf of the NEC statement, which now committed the Party to the unification of Ireland, 'by agreement and consent'. The statement was agreed overwhelmingly and represented a major policy shift.[22]

An enthusiastic audience of over 400 listened to Joan addressing a LCI fringe meeting at the conference. Whilst the NEC statement was to be welcomed as a 'significant step' she stressed the need to campaign across the labour movement for full British political and military withdrawal from Ireland.

*

The General Election of June 1983 saw the Conservative Government increase its overall majority to 144. Sinn Fein's candidate Gerry Adams won West Belfast with a majority of 5,000, ousting the Independent MP Gerry Fitt, who had resigned from the Social Democratic and Labour Party (SDLP) in 1979. Jeremy Corbyn's invitation to Gerry Adams to visit the House of Commons provoked media uproar – and fury in the Conservative Party and among the Labour leadership. Four days before the visit Joan was arguing for a united Ireland on the floor of the House of Commons; she had been riled by Don Concannon's bipartisan question to James Prior, Secretary of State for Northern Ireland: 'Sinn Fein having gone political, is he getting any expressions of condemnation of terrorism from this new political party?'[23] Prior replied: 'Far from it. Quite the reverse, in fact and I do not think that is something that ought to be lost on anyone who seeks the path of peace . . . It's no good saying a united Ireland was the answer to the problems of Ulster when that was known to be unacceptable to the majority of people in the Province.'

Howls of Conservative derision greeted Joan's response, 'It is time we stopped treating Northern Ireland as a colony. We must also withdraw the Unionist veto so that we can get down to discussing the politics of the situation and how we can bring about a united Ireland. Until that is done the killing and violence and the whole hellish situation will continue.'

James Prior disagreed:

> The one certain way to increase the violence and lead to civil war would be to try to make the majority there act contrary to their own views. We have to seek agreement peacefully. It is no good saying that a united Ireland is the answer when we know it is unacceptable to the majority. We have to try to move forward rather more sensibly than that.

Jeremy Corbyn appreciated Joan's staunch backing of Gerry Adams's visit, 'It caused a lot of annoyance in the Party leadership at the time, not from Michael Foot individually, but from the Leader's Office and from the then Chief Whip, Michael Cocks. Joan was very supportive and came to the meetings with Gerry Adams.' Corbyn deeply respected Joan as 'someone coming from a rural area representing a traditional inner-city white working class constituency who had radical views on international issues and who was prepared to see Ireland as an international issue.'

For Joan, Jeremy Corbyn was 'a very close friend because of the Irish issue and his Socialism in general'. On his website in 2001 Corbyn stated: 'A peaceful, political solution would only be found by engaging in democratic dialogue and contact with Sinn Fein and others in Northern Ireland. Those of us who took this position were attacked and demonised in many quarters. Our long-held views are now Government policy.'

*

On 22 February 1984 *The Times* reported 'Labour leaders tried yesterday to limit the damage they fear may have been done to the Party at the Chesterfield by-election by Miss Joan Maynard who said on Monday that she would not consider the IRA to be terrorists.'

Joan recalled the incident, 'breaking when Tony [Benn] was trying to get the Chesterfield seat, unfortunately. Not that he repudiated me but they knew we were buddies'. Joan had been in Chesterfield the previous Tuesday and Wednesday supporting Benn's election campaign.

She expressed her views after a meeting at the House of Commons on 20 February called to protest about the use of 'show trials' in Northern Ireland. Asked her opinion on IRA violence she said:[24]

> I do not condone violence, but if you take away every democratic right, they have no hope of ever winning a majority in Northern Ireland. I believe that the courts have become an adjunct to the military power and they do not feel any longer that there is any justice in the courts. I would not call them terrorists because I know that word is used in order that everyone will switch off and say there is nothing you can do with the Irish except bomb them. I think 'terrorist' should be avoided in general. The word is used in the case of Ireland so that people will stop looking at the issue and what is causing it.

She then posed the question, 'How would you feel if there was an occupying army in this country? If you take away people's democratic rights and tie the legal system to the military power, which we have done, so they do not feel any confidence in the courts any more, that drives people into a corner and produces violence.'

Asked whether the IRA were justified in that violence, she replied:

> What would you do in a similar situation? You did not call the Americans terrorists when they dropped napalm on little children in Vietnam. You call people terrorists when it suits you and when it doesn't they are fighters for freedom and democracy. They are fighting to get an occupying army out of their country. It is an occupying army that represents a country that divided their nation without their consent.

Labour's big guns were brought out to limit any damage. Peter Archer, chief spokesman on Northern Ireland, told the *World at One* that Labour unhesitatingly condemned the IRA as a terrorist organisation. Choosing his words carefully he said Joan had condemned violence and she was probably saying that if there was no obvious redress for people's grievances within the constitutional system, some people, unhappily, would take to violence.

Barnsley MP Roy Mason, former Northern Ireland Secretary and old adversary of Joan was scornful 'People who entertain followers of terrorist organisations are politically naïve in the extreme. What is more they are giving credence to their case – they ought to have more sense.'

David Blunkett, Sheffield City Council leader and NEC member, felt Joan's views would not damage Tony Benn's election chances as he'd made his position on Northern Ireland quite clear, 'she spoke as an individual and is entitled to her views'.

Benn refused to comment.

Joan claimed her position was supported by a growing number of Labour MPs and, if accurately reported, would not damage Labour's chances of winning the Chesterfield by-election. Later, speaking in the Commons, she stressed she was not a supporter of the IRA.[25] She was greeted with brays of 'shame' and 'oh-ho' from the Conservative benches when she added she was not in favour of terrorism 'on the other side'. Conservative MP Robert Adley asked James Prior, Secretary of State for Northern Ireland, to reject Joan's views.

Joan argued that she had been misrepresented:

> In one newspaper there was at least one untrue statement. I repeat what I have said before, that I am not in favour of violence here or anywhere else. I have certainly never been and am not a supporter of the IRA or any other warring groups in that unhappy country.
>
> [James Prior] . . . I hope in that case that she will go one step further and say she is not in favour of terrorism and does not believe they are freedom fighters.
>
> [Joan Maynard] . . . I am not in favour of terrorism but I am not in favour of it on either side.
>
> [John Taylor, Ulster Unionist MP for Strangford] . . . Will the Prime Minister assure the people of Chesterfield that the people of Northern Ireland consider

> that those responsible for the murder of a British Army sergeant two days ago to be terrorists and not freedom fighters? (cheers)
>
> [Margaret Thatcher] . . . I warmly endorse what he says and thank him for it.

Letters from Labour activists were stinging. Robert Sharp wrote from Durham:

> Dear Joan
> Are you really trying to sabotage Tony Benn's chances at Chesterfield. Your remarks about Ireland couldn't have come at a worse time for Tony Benn and were latched on to as manna from heaven by the Tory press... If Tony Benn loses badly at Chesterfield some of the blame must surely lie at your door.
> PS You, Ken Livingstone and others making similar remarks on Ireland have cost the Labour Party hundreds of thousands of votes.

Joan was mightily relieved when Tony Benn won Chesterfield with an increased majority of 6,264.

A week later, (8 March) Tomas O Briain, member of the London Branch of the Celtic League, wrote to Joan to express his appreciation: 'Though you are not one of the most prominent politicians, you are always there . . . I welcome the return of Tony Benn to the Commons, but feel he needs to be under constant daily agitation from sensible politicians like yourself. Not being a Party hack, I don't see any real advance in a Labour Government led by Neil Kinnock.' Reflecting on the many letters she received from the public, Joan concluded: 'The interesting thing about them is that maybe over 30% of them were on my side which, in the climate, was quite amazing really, I thought.'

The 70% made tough reading:

From Paul Mosby, London, 9 March 1984

> Dear Miss Maynard
> Do you still consider the IRA to be 'freedom fighters' and not terrorists. Yesterday they murdered a man in front of his wife and 3 year old daughter. Today they threaten to poison food in a chain of supermarkets. I cannot understand how you are sympathetic to these loathsome people.

From Kathleen Cronin, Birmingham, 25 February 1984

> It is an undeniable fact that thousands of Irish men and women – including my own parents – have voluntarily chosen to make their homes in the UK, thus preferring to exchange the 'freedom' of the Irish Free State, as it was then called, for the 'captivity' of the UK.

From Willard Weiss, London, 23 February 1984

> Dear Miss Maynard
> I am only sorry that it was not you at Harrods, or at any of the other bombing sites, instead of the innocent victims of your friends from the IRA.

from a former bandsman

> I have particular nausea concerning the murder of innocent musicians entertaining the public in Regent's Park. Do you still consider these people to be 'freedom fighters'?

From John Bennet, Strangford, Northern Ireland

> Thank you for reminding me that Orwell's 1984 was a sound prophecy: 'Terrorists are freedom fighters' . . .

Letter in the *Land Worker* April 1984

> From: B Houlden. Ranby Branch.
> Having just read Joan Maynard's comments on the IRA in the national press, I am withdrawing my political levy until such time as Miss Maynard resigns her position as MP, emigrates to Siberia, joins the Politburo and becomes the first female president of the USSR. This is where her true colours lie.

'Some people, I thought, were beyond the pale. But anybody who wrote a reasoned argument against me, a reasonable letter, well, I thought, it's worth trying to put my point of view to them, so I wrote back.' In some cases she met her critics face to face:

> I got into awful trouble with a woman in Sheffield; I can't remember if it was her son – I think it was – who was killed. He was in the British army, you see. The *Star* newspaper was the evening paper in Sheffield and they had a huge spread on this woman having a go at me. I can't remember whether she challenged me to meet her, or if I thought of the idea. Anyway I arranged to meet her; I thought that was the best thing. I didn't believe in running away. I felt so strongly that I was right, and I did meet this woman. I don't know that Jock agreed with me meeting her, but he went with me. We let her choose the ground where we would meet. What I tried to explain to the woman was that if the policy I believed in had been pursued, then her son wouldn't have been involved at all. I don't know if I succeeded, there was some relative there who was quite understanding. You could understand the woman in a way. If you've lost your son it tends to make you pretty irrational, I suppose.

*

'Another one to go in the success file' was how Jock Sturrock described Robert Boyle's letter to Joan from Her Majesty's Prison Ranby, Nottinghamshire:

> 25 October 1981
> Dear Miss Maynard
> As you can see I have now been granted my transfer so would like to thank you very much on behalf of myself and on behalf of my family for everything that you have done for me. I feel I owe everything to you and I would just like to say how grateful I am so thank you very much.

As well as speaking in Parliament and on platforms across the country Joan felt that providing assistance to Irish prisoners detained in Britain, and their families, was something 'practical' she could do. (This was typical of her politics – whether it was housing a family evicted from a tied cottage in her own home or providing wire cutters for the women of Greenham Common.)

Joan's 'practical work' involved her in campaigns to overturn wrongful convictions of Irish prisoners in Britain, and to provide support for their families. Because of the closeness she had enjoyed in her own family life, Joan had an abhorrence of families being torn apart. But in the climate of fear, violence and retribution, such campaigns were deeply unpopular.

NICRA's opposition to discrimination in Northern Ireland had received some support from back-bench Labour MPs, particularly after Bloody Sunday; but in her book, *No Faith in the System* Sister Sarah Clarke wrote of those who were 'wonderful at the beginning but, like so many others as the situation became increasingly repressive, particularly after the passing of the P[revention of] T[errorism] A[ct], they were unwilling to associate with the Irish cause (Clarke 1995, p. 36).

Sister Sarah was working in North London and recalled:

> After the PTA, terrible things happened. They took in people for seven days and under the pressure people admitted to things they didn't do. People were badly treated and that's when we needed MPs. But all our MPs, including mine, didn't want to know. He wouldn't come out to me although up till then he'd been up at the convent having lunch. He would just say to me, oh you'd better mind yourself. So it was pretty tough. We had nobody. The only one we had was Joan Maynard. I thought at the time MPs were told not to bother. And some of them gave the excuse, those that we used to know and used to lobby, that it was a matter for their constituency MPs. So we were left with nobody. It was then that Joan Maynard always took the right step. She was a lovely lady, even though her enemies used to call her grandmother of Stalin.

Attacks from her enemies failed to deter Joan. Sister Sarah wrote: 'She was exceptional. Right from the start she would chair meetings for us and ask questions in the House – she and Fenner Brockway participated whether it was popular or not and did what was right and just.'[26]

Sister Sarah went onto say of Joan:

> I always had her at a distance; I wasn't terribly close to her. But I just admired her, that she had the courage. She knew awful things were happening and she was prepared to listen, which was wonderful. Another thing I admired about her

> was she had this high office in the Labour Party as a member of the National Executive Committee and she had a lot to lose by going against the grain.

Joan 'went against the grain' both as an NEC member, requesting Brynmor John to look into the cases of Irish prisoners in Britain,[27] and as an MP by putting down questions in the Commons. She asked the Home Office (April 1985) about the use of the Greiss test in the detection of nitroglycerine and was informed that it had been largely replaced by 'new and more sensitive techniques, though the Greiss test may still be used for screening purposes in conjunction with other techniques . . . The weight attached to the Greiss test is now somewhat less than 10 years ago, but this should not be interpreted as loss of confidence' (Mullin 1997, p. 272). The Greiss tests, carried out by the discredited forensic scientist Dr Frank Skuse, had been used as evidence by the prosecution in the Birmingham Six, Maguire Seven and Judith Ward convictions.

On 24 July 1984 Joan chaired a meeting about the Birmingham Six at the House of Commons;[28] seventy MPs were invited but only Clare Short turned up. Sister Sarah recalled:

> Clare Short sat in the corner and did not contribute. I said to her afterwards, why didn't you come and say something. And she said, oh I know they're innocent but it's my constituency. She was putting politics first, but Joan Maynard put what was right first. We had nobody, they just walked away. We were frightened. I never saw her losing her cool. Then, you see, the Maguires were in, the Guildford Four were in and the Birmingham Six were in.

It was through Sister Sarah that Chris Mullin, then a journalist, was put in touch with the Birmingham Six. Chris Mullin and Joan had become close friends since their first encounter at the High Peak selection conference in 1974. He related how

> from about 1977 onwards I began to take an interest in the Birmingham Six pub bombing case and I started putting down a lot of questions about it through Joan. She had a research assistant's pass, as any MP is entitled to,

> and since I needed to come and go to the House of Commons for all sorts of purposes, lobbying MPs on behalf of the Campaign for Labour Party Democracy, for example, she gave me the research pass. One of the great advantages of being able to say that I was Joan Maynard's researcher was that I could get access to the prisons because at that time as a journalist I couldn't have done – the prisons have since got a bit more relaxed about allowing journalists in. But at the time it wouldn't have been possible for me, as a journalist, to actually meet the Birmingham Six and, indeed, the Guildford Four. But as Joan Maynard's researcher I had a little stock of House of Commons notepaper and I would say, I am writing on behalf of Joan Maynard, who is taking an interest in these cases. I'd write to the governor 'could I please have a pass to come and see so-and-so'. And lo, the gates opened. So I interviewed all six of the Birmingham Six, several times over in some cases, as Joan Maynard's researcher. And that really enabled me, wearing that hat, to get access which simply wouldn't have been available to me. It was invaluable as far as overturning the convictions was concerned. I think it was perfectly legitimate, provided the MP knows what's going on and sanctions it. It eventually bore the spectacular results that we all know about.

Chris Mullin would carry a small tape recorder, a practice not permitted in some prisons. After he interviewed Paddy Hill in Gartree and handed the tape to television's *World in Action* he was banned from the prison for a short time by the prison governor Richard Tilt. In the late 1990s, as head of the prison service, Tilt would find himself interrogated by the chair of the Home Affairs Select Committee, Chris Mullin.

Joan wished she had been present in court the day the Birmingham Six were released; she hoped there would be a big celebration. 'Chris did a wonderful job, you know. They'd never have got out if Chris hadn't done what he did, never.' In retirement, she was thrilled when Dennis Skinner informed her that the Campaign Group of Labour MPs had formally recognised her and Chris Mullin's contribution to the release of the Birmingham Six. At their meeting on 20 March 1991 the Group agreed the following Early Day Motion: 'This House wishes to put on permanent record its gratitude, admiration and respect for the untiring work of Mr Chris Mullin, a member of this House, who inspired by Joan Maynard, former MP, has worked unceasingly to prove the innocence of the Birmingham Six, and by doing so, played a central role in securing their release.'

According to Sister Sarah:

> The case of the Guildford Four was the hardest nut to crack. But once we had cracked it, it made a big difference. People then believed that the police can do wrong and now it's not so hard to say police have tampered with things or have falsified evidence. You are believed. But up to the Guildford Four it was unbelievable.

The Guildford Four – Patrick Armstrong, Gerry Conlon, Paul Hill and Carole Richardson – were convicted of causing explosions which killed five young people in two Guildford pubs, five days before the October 1974 General Election. They were the first people to be detained under the Prevention of Terrorism Act.

Ten years later Paul Hill's aunt and uncle, Theresa and Errol Smalley approached Sister Sarah for assistance with the 'Free the Guildford Four' campaign. Sister Sarah described Joan as a 'wonderful support' for the committee established by the campaign. In the 1983 General Election Jeremy Corbyn was elected an MP; Sister Sarah remembers Joan and Jeremy being the only two in the House of Commons who supported the campaign. Joan valued Jeremy's contribution enormously: 'Eventually Jeremy helped a lot and visited Paul Hill too. He was wonderful, was Jeremy.'

She felt similarly about Chris Mullin. Yorkshire Television was making a programme about the Guildford Four; Chris Mullin recalls: 'They couldn't get access to Gerry Conlon, but I could as Joan Maynard's researcher. So I went to see Gerry Conlon, taking with me the questions they wanted asked, and I brought back the answers. It was very useful.'

Joan did not visit Paul Hill but she put down a number of questions about his case in the House of Commons. She worked closely with Alastair Logan, who would telephone her office with questions for Joan's secretary Marian Neville, to prepare and forward to the tabling office. Logan was the Guildford solicitor on duty when the Guildford Four were taken in. After two or three times of listening to them, he was convinced they couldn't possibly be responsible for the outrage. He wrote newspaper articles, spoke at conferences and appeared on television and radio programmes to keep the Four in the public consciousness. His tenacity over the fifteen years lost him a lot of business. Marian Neville has said how, despite his unstinting work, Logan was 'airbrushed out' over the Guildford Four case. When the convictions were quashed at the Old Bailey, 'he didn't get the credit. It was these big London people, wasn't it, who took over at the last minute'.

Joan assisted Paul Hill's mother in obtaining funds to visit her son in England. The Home Office ensured prisoners were moved around, and there was strong resistance to them being transferred to Northern Ireland. Joan said: 'The thing these devils did, was, they made it very difficult for families to travel from Ireland and get entrance visas; you see, it's a hell of an expensive job.'

On 22 October 1981 Paul Hill's mother wrote to Joan:

> I received a giro of £17.20p off Falls Road social security for prison payments to Wormwood Scrubs to visit my son Paul. So once again, Joan I am deeply indebted to you for your help and concern in this matter because without your help I would never have received this payment. My son Paul was sentenced to a recommended natural life on the date of this letter in 1975. Other people have admitted to this crime and my son's appeal was turned down in Oct 77. He has been moved 27 times and has spent 828 solitary yet they refuse to move him back to this country to serve his sentence . . . My son told me you have helped him with some matters. So I want to say thank you on my son's behalf and for all the help you have given me. I hope to visit Paul again around Xmas so I hope I don't have the same trouble again. I will write and let you know if I have Joan. I will close now so hoping this letter finds you in good health. Many thanks for your help in this matter.

In 1989 Lord Lane pronounced the convictions of the Guildford Four 'unsafe and unsatisfactory' and in his concluding remarks declared: 'The officers must have lied.' At the original trial fifteen years before, the judge had made it clear that had the death penalty been available the four young people would have been executed.[29]

During the brutal interrogation of the Guildford Four, members of the Maguire family were implicated when Anne Maguire's nephew Gerry Conlon said he had stayed with his aunt in London. Anne Maguire's account of her family's arrest, interrogation and imprisonment is movingly recorded in her book (Maguire 1994).

Joan was quick to support the Maguires' solicitor, Alastair Logan, in his work for their release. 'I was struck by Mrs Maguire's conservatism. It was absolutely crystal clear to me that she wasn't a terrorist; you've never seen anybody look more like an ordinary housewife.' Her view was backed by Cardinal Hume's assessment: 'To have met her and to have sat with her in conversation adds to the total improbability of her, or any of her family being involved in the terrible crimes of which she was accused.'[30]

In 1974, Judith Ward was convicted of a series of bombings including that of a bus carrying soldiers and their families along the M62 to their base at Catterick, North Yorkshire. Twelve people, some of them children, were killed. Judith Ward was convicted primarily on the basis of her own confessions and scientific evidence produced by Frank Skuse. She was sentenced to thirty years' imprisonment and after her conviction did not apply for leave to appeal.

Joan visited Judith Ward, a category A prisoner in Durham prison's infamous 'H' wing; she remembered it as a terrible, stark place where she was photographed and accompanied by a prison officer throughout her visits to the frail young woman. Judith Ward never pleaded her innocence to Joan, 'so I assumed at the time she maybe wasn't'. Later Joan was shocked to learn Judith Ward thought her chances of getting parole would be improved if she kept quiet.

Following one visit, Joan received a letter from Judith Ward:

> HM Prison Durham, 21 February 1983
>
> Dear Joan
>
> I hope you don't mind me addressing you like this but I didn't know if you were a Miss or a Mrs and I don't like Ms, I think its quite stupid!! Well, I would just like to say thank you for using some of your very valuable time in visiting me. I was grateful and it cheered me up a little to know that at least someone was interested enough to ask for me! I did mean to write sooner but

> this last week I've only just been able to have enough to buy stamps, plus the fact that I'm having considerable trouble with in-coming and out-going mail and it has put me off writing letters a little.
>
> PS Keep up the good work you're doing a great job.

After fifteen years of imprisonment, Judith Ward's conviction was quashed in 1989.

In *Error of Judgement* Chris Mullin writes: 'Judith Ward's release brought to eighteen the number of innocent people wrongly convicted of terrorist offences committed in 1974.' (Mullin, 1997, pp. xi–xii)

Though in no way a supporter of Joan's politics on Ireland, Roy Hattersley has observed that the 1974 Prevention of Terrorism Act, whose swift passage through Parliament Joan had so fervently opposed, was a 'response to the anxieties of the British people – whose traditional lack of concern for civil liberties the Government chose to endorse'. (Hattersley 1997, pp. 247–248).

In the face of unremitting political and media censure, Joan continued to pursue related civil rights issues: Diplock (non-jury) courts, the use of plastic bullets and strip searching. How starkly her approach contrasted with the approach of Labour's front bench – 'always one of cautious criticism' (O'Donnell 1997, p. 102)

Joan would become completely exhausted by the incessant demands. Producers of television current affairs programmes were alarmed when she fell asleep between 'takes'. Marian Neville tried to protect her. In a note to Joan she wrote:

> I have rung this comrade from the Celtic League and explained that you will not be in London for this demo. He was disappointed and asked me to let you know this. He said it was the first demo in this country for a very long time and that if you could go they would appreciate it – especially after the violence at the weekend. I did explain to him that you are doing miners meetings as well as trying to get a bit of a holiday.

Despite the initiatives of the 1980s – the New Ireland Forum and the Anglo-Irish Agreement – Joan held firm to her original position, resolute in the face of death threats, media vilification and attacks from inside her own party. For Joan, the internecine complexities of Irish history could be reduced to a single fact – Ireland had been colonised by the British; therefore the only way to achieve lasting peace was for Britain to withdraw and for Ireland to be reunited. In 1997 she said: 'The only solution to the problem is a united Ireland. Ireland is one country, there will never be peace until it is reunited. When you deny people every democratic outlet, they turn to force. We must help find the political solution to this problem of which we are so much a part.'

ELEVEN

House of bondage – the tied cottage

In her introduction to, *A Hundred Years of the Farm Workers Struggle* Joan wrote:

> As a group they have been oppressed for longer than any other workers, isolated and of course confined and restricted by the tied cottage system. Their contentment, a blessing in one sense, has also been their greatest enemy. The tied cottage system has kept them quiet and it has held down wages in the industry. (Maynard c.1974)

As a girl, Joan had witnessed the injustices of the tied cottage system. Friends at her all-age village school in Ampleforth were children of farm workers living in tied housing, under the pall of eviction. In later years on postal rounds and collecting Union contributions she would learn much more about life in a tied cottage. If the farm worker fell ill or fell out with the boss, the whole family could be summarily evicted, their possessions literally dumped in the lane; if they were 'lucky' they'd be given a tarpaulin. Living under the constant threat, if not reality, of eviction enforced compliance and subjugation; little wonder Joan emphasised the role of the tied cottage system in maintaining low wages. How could a farm worker demand more pay and better conditions, let alone take any sort of industrial action, when the family home was at stake?

Wives of farm workers could be compelled to undertake domestic work in the farmhouse, particularly as domestic labour in rural areas grew scarce. In Kent, for example, where light industry offering good wages developed on the Isle of Thanet, women were afraid to leave the farm. In August 1955 Eric Atkinson, housing officer to the Dorking and Horley RDC, presented a paper to the National Housing and Town Planning Conference in Canterbury. Referring to the tied cottage, he told delegates the growing shortage of domestic workers 'had led to an increase in employers saying to the worker that unless your wife works two mornings a week for the farmer's wife the worker himself will be dismissed, and then lose his job and house. A most distasteful and distressing demand'.

Joan would read about the inequities of the tied cottage in the Union journal, *The Land Worker*. It published a letter from an Essex branch member in April 1952 to the East Essex organiser:

> I have recently put in for a council house. I don't mind where it is in reason. My reasons are that the house I am living in is very damp and the rain comes in the bedroom during wet weather and runs down the walls, and we cannot leave anything in the rooms for if we did we could almost wring the wet out of them. Also the drainage from the house runs into a ditch right outside the back door and causes a terrific smell. The children are always suffering from colds. Now you know how it is with these tied cottages. We have to be careful what we say. I am not complaining about the job or the boss. He is very good in other ways but will not do anything about the house. I don't wish to be turned out for complaining but I have told the sanitary inspector of the conditions. He is coming some time when he is this way to give a general inspection. I am wondering if I have put my foot in it. As you know, I don't wish to be turned out especially with the two children but I should like to get a council house or a house that's not tied. I should appreciate it if you could help us in any way.

The same month, a branch member from County Durham who had worked for twelve years for the same farmer broke a leg in the service of his employer. The compound fracture required a month in bed. 'The employer notified him that he would want the cottage for another worker who would fill his place . . . despite all the efforts of the Union we could not get the family re-housed before the court order expired and on 9 April the bailiff arrived with an order to evict.' (*Ibid*)

When Joan joined the Union in 1947 it was nearly forty years since farm workers' leader George Edwards had first raised the matter at the TUC in 1909. Then farm workers were obliged to sign draconian contracts – 'I the undersigned . . . agree to give the cottage up held by me, with all its apartments, to the landlord or his agent, at a week's notice'. (Groves 1949, p. 125)

Joan and the Union had high hopes that the 1945 Labour Government with its resounding majority would honour its pledge to abolish the tied cottage system. Earlier minority Labour Governments had failed to do anything, mindful of the powerful farming lobby.

Despite successful resolutions to Labour Party Annual Conferences calling for abolition of the tied cottage, the 1945 – 1951 Labour Governments failed to deliver. As the second half of the twentieth century opened, the feudal relic of the tied cottage system continued to flourish.

To Joan's consternation, some in the Union leadership appeared sympathetic to the Labour Government's inaction. The editor of the *Land Worker* Arthur Holness, told Labour Party activists:

> The Union was, of course, disappointed that the Labour Government had not found it possible to carry out its pledges to abolish the tied cottage. But we must have a sensible appreciation of the facts. In the old propaganda days no one anticipated that Labour would take office following a war which accomplished a wider devastation than was ever before achieved in human history… We should be foolish indeed to join the pack which had no understanding or appreciation of the nature and necessity of the burdens which the Labour Government, in the face of appalling difficulties had been carrying since 1945. Some members had said that the abolition of the tied cottage was one of the first things the Labour Government of 1945 should have done. That was to reason from immature experience and the half knowledge which is indeed a dangerous thing… However important the tied cottage question might be, and he [Arthur Holness] was certainly not attempting to belittle its importance, it could not reasonably be argued that it should come before decent wages and working conditions, and the rehabilitation of agriculture to make it possible to meet the demands the workers rightly made upon it. . . . Unfortunately, at the

> last election there was a victory which only just bettered a defeat. To abolish the tied cottage would need a Government with a comfortable majority and strong backing in the country.[1]

As members of 'the pack which had no understanding', Joan, Jack Bowen, Bert Waind and Tom Gascoyne demanded abolition at the Yorkshire county conferences and called for militant action on the doorstep to prevent evictions. At 'Brains Trust' meetings arranged by local discussion groups in school and church halls, Joan and Tom Gascoyne spoke of the insecure hovels inhabited by many of their members. Dark theories were voiced that the anguished accounts and images of evicted families in the *Land Worker* functioned effectively to recruit and maintain the membership. At the other end of the country, pack member Jack Dunman cast doubt on the integrity of the Union leadership for not pressurising Labour to abolish the system.

Understandably, such criticism was too much for the editor of the *Land Worker* who retaliated – attacking Dunman's 'unwarranted impertinence' for suggesting the leadership was playing a 'double game'. But pressure from the pack was growing, and at Union Biennial Conferences throughout the 1950s resolutions called for the leadership to be more proactive. At the 1957 Biennial Les Shears proposed the leadership be given 'a kick in the pants' if it did not exert more pressure on Parliament, the PLP and the TUC. President (and Labour MP) Edwin Gooch MP attempted to respond to the criticisms, but the resolution was carried unanimously. So too was a resolution seconded by Joan, calling for the Labour Party, when returned to power, to introduce legislation to put all tied cottages under the Rent Restrictions Act; this would place responsibility for providing suitable alternative accommodation on farmers and local authorities.

Detecting a slight shift to the left at the 1956 Labour Party Conference, Joan felt less depressed than in previous years. She was heartened to hear Frank Cousins, general secretary of the TGWU, say in quiet and measured tones that he and his members believed in nationalisation and in 'old-fashioned Socialism'. Joan had studied Gaitskell's face closely and remembered him looking, 'somewhat shattered during this disclosure'. After the debate on the tied cottage she spoke briefly with NUAW general secretary Harold Collison, who appeared pretty well satisfied with Labour's proposals. Joan was surprised; she couldn't accept Labour maintaining that the nature of people's jobs meant they should live on the premises or near their work. She recognised this could be the case, but it did not justify houses being tied. Labour's proposal required the tied house to be registered with the local authority. In return for the registration fee the local authority would provide housing for a tenant on retirement due to age or health, or if they left the house through no fault of their own. From her own local government experience Joan was concerned how, 'no fault of their own' might be interpreted by rural district councils dominated by farmers – 'you could imagine![2] She told Harold Collison the Union should press for nothing short of abolition, as decided by that year's Union Biennial Conference.

Through the Union Joan worked to support Yorkshire members threatened with eviction. After the death of her parents she would offer them her own house as a refuge. John Gascoyne recalls:

> Her devotion went to ridiculous lengths in that we had a lot of tied cottage cases and evictions, and when it came to it, and the people evicted had nowhere to go, Joan would put them up. You weren't always talking about the pleasantest or nicest families. It would be women with a lot of kids and harassed and no money and no hope and not used to sharing a house or being tidy. Not used to controlling the kids because they'd lived in a tied cottage in the middle of nowhere. In Joan's house there was nowhere for them to roam and run about – imagine having kids like that in your home. There were only two rooms downstairs and she had piles and piles of books, forms, leaflets and the typewriter, and she had all her work to do and she had all these people in her house. Sometimes she didn't like it. I don't know anybody else that would do that, and I don't know anybody else that having done it once would do it twice... they would stay there for months.

By the time the Labour Party was returned to power under Harold Wilson in 1964 it had revised its position on the tied cottage. On 17 July 1963, George Brown pledged security of tenure: 'We will ensure that no occupant of a tied cottage is evicted until alternative accommodation has been provided.' The new Government with Richard Crossman as

Minister of Local Government and Housing moved quickly. Within forty days of being presented to the House of Commons the Protection from Eviction Bill received the Royal Assent on 17 December 1964, bringing the tied cottage on to the statute book for the first time (Jones 1975, p. 24). Its prime purpose was to put an end to summary evictions. During the course of the legislation, Union sponsored MP Bert Hazell said the Minister had bent over backwards in trying to meet the wishes of the farmer. Crossman made it clear there would shortly be further permanent legislation giving security of tenure to the agricultural worker. George Hook, head of the Union's Legal Department, concluded the Act provided 'greater measures of potential protection than the bulk of tied cottage occupants on farms have ever before enjoyed, and the Government should be given full credit for taking this initial and early bite into the tied cottage system'.[3]

The Labour Government had a slim majority and Richard Crossman was subject to increasing pressure from the powerful farming lobby opposed to further tied cottage legislation. Crossman's diary reveals his own frustration, his relationship with Harold Collison and the valiant efforts of Denis Hodsdon, assistant general secretary:

> I had a sudden call from the National Union of Agricultural Workers – they had to see me that afternoon. At 3 o'clock young Dennis Hodson [*sic*], the secretary of the Union, came in with my old friend Collison, who is his chairman. The trouble, of course, is the tied cottage and the longstanding party pledge never to throw a man out of a tied cottage unless the local authority can provide him with a house. This is impossible to implement because if farmers knew that anybody they evict would automatically get a council house, they would evict all the more readily. Now Collison understands why I had to implement the spirit of the party policy but couldn't implement the letter of the resolution. I was furious, therefore, when Mr Hodson came to tell me that the Agricultural Workers' Union were not prepared to consider my reasonable compromise and had reverted to their irreconcilable original position. I sat down to it and argued it out, and about every ten minutes Mr Hodson said to me 'You're wasting your time Minister'. And I said, 'No I'm not'. Finally I told him that if the Union are serious about

> this I shall simply not include the topic in the big Bill at all. He replied that in that case I will be hounded and harried in every rural constituency for failing to keep the party pledge. That really did rile me and when I got to Paddington for the 5.10 train I was still hot under the collar in a way I haven't been since I became Minister.[4]

The following month Crossman explained to the House of Commons (5 April 1965):

> We as a Party have an election pledge to guarantee alternative accommodation to farm workers. The more I looked at this the more I realised that we could not fulfil that guarantee in terms of writing it into the Bill, for if we had written it in and said that local authorities must give alternative accommodation to evicted farm workers, we should have been urging farmers to evict the farm workers they liked best so as to ensure them council houses.

The bill proposed clauses stipulating that the court, in considering the farmer's application for possession of the tied house should not only consider the availability of suitable alternative accommodation, but also whether the efficient operation of the farm would be seriously prejudiced unless the house was available for another employee.[5]

Joan felt Crossman's Rent Bill sold farm workers short of security and was further capitulation by Labour to the farmers' interests. She immediately wrote to comrades in Dorset, Hampshire and Norfolk proposing County Committee delegations to the Union Executive in London to persuade it to oppose the proposed legislation.

Organiser Jack Boddy shared Joan's concern:

> You will appreciate that we officials are in a difficult position as it appears that the powers that be are soft pedalling on it, no doubt in order to save embarrassment! We are under very definite instructions. Our brief is to state that the clauses concerned do not fulfil the pledge but that the Bill contains certain features which are to be welcomed. I personally feel disgusted with both the Labour Party and our own leaders. I have had a word with one E[xecutive] C[ommittee] member and our Acting President, they are well

aware of my feelings and claim to share them. I should have thought that the latter would have felt constrained to resign from the Labour Party Executive in view of his own personal commitment to this . . . I feel the present position is to some extent of our own making. We have gone to town on the matter of evictions which are obviously few and far between, and have failed to highlight the far greater menace in the accursed system – the insidious undermining of the workers' independence of thought and action, and its influence on the normal employer/employee relationship. Crossman now states that given a year's trial of the new arrangements and we shall see that few evictions take place. He may be right, but the worst features of the system will remain untouched. What a pity this is not a Biennial year! (12 April 1965)

From Norfolk, Wilf Page wrote to Joan on 13 April:

The two Jacks and I have had a number of discussions on the dirty work done by the Gov[ernment] and the E[xecutive] C[ommittee]. They are both very angry about this and their attitude is naturally developing a widespread reaction against the EC. I have suggested to a number of Secretaries to send letters of protest to the County Committee and the EC.

Ted Parry informed Joan he had raised the issue of the tied cottage at a district meeting in Hampshire and made reference to Labour's pre-election pledge, amendments to the Rent Act and the attitude of the Executive Committee on these matters. 'There are so many of our people, from the Executive Committee down, who having rid themselves of the shackles associated with the tied cottage, seem to have so little genuine consideration for rank and file members.' (20 April 1965)

Joan wasn't surprised that Les Shears was 'hopping mad about being let down by Collison and the Labour Party'. He wrote from Dorset on 14 April 1965 that his Executive Committee member described how, just before the bill was presented to the House, the Executive Committee members received a telegram calling them to an urgent meeting. Only when they arrived were they informed it was to approve the section of the bill about the tied cottage. Collison tried to persuade the executive to agree and eventually a compromise was reached. Whilst they could not accept the proposals they would not vote against them because Crossman had threatened to withdraw the whole section if the bill was opposed by the Union. It was a pragmatic decision to save the little protection offered by the bill.

For Joan it was all a fudge. In a letter to Harold Wilson she warned Labour could not expect farm workers' continued support unless he kept his pre-election pledge that no farm worker would be evicted unless suitable accommodation had been made available. Northallerton and Cleveland District Committees proposed the Union's Yorkshire members should contract out of their penny-a-month levy to the Labour Party. If taken up on a national scale it would cost the Labour Party over £6,000 a year. The Northallerton Committee urged the Union's national membership of around 130,000 not to vote Labour until the Party kept its oft-repeated pledge on the tied cottage. On 24 April Joan organised a meeting of farm workers in York where they threatened not to pay affiliation fees to the Labour Party in protest at Crossman's bill.[6]

She told the local press, 'The Union has been incensed about the tied cottage for sixty years. We are not going to throw the towel in now. The system is still the curse of the countryside, and the Labour Party above all others ought to know that.'

The Union Executive was furious. General secretary Harold Collison rounded on Union Organiser Jack Brocklebank; Joan was stoking up the opposition – he must control her. As a lay member of the Union Joan couldn't be touched by the Executive. In May Jack Brocklebank was threatened with dismissal.[7]

The Executive stuck to the compromise hammered out with Crossman. In the House of Lords, Acting President Lord Hilton began his speech by criticising the bill for failing to provide the farm worker with the full protection as promised by Labour before the General Election; 'however, we realise that the Bill is a great improvement on the past situation, so we do not at this stage intend to oppose it.'[8]

During the housing debate on the first day of the 1965 Labour Party Conference at Blackpool, Joan (delegate from Thirsk and Malton) moved: 'This Conference demands that the Labour Government abolish the tied cottage system immediately, because of the power it gives the farmer over the worker, reducing him to only half citizenship.' She told delegates it shouldn't be necessary to move such a resolution yet again from a Labour platform; on at least two occasions the Labour Party had promised to do away with the tied cottage and had failed to do so. As she was making her speech a member of her Union, his wife and three children were being threatened with eviction from their cottage in Barton, Richmond, the constituency adjacent to her own.

She explained how clauses in the Rent Bill proceeding through Parliament defeated the commitment not to evict a farm worker without there being suitable alternative accommodation available. The clause, which stated the judge should take into account whether or not the farm could be properly run without the cottage, brought the farm worker back to square one. It was the same old argument farmers always used – they couldn't run the farm without the cottage. She maintained farmers would argue this even when there were a number of empty cottages on the farm. It was not the cottage they needed to run the farm, it was the need to retain power over the farm worker.

She attacked another clause which stated courts had to take into account who would suffer the greatest hardship, the farmer or the farm worker, if the possession order was not granted. For years she had heard in the courts 'sob stories' of the hardships farmers would face by not getting their new employee into the cottage. In her experience of such cases the county court judges were not particularly sympathetic to the farm workers.

Her argument was that the farmer could get all the labour required if farm workers were paid the wage they were entitled to as skilled workers, and if they worked the forty-hour, five-day week pertaining in many other industries. Nobody had been more loyal to the Labour Party than the farm workers and it was time for loyalty the other way around. The tied cottage was a festering sore on the countryside.

She acknowledged Crossman's undertaking to look again at the problem if evictions continued, but this still left untouched the underlying problem: the power of the farmer over nearly half of all farm workers. Joan concluded 'The power is subtle and insidious; it is not so much whether the farmer uses the power; it's the mere fact he has it. The farm worker can't speak his mind for fear; often our people can't stand for local authorities for fear of being removed from their homes. Often they have to work over 65 years of age to keep the house.' In case the Party was worried legislation to abolish tied cottages would lose it seats in rural areas, she reminded delegates 'We have never had any votes from farmers in rural areas and we are not likely to get any.'

As Joan had predicted, her motion placed General Secretary Harold Collison in a very awkward position. Anxious discussions had taken place with his Executive the previous evening, how could he not support Joan's motion at the conference? He went to the rostrum to explain the Union's position and outlined the history of the negotiations with the Labour Government; how the Union had made it plain to Dick Crossman that it did not consider his legislation honoured the Party's pledge to make an eviction from a farm tied cottage impossible unless suitable alternative accommodation was available; how the Union had nevertheless recognised the legislation was an improvement and would not therefore oppose it; and how the Minister himself had acknowledged it did not meet the pledge in words, but he felt it would in practice, and he would be prepared to look at the matter again if proved to be wrong.

Collison said the Union would support Joan's motion, if pressed, but it wasn't happy with the wording. Joan could hardly believe her ears when he told delegates the Union had never sought the abolition of the tied cottage but a change in the law to prevent evictions unless suitable alternative accommodation was available.

The press reported Collison saying:

> The Union supported the motion demanding the abolition of the tied cottage system but he pointed out that the words were open to misinterpretation. His Union did not ask, and had never asked, for the abolition of the tied cottage as such. What they had done consistently over the years, and were still doing, was to say that no worker should be evicted from a tied cottage unless other suitable accommodation was available to him. The Rent Bill did not fulfil Labour's pledge and fell short of the undertaking given to them. They would not oppose the Bill, but they felt strongly that they had the right to ask the party to recognise that the pledge had not been fulfilled. Mr Crossman believed that what he and the government were doing would stop evictions

> from taking place without suitable accommodation being provided, but he believed there would still be evictions. If so the Union had made it clear that they would come back to the government and the government had promised that in those circumstances they would give further consideration to the matter.[9]

In the ensuing debate Crossman repeated his undertaking to probe more deeply into the issue if it proved necessary and he proposed remitting the resolution to Labour's Executive. Whilst Joan reluctantly accepted Crossman's proposal she was adamant that the main issue of employer power remained unaddressed.

Her conference speech provoked an angry response from the farming correspondent of the *Hull and Yorkshire Times*. She wrote back straight away:

> I don't know why your correspondent said my speech got a cold reception, for it was greeted with warm applause and widely reported . . . Perhaps he was thinking of the reception it got from the General Secretary of our Union who got up to say they supported the resolution and then proceeded to attack it. In fact he said, and I quote, 'My Union did not ask and had never asked for the abolition of the tied cottage as such.' This is news to me (and all members) as our Union has been for the abolition of the tied cottage system since it was first formed. I quote now from the Union's policy statement issued this April on tied cottages. It says 'Ever since its formation, this Union has consistently demanded the abolition of the tied cottage system'. Our previous policy statement Health and Wealth Under Our Feet carries an almost identical statement. When Lord Collison said that once the Rent Bill was law, no farm worker could be evicted without suitable alternative accommodation, he failed to point out that two further clauses in the Bill cancel this pledge out. They are as follows: The county court judge must also take into account whether or not the farm can be run without the cottage, and also who will suffer the greatest hardship – the farmer or the worker if the order is executed. As I said at the Labour Party conference, this brings us back to square one, because these are the two arguments we have always had to face in the courts – even when there have been empty houses

> on the farm belonging to the farmer who was pressing for a court order to get possession. Lord Collison also said that the new legislation will give occupants of tied cottages a chance to state their case, a chance they did not have before – and that we had therefore gained a step forward. Our people always had a chance when they got to court to state their case. Much good it did them, I must say, so where is the step forwards? Dick Crossman said the new legislation would remove the real objections to the tied cottage. This is where he is wrong. Our main objection is to this system which gives the farmer so much power over the worker, making him dependent on the farmer for his house as well as his job. It is this power which reduces the farm worker to only half a citizen. It restricts his freedom of speech, and it is this to which we object and it is this power we want removed. It is not material whether this power is used or not, the mere fact that it is there is sufficient for the farmer's purpose. As I have said before, it hangs over the heads of our people like the sword of Damocles, always poised ready to fall. Another criticism is the cost to the Union going back to courts for second and third applications for extensions of time. What then, have we gained from the new Bill – just a tiny bit more time, that is all, but the main evil remains.[10]

The Rent Act was given the Royal Assent on 8 November 1965. In the same year Harold Collison was elevated to the peerage.[11]

Within a year of the 1965 legislation, urgent talks were taking place (19 September 1966) between the Union (Lord Collison, Jim Watts, head of the Legal Department) and Anthony Greenwood, the new Minister of Housing and Local Government.

The *Land Worker* assured readers the Minister had been left in no doubt about the anger and deep concern felt by the Union at these evictions, especially in light of the earlier optimism about the 1965 Rent Act expressed by his predecessor Richard Crossman. Whilst Anthony Greenwood synpathised with the Union's attitude and the distressed families, he felt the Act needed to be given more time before a further review could be justified. At the same time he undertook to press the local authorities to do everything possible to help the evicted families – these were the first evictions to be reported under the 1965 Act.

Meanwhile, Joan had been elected as vice-president of the Union and was denouncing the Union leadership. During her vice-presidency she retained her position as secretary of the Union's Yorkshire County Committee and in this capacity sought backing from the Northern Region Group of Labour MPs in campaigning for abolition of the tied cottage. Through the group she wanted the matter brought before the PLP because she felt Union members were getting nowhere relying on discussions between leaders of the Union and leaders of the Party. Encouraged by the initial positive response in July 1967 from Tom Urwin MP, secretary to the Northern Group, Joan invited him to come and meet the Yorkshire County Committee to deepen his understanding of the tied cottage problem. Committee members had personal experiences of the tied cottage and expended considerable time and effort in court supporting Union members threatened with eviction. Despite expressing willingness to meet at a later date, Urwin failed to give a firm commitment. Several invitations ensued. Eventually he responded to Joan's invitation of March 1968:

> This matter has been discussed with the Northern Group, and I have also had private discussions with Mr E Wainwright MP and Mr Bert Hazell MP and in view of the fact that the National Union of Agricultural Workers is dealing with the matter on a national basis, I frankly cannot see any further purpose being served in my coming up to Yorkshire.

Following the County Committee's discussion of Urwin's letter, Joan wrote to him (May 1968): 'We are of course well aware that the Union are dealing with it on a national basis; in fact our Union has been for the abolition of the tied cottage system for over 60 years.' She assured him that only good could come of a visit from members of the Northern Group of MPs so they could see for themselves how tied cottage tenants suffered under the system. After such a meeting the MPs could put pressure on the Government to get rid of the system if they felt the case to be 'good and urgent.'

Probably with some relief, Urwin informed Joan that since his recent ministerial appointment he was no longer secretary of the Northern Group of Labour MPs. His successor Gordon Bagier wrote crisply to Joan (20 June 1968):

> Your letter concerning tied cottages was considered at the last meeting of the Northern Group of Labour MPs. All points made have been noted by Members of the Group and it is understood, after consultation with the NUAW at a national level, that the matter was being effectively handled and that the Group should not attempt to intervene in local matters.

Bagier's letter was received with scornful disbelief by the Yorkshire Committee, on whose behalf Joan replied in September:

> You say that our Head Office are handling the matter effectively and that as a Group you should not intervene in a local matter. First of all, if as a Union we had been effective the tied cottage would not still be with us, secondly this is not a local matter it is a matter which affects our members from one end of the country to the other.

She pointed out that some Union members advocated the NUAW withdrawing its affiliation fees from the Labour Party because of its failure to carry out its pledge on the tied cottage. Whilst Joan herself would be opposed to such action, believing more good could be done for Union members within the Party than outside, it would be hard to maintain this view if the Group continued to refuse meeting members of the Union who had suffered under the system. 'It grieves me that I as a member of the Party for 22 years have to plead with Labour MPs to understand and help workers to overcome something so obviously unjust as the tied cottage system'.

Joan maintained pressure on the Labour Government at both the 1968 Annual Labour Party Conference and the TUC. To loud applause she told Labour Party delegates it was a scandal that her Union was still having to come to the rostrum to move a resolution on the tied cottage. In her denunciation of the tied cottage and its attendant suffering, anxiety and fear, she described how 800,000 people lived in a system that made them into 'bondsmen' of feudal times. The Housing Minister, Anthony Greenwood, sympathised with the points made and said the Government was reviewing the present legislation to see how it could be strengthened.

Again Joan's speech provoked correspondence in the local press:

> It is too well known that farms in remote areas would grind to a halt unless houses were available, provided by the farmer, for men who could neither build nor rent quickly on taking up employment, nor expect instant council accommodation. What one deplores is Miss Maynard's attitude and her use of provocative and vicious language. And more important, the fact that she keeps well clear of the subject of a remedy. Isn't one just sick of hearing this sort of thing, in connection with management–labour relations today?... The country is crippling itself internally with this type of nonsensical conflict. All this leads to anarchy, total breakdown of our social structure and Communism. Maybe that is what Miss Maynard is really seeking.[12]

Joan was well accustomed to accusations of being a Communist or anarchist; they usually substituted for argument. Nevertheless, she replied in measured tones the following week, asking how all the other workers in remote areas managed to either build or rent a free house. When farm workers were paid a wage that compared to their skill and importance as workers, farmers would have no labour problems. Far from asking for anarchy or Communism, she was merely asking that farm workers be treated as ordinary citizens entitled to elementary justice.

Seconding a Society of Graphical and Allied Trades motion on the tied cottage at the TUC Conference, Joan placed her argument within the context of Human Rights Year. Angrily she quoted Anthony Greenwood's speech at a local government conference the previous year: 'No man is free if his choice of employment is restricted by considerations of accommodation.' Talk, said Joan, was cheap; action was needed.

Farmers were up in arms about Joan's proposals to the Labour Party and TUC, accusing her of discriminating against them as employers of farm workers.[13] What about employees in other tied housing? Joan pointed out the specificity of the farm workers' situation: in few other industries were the houses owned by an individual employer; in miners' or railway workers' homes, for example, the houses were owned by the company, and the employees could collectively oppose threats of eviction. In no other industry was there such a history of bitterness with its record of court orders and evictions. Whilst farmers might claim there were now few evictions, Joan would remind them it was largely because of the all the work put in by Union officers in preventing each threatened eviction. When accused by farmers of being emotional – a criticism so frequently directed to women, Joan replied:

> It is an emotional issue, it involves people, it involves humanity, it involves a home, a marriage is a stake, health is at stake. I have just left one of the tied cottage cases referred to in my TUC speech, they are sick with worry, they can't sleep at night, but they are also angry, I am glad to say, at the indignity to which they have been subjected through no fault of their own. They cannot help the man being ill, they wish with all their hearts that he were well, they have three children to bring up. I am angry too, I hate all that the tied cottage system stands for because of what it does to my people; I shall not rest until it is abolished for ever.

In its 1969 Agriculture Bill Labour sought to amend the 1965 Rent Act by allowing the farm worker six months' security of tenure in his tied cottage following termination of employment. Whilst the Union opposed various discretionary clauses in the bill, Joan considered the entire bill served little more than to prolong the agony of the threatened tied cottage tenant. At meetings of the Executive she stressed the Labour Government should legislate for nothing less than its pledge to abolish the tied cottage system. Convinced the Executive Committee's efforts in meeting Ministers behind closed doors were getting nowhere, she advocated a public campaign supported by the TUC and the Labour Party. The Labour Government should be compelled to abide by its own Party Conference decision. She proposed taking a leaf out of the farmers' book; on the training board issue, they had campaigned publicly and successfully against Government proposals to pay a training levy.

The landowning interests in the Lords amended the Bill by removing the six months concession. Joan was contemptuous; the tied cottage system ruined the lives of farm workers' families, yet the landowners in the Lords were the very people who claimed to uphold the sanctity of family life. The Government's promise to restore the concession in the Commons was denied when Labour was defeated in the General Election. Joan judged the

1970 Agriculture Act to be worthless.[14] The Union's experience of more than 2,000 cases heard in the courts over the previous five years had left her in no doubt that as long as discretionary clauses remained in Acts of Parliament, county court judges would decide in favour of the farmers.

Proponents of the tied cottage system in agriculture would argue that several other industries and occupations provided tied housing, and the glib point was often made that the Prime Minister occupied a tied house. Harold Wilson's defeat prompted a farmer to write gleefully to the *Yorkshire Evening Press*: since Joan's Party leader had been forced to move from his tied house would she redouble her efforts for the abolition of the tied house system? Yet again Joan patiently rehearsed the argument:

> There is clearly no comparison between the situation of an ex-prime minister leaving number ten and a farm worker leaving a tied house. Because of the farm worker's low wage, to a large extent due to the tied house, he has no freedom to choose where he will live. Circumstances and stark economic reality force him either into another tied house, or through the courts he may get a council house.

With feeling she added: 'As I have always done everything I could to get rid of the tied cottage system it would be hard for me to redouble my efforts.'[15]

For years Joan had been concerned about the quality of legal representation available to farm workers threatened with eviction. Controversially she argued that local rural solicitors were in league with the landlords and that the courts, and RDCs were dominated by farmers and their friends:

> Our Rural District Councils, the housing authority, are controlled by farmers. A farm worker on an eviction notice has a poor chance of a council house even if he could afford one, if his boss is on the Housing Committee, and if he isn't, his friends are. Where there is no Labour councillor to speak for the worker, the power of the employer is complete. I heard the Housing Inspector of a Rural District Council saying he hadn't much sympathy with the claim of an agricultural worker for a house because he refused to work overtime and that is why he is being evicted. Did you ever hear such impudence?[16]

She would quote a county court judge telling a Union member in her presence in 1967 'It may seem a hard thing for me to say to you, but land is more important than people. I give you three weeks to get out. The judge in giving judgement for the farmer against the worker indicated once again that county court judges are not notorious for their sympathy with my people but for their sympathy with the other class.'

In responding to Joan's concerns about the earlier 1965 legislation, Lord Collison did acknowledge that unfamiliarity with pertinent sections of the Rent Act resulted in some solicitors engaged by the Union failing to deploy all the arguments available to them:

> Unfortunately, we are in no position to pick and choose as a great many rural solicitors are not disposed to take on this kind of representation, and in other cases the nearest competent solicitor is already acting for the farmer. We are attempting to resolve this particular problem by ensuring that our instructions contain the best possible brief to solicitors, having regard to the circumstances of any particular case.[17]

As Yorkshire County Secretary, Joan wrote to Anthony Greenwood (10 March 1970) about proposals in the 1970 Agriculture Bill:

> So far as the new legislation is concerned, first of all we have no faith in the County Court Judges. In our long History and long experience we have hardly ever found them to be on our side. Because the new proposals are edged [*sic*] round with all sorts of qualifications we do not think that many of our people will get the 6 months grace allowed in the Bill.

Anthony Greenwood's response was curt. 'If you wish to take further your remarks about the judiciary, this would be a matter for the Lord Chancellor. Certainly I do not accept the suggestion that the county courts are biased one way or the other in this – or any other – matter.'

The Executive Committee of the Union had met with the Home Policy Sub-committee of Labour's NEC over several years to thrash out the tied cottage question. In Opposition the Labour Party championed the issue in pledge after pledge. In Government the legislation was a messy compromise.

When Joan was elected to the Labour Party's NEC in 1972 she resolved to overcome her feelings of hurt and betrayal arising from the abolition of the Union vice-presidency earlier that year. In the interests of the members, she determined to cooperate with the general secretary, Reg Bottini, and the Union Executive in ensuring a commitment to tied cottage abolition would be included in the next Labour Party manifesto. She worked closely with Jim Watts, head of the Union Legal Department, to ensure agreements reached with the Party earlier in the year would be translated into the Labour manifesto for the next General Election.

Joan firmly maintained that without her presence on the NEC, abolition would not have figured in the two Labour Party manifestos of 1974. She had to argue the case persistently and hard in committees and correspondence, not because NEC members were unsympathetic, but because 'everybody was fighting for their own bit, foreign policy, civil liberties, housing, and I was the only person who had direct knowledge and experience of the problem.'[18] Labour was very much an urban-based party with urban concerns and priorities.

The General Election of February 1974 produced a minority Labour Government. Wilson boldly set about settling the miners' strike and tackling pay policy, but at the Union's May Biennial Conference in Clacton anger was mounting that the Government was dragging its heels on the tied cottage. Delegates were unimpressed when Norman Buchan, Minister of State for Agriculture, explained the tied cottage could not be addressed at a stroke, the Government was considering setting up a working party. Joan acidly observed that action after thity years of Labour promises could hardly be termed 'at a stroke'. She reminded him that during the previous three years over 3,000 cases had come before the courts in which farmers had sought possession of their workers' cottages. Eighty delegates travelled to Westminster on the evening of 9 May to lobby MPs in the House. Stan Newens MP chaired the meeting, which was attended by a small group of Labour MPs including Dennis Skinner, Martin Flannery and Bob Cryer. Joan forcefully reminded the meeting of the manifesto pledge.

On 7 June she wrote to members of the NEC Home Policy Committee:

> At the meeting of the Home Policy Committee you will have a letter from my Union the NUAAW. I share their disquiet that so far our Labour government

> has made no move towards carrying out the firm promise in the manifesto to abolish the tied cottage system . . . The system is costing the Union around £10,000 per year defending our members in the courts, this in addition to all the heartache and hardship it causes... Farm Workers cannot fight for decent pay when they are bound and gagged in tied houses. I ask you to support our Union in the approaches they are making to the government for implementation of the manifesto promise.

A fortnight later (20 June) Reg Bottini led a deputation of the Union Executive and a member of the TGWU to a joint meeting with the Housing and Construction Minister and the Minister of State for Agriculture. There they were advised that although the Government was committed to the abolition of the tied cottage system, the Parliamentary timetable and the absence of an overall majority did not permit the Government to implement its manifesto undertaking in the present session of Parliament.

Earlier in the year the *Farmers Weekly* had published an article by Joan criticising the tied cottage. The editorial in the June issue of the *North Riding and Durham Farmer*[19] declared: 'The political pressure is building up once more, and "our dear friend" Miss Joan Maynard is once again leading the campaign. Your Union is pledged to resistance by sensible and reasonable argument, to this political manoeuvring.'

A subversive contributor to *Farmers Weekly* was farm worker George Scales (NUAAW Essex); he reported to Joan how as a tied cottage dweller he had cheated a little by responding to the *Farmers Weekly* questionnaire on the tied cottage and found inadequate space for all he wanted to say. Joan was highly amused – the questionnaire was designed to be completed by farmers. Unsurprisingly it came out in favour of the system.

In September 1974 George Scales was in touch with Joan again:

> Since we learned of your adoption as the Labour Candidate for Sheffield Brightside there are some among us of the NUAAW in Essex, who, although quite aware of the wisdom of your selectors, are somewhat perturbed as to how things will shake down after you are elected, when, as their chosen parliamentary representative, the people of Brightside will claim your undivided loyalty to their particular causes; which of course will be industrially rather than agri-

> culturally oriented... Will the Brightsiders' gain be made at the expense of the tied-cottagers?

He needn't have worried. It was said in the Commons that Joan could hardly wait to hang up her coat before tackling the tied cottage. Within hours of her election she was asking other Labour MPs, 'who is responsible for the Queen's Speech' On learning it was the Cabinet she contacted all the Cabinet ministers she knew to be sympathetic, ten in total, and urged them to fight to get tied cottage legislation into the first session of Parliament. When there was no reference to the tied cottage in the Queen's Speech she raised the issue at the next meeting of the PLP and tabled an Early Day Motion urging the Government to bring forward a bill. At her request the Tribune Group wrote to the Prime Minister. With Tom Torney MP, former chairman of the PLP's Agriculture Group, she took a petition signed by over 140 MPs to 10 Downing Street. It denounced the tied cottage as a system of bondage subjecting farm workers to anxiety, hardship and indignity. Appreciating that townspeople were unaware of what was happening all over the countryside, Joan invited farm workers to the Commons to describe their experiences to MPs and advised Union branches to invite MPs to meetings to learn about the tied cottage at first hand. Every branch should demand to know what its MP was doing about the tied cottage. 'I literally never let the matter rest until I got it into the Queen's Speech, where it has to be before you can have a bill at all.'

Joan was determined to make her maiden Parliamentary speech as soon as the timetable allowed. On the evening of 6 November, nervous yet decisive, she informed the House that as well as representing Sheffield Brightside, an industrial seat in the great city of Sheffield, she was the sole sponsored member for farm workers. With the full backing of her constituency she would put forward the farm workers' case concerning the tied cottage system in agriculture. Drawing on nearly thirty years' involvement in hundreds of tied cottages cases she spoke movingly of the fifty per cent of farm workers who lived in tied cottages, how their job and the roof over their head was in jeopardy if they disagreed with their employer or if they were ill, had an accident or were too old to work. She described how they were dragged through the courts to enable their employers to obtain possession of their home. Never mind that they had given years of honest work. Pointedly she told MPs, many of whom were members of the legal profession, that defending members in the courts was costing her Union £10,000 a year, money it would rather put into its own funds than the pockets of lawyers.

Emphasising the connection between the tied cottage and low pay in agriculture she said:

> If the farmers were not able to offer the bait of a cheap house at the time of a housing shortage, they would have to pay the rate for the job. That is why the tied cottage issue is so important to farm workers. It is clear that it is closely related to low pay in agriculture... Agriculture has a twentieth-century approach when it is considering new techniques but an eighteenth-century approach when it is considering wages. Part of its eighteenth-century approach is the persistent fight which is put up to retain tied cottages and low pay. I say that tied cottages must go and that they will go when a Labour government – I hope it is this one – have the political will to do away with them. (Hansard, 6 November 1974, cols.1135–1137)

The Union leadership was also exerting pressure on the Government through direct discussions with the Secretary of State for the Environment and the Minister of Agriculture. Bottini was given unequivocal assurance that the necessary amending legislation would be high among the Government's priorities for the second session of Parliament and discussions would take place between the Government and the Union to develop a consultative document.

Joan's calls for action against the tied cottage and the Union's discussions with the Government provoked angry responses from farmers and country landowners, who campaigned to force the Government to change its mind. Soon there were reports of divisions in the Government over the proposed tied cottage legislation and the Department of the Environment was accused of delaying tactics. It was Gavin Strang, Parliamentary Secretary to the Minister of Agriculture, who reassured the Union at its June rally in Skegness that the Government had made an unequivocal promise to end the centuries-old injustice of the tied cottage. Ted Short, the Leader of the House of Commons, had stated categorically it was the Government's intention to introduce legislation in the next session of Parliament.

In August the government published the consultative document 'Abolition of the Tied Cottage System in Agriculture'. It specifically distinguished agriculture from other tied housing: 'There is no other major industry where the fact of unfurnished accommodation provided by the employer/landlord enters so extensively and controversially into the relationship between employer and employee.'

The document further fuelled the opposition of farmers and country landowners, who claimed legislation would inhibit the mobility of labour, lead to an exodus of thousands of workers from agriculture and have terrible consequences for food supplies and prices. Two thousand farmers came to London in September to protest.

In the Commons Joan denounced their criticisms and welcomed the Government's firm commitment to introduce legislation in the next session. She provoked laughter when she countered claims that stock and dairy farmers would find it impossible to carry on without tied cottages: 'Vet surgeons do not live in tied cottages and midwives do not live in the houses where children are born . . . nevertheless we manage to survive.'

John Wheaton (NUAAW branch secretary Old Windsor, Berkshire) was delighted and wrote to the *Morning Star* calling on trade unionists and local Labour Party leaders to send letters of support to

> that sterling character Joan Maynard without whose valiant effort and determination this [tied cottage] issue may well have been passed over for another seven or eight decades. It will not be news for Joan to learn that she does not command the respect of all NUAAW officials, and members. This is to be regretted for she is by far one of the staunchest and most progressive leaders the Union has had since the days of Joseph Arch.

The pledge was at last included in the Queen's Speech on 19 November 1975. Speaking in the ensuing debate Joan congratulated the Government and looked forward to action after thirty years of promises. She expressed astonishment at Conservative claims that abolition would increase the price of food; 'nearly 50% of farm workers already live in rented property and we don't hear the farmers for whom they work saying that they find it impossible to run their farms'. On the shortage of houses in the countryside, it wasn't the fault of the workers, 'to some extent it is the landowners who have sometimes been unwilling to sell land or have been willing to sell only at very high prices. Many of the people concerned have not only been the owners of the land but have dominated the local authorities'.

On 3 December 1975 the Union lobbied MPs against the tied cottage; several hundred farm workers from across the country travelled by coach to London, forgoing a day's pay to do so. Carrying placards saying 'Tied Cottages – the Workers Man Trap' they were welcomed by Joan to Westminster, where they told MPs about the tied cottage – how the farmers tell you how to live; how when you finish a day's work they still come round in the evening; how you daren't speak out. Joan said the lobby killed the lie put about by farmers that workers didn't really want abolition of the tied cottage system.

Gavin Strang assured the lobbyists that legislation would be introduced to give them the same security of tenure as other workers; progressive farmers would regard it as a practical and sensible implementation of timely reform. For Union President Bert Hazell, such legislation would be 'the greatest social advance of the past century for our people in the countryside, and it cannot come too soon'. Reg Bottini was cautious, rightly predicting that legislation would be bitterly opposed in the House and elsewhere.

At the NFU annual general meeting in January delegates were hostile. the *Land Worker* reported allegations of NUAAW policy being inspired by 'reds under the bed' and neo-Communist activists. It carried reports of the *British Farmer and Stock Breeder* saying the general feeling was that Joan alone had organised the tied cottage plot, she was the femme fatale of the NUAAW. Just who did Joan Maynard think she was? Indignant and ignorant, a farmer wrote to the *Guardian* (19 April 1976), 'Do you know that the great anti-tied cottage legislator Mrs [*sic*] Joan Maynard MP has not one tied cottage in her constituency? So who is she representing?'

On Monday 12 April 1976 the Government published its bill to extend Rent Act security of tenure to workers living in agricultural tied cottages.

Joan was angry – this wasn't abolition of the system. But the *Land Worker* described it as 'a watershed in the long struggle of farm workers to get the same kind of security as other workers who are tenants protected by the Rent Acts'. Its main proposal was: 'Unless and until suitable alternative accommodation is proved to be available, an agricultural worker whose employment has ended will have security in the cottage like any other Rent Act protected tenant.'

In the *Land Worker*'s words 'qualified expectation' suffused the Union Biennial Conference at Malvern in May 1976; the Second Reading of the Rent (Agriculture) Bill had just been secured in the House by 33 votes. Delegates listened to Ernest Armstrong, Parliamentary Under Secretary of State for the Environment, warmly acknowledge the work of President Bert Hazell, General Secretary Reg Bottini, Head of the Legal Department Jim Watts, and Joan. Bert Hazell had steered the campaign with firmness and shrewdness born of long experience, Reg Bottini had masterminded tactics with great skill and Jim Watts's first-hand knowledge of the problem had been invaluable. Joan was praised for her vigorous campaigning in Parliament and the Labour movement.

In Parliament the Secretary of State for the Environment, Peter Shore, opened the debate on the Rent (Agriculture) Bill, describing the distress and humiliation of eviction; each year over a thousand families faced eviction with nowhere to go when farmers obtained court orders for possession of the tied cottage. Opposition spokesman on agriculture, Francis Pym, declared an interest as an owner of tied cottages and assured the House the agriculture industry had a good record and reputation for looking after its workers' families no less than its workers. Joan condemned widespread scaremongering about the effects of the bill; all went well until there was difficulty about a tied cottage – disagreement with the employer, illness or old age. Everything changed when a man could no longer work on a farm, 'bang goes goodwill'. Union members had been dragged through the courts like common criminals. The tied cottage was feudal and inhuman and caused untold suffering for farm workers.

During the course of the bill Joan was constantly approached by farm workers concerned to know if and how the legislation would affect their situation. She took great care to respond to the specifics of every case, and in complex circumstances entered into detailed and careful correspondence, enlisting, where appropriate, support and information at all levels of government.

Whilst in Joan's view the tied cottage was a key obstacle to increasing farm workers' pay, the other obstacle was the Agricultural Wages Board (AWB). Her motion at the Malvern Biennial to withdraw from the AWB had been heavily defeated. Undeterred, she introduced a Private Member's Bill, The Farm Workers' Collective Bargaining Bill, whose purpose was to amend the Employment Protection Act 1975 to provide for conversion of the AWB to a statutory Joint Industrial Council. Aware that most Private Members' Bills never reached the statute book she thought it would nevertheless put the issue of farm workers' low pay on the Commons agenda.[20]

Reg Bottini was enraged by Joan's bill. He believed in the AWB and accused Joan of acting counter to Union policy as agreed at the Biennial Conference. On 26 May the Executive Committee issued a press statement saying it had considered the bill and, 'bearing in mind the overwhelming rejection by the Union's National Conference of a motion moved by Miss Maynard calling the Union to withdraw from the AWB, decided to dissociate the Union from the Bill as being inconsistent with Union policy as decided by National Conference'.

Joan was adamant the bill did not contravene Union policy. It was an enabling bill seeking to give the Union the right, if it desired at some future time, to convert the AWB into a statutory Joint Industrial Council. The Council would allow direct negotiations between farmers and workers – without independent members.

The distinction was lost in many quarters, not least because of the Union Executive's press statement. North Devon County Committee met on 30 May and proposed a warning be issued to Joan that Union sponsorship would be withdrawn if she continued to contravene Union policy. Joan sought to meet with the Union's Political Committee and Executive Committee to explain her case, but Bottini informed her on 23 June that the Executive had agreed he should meet alone with her and report back. Joan was frankly frightened of meeting alone with Bottini; she would follow Jack Brocklebank's example: 'When Bottini had him on the carpet he always made sure he had somebody with him.' So she wrote (8 July 1976):

> When we meet perhaps you will be able to explain to me how my Private Members' Bill runs counter to union policy . . . I will have a copy of the Bill with me. I am quite willing to meet you, I only make two stipulations – one that I may bring my secretary to take note of the proceedings and two that we should alternate meetings between Gray's Inn Road and the House of Commons.

An exasperated Bottini saw no need for a secretary to be present to monitor their conversation, 'and the implication is so serious that I am not prepared to meet you on that basis. Neither do I understand, if there is to be series of meetings, they should alternate between this office and the House of Commons.'

Joan answered (26 July 1976):

> I suggested bringing my secretary because I thought it sensible to have a note of our discussion and the points raised, rather than having to keep all in my head. No doubt you may well like to have your secretary too. I have been trying since April to meet the Union to discuss with them issues which affect our members. I have two jobs, one to look after the interests of farm and rural workers, two my responsibility to my constituents . . . I am anxious to work with the Union and I have worked with Jim Watts on the recent Committee Stage of the Tied Cottage Rent (Agriculture) Bill. I am willing to meet the Political Sub Committee of the Union, or the full Executive. I am equally willing to meet you if my secretary can be present. I suggested alternative meetings at Gray's Inn and the House of Commons because we are both equally busy people and we should treat each other as equal human beings… The only people who will suffer whilst this wrangle is going on is the membership whom we are here to serve.

The two were unable to reach agreement. In August Joan coldly acknowledged Bottini's letter of 30 July: 'The House is in recess but I will be in touch with you when we come back in October.'

As ever, Joan was supported by Jack Brocklebank. He had addressed well-attended meetings in Yorkshire and Durham to explain the Rent (Agriculture) Bill and the Farm Workers' Collective Bargaining Bill. Nowhere, he assured her, did members see any conflict between the bill and the Biennial Conference decision on the AWB.

Others of Joan's supporters were worried that her opposition to Government economic policy might contribute to Labour's downfall and with it the tied cottage legislation. The *Land Worker* published a letter from George Scales (June 1976) criticising her action: '[There is] no one in this country who wishes the Labour government keeps afloat more than the tied cottager.'

Smarting, Joan acknowledged his right to criticise her (11 June 1976),

> but for God's sake do not give them sticks to beat me with. Couldn't you have sent the letter direct to me? . . . I was refusing to support the government who were once again breaking their promises which they were elected on, as a consequence workers will pay more for food, higher rents, workers' children will be taught in larger classes, public transport – which affects workers – will become worse, one could go on... Are you really saying that in order to get the tied cottage Bill through and maintain the Labour government I should vote for anything and everything no matter how anti-worker or evil it is?

Six days later she added: 'It is not the warring factions within the Labour Party who gave Maggie Thatcher the opportunity to lick her lips, it is the disastrous policies of our own government. I can assure you that on the night thirty-seven of us abstained we were not being clumsy, we knew full well what we were doing.'

Bottini had been correct in predicting the farmers and their friends in Parliament would try to cripple the Rent (Agriculture) Bill. The main attack came from the Lords, whose amendments removed security of tenure proposed for tied cottage occupants employed in grazing and meadowlands, dairy farming, livestock-keeping, pasture land, orchards and forestry. Speaking during the Commons debate on the amendments Joan accused their lordships not only of wrecking the bill but ripping it apart; they were people who never lacked security themselves yet were determined to deny it to farm workers. To argue that it was essential for stockmen to live on the farm was to ignore completely that there were such things as telephones and motorcars.

In Yorkshire, County Conference delegates were contemptuous of the Lords' attempts to wreck the bill. Joan was delighted when they adopted an emergency resolution proposed by Roger Fieldhouse (Hampsthwaite Branch) declaring the House of Lords to be undemocratic, unrepresentative, farmer – and landlord – dominated and anti-working class. Joan wrote to Reg Bottini on 27 October: 'Actually the House of Lords is like the tied cottage system, both are equally archaic and should have been done away with many years ago' – a little swipe at Union leaders Hilton and Collison as well as Bottini's own (unrealised) aspirations.

The Government held firm and reversed the Lords' amendments by use of the guillotine procedure. On the bill's return to the Upper House, the Lords accepted their defeat and did not insist on the amendments.

Marian and Richard Neville were present during one of the debates; they had experienced living in a tied cottage and had campaigned hard for abolition. 'Joan sent us a note and got us tickets. We were so excited we got turfed out of the gallery. There were people on the Tory side saying it was to the benefit of the farm workers. I shouted out, no it is not, it's in lieu of wages! Anyway she eventually got it through and we were overjoyed.'

Politically this should have been a crowning moment for Joan, yet she was being rubbished in the editorial of her own Union journal the *Land Worker* and in the tabloid press for her other political activities. The December issue of the *Land Worker* refered to 'a celebrated MP, who had a go at the platform speakers at the Tolpuddle rally' (she didn't) and in the *Sun* under the headline 'Rebel Joan, the Left's smash and grab raider', its political editor Roger Carroll excoriated her 'chilling opinions', the deselection of Eddie Griffiths, the lifting of the ban on Left groups joining the Labour Party and her 'Northern Ireland activities', especially inviting the leader of Sinn Fein to the Commons. (2 December 1976)

Labour Weekly (3 December 1976) carried the headline 'Joan Maynard in attack on leaders of trade unions'. Speaking in Dronfield, Sheffield, Joan had attacked the Social Contract: 'Workers' standard of living is going down all the time, yet only when we can persuade the trade unions to break with the Government's policy on wage restraint can we expect things to get better.' The following week Joan wrote to *Labour Weekly*:

> Your headline representing my speech at Dronfield says I attacked leaders of the trade unions. In fact I was attacking the policy of wage restraint, as I always have, pointing out that it was lowering the standard of living of working people. I then posed the question, how much longer will trade unionists pay their contributions when the wages question is really not being handled by their union, because it has been taken out of their hands by the TUC and the government. I deplore attacks on people and prefer discussing politics.

On 7 December 1976 County Secretary G.H.J. Gilbert sent a letter to Bottini; the Wiltshire County Committee had instructed him to write 'deploring the adverse publicity gained by the activities of the Union sponsored MP for Sheffield Brightside, and viewing with grave concern the effect this will have on the membership.'

The TUC general secretary, Len Murray, wrote to Bottini to complain about Joan. Bottini replied (20 December 1976): 'My Executive Committee asked me to inform you that they dissociate themselves from the remarks made by Miss Maynard in regard to trade unionists not continuing to pay their subscriptions.'

In January Joan learned that the Bedfordshie and Buckinghamshire County Conference had passed a resolution calling for the Executive to drop her as its sponsored MP. She also heard talk of similar emergency resolutions being put to delegates at other county conferences.

Joan was convinced opponents were trying to discredit her among the membership. She didn't suspect the members – they were 'the salt of the earth'. Her friend George Scales had a less romanticised view and told her (22 January 1977): 'The only connection we have with salt, is the way we run when a little of it has been sprinkled on our tails.'

He wrote to the editor of the *Land Worker*:

> The Bucks and Beds conference delegates' rounding on Sister Joan Maynard was an act, so contemptible, it makes me feel ashamed of my class, my Union

and the name – farm worker. Have they no sense of history? Do they honestly believe we would have progressed as far as we have if our destiny had been left to the reforming aspirations of the right-wingers and the middle of the roaders?

*

The Rent (Agriculture) Act 1976 came into effect on New Year's Day 1977[21] Joan acknowledged that whilst abolition of the tied cottage system had not been achieved, farm workers now had the security of knowing suitable alternative accommodation would be provided; they would be more independent and this very independence would increase their stature and dignity as people. She would always maintain Union policy had been for abolition and Labour Party policy was 'suitable alternative accommodation'. Had Labour leaders not been so close to the farmers, and had the Union leadership campaigned more vigorously, she believed abolition could have been achieved; 'unfortunately the pass was sold in high places'. She paid tribute to Gavin Strang for all the help given to her as 'a new raw MP.' Indeed Gavin Strang was regarded by both right and left within the Union as key to ensuring the legislation progressed through Parliament – a considerable achievement given the Government's fragile majority and the powerful elements of internal opposition.

Whilst Joan's contribution was unacknowledged among the Union leadership – to her lasting sadness she wasn't even mentioned or allowed to speak at the celebration dinner in London – it was warmly recognised by other Union and Labour Party members. She received scores of letters from farm workers: 'I am sure many will sleep sounder from now on and will no longer be trodden on as in the past. At last the black cloud has been brushed aside forever. Thanks, from one of the old plough boys.'

Audrey Wise said of Joan's contribution to the tied cottage legislation: 'It is to Joan's credit more than any other single individual. The rest of us were willing supporters and everybody came behind her on that issue on the Left. The Left didn't really take up rural issues, they did with the tied cottage, but they wouldn't have done without Joan.'

Wilf Page's assessment was similar:

She'd be the first one to agree she wasn't the only one; we were all campaigning on the tied cottage. When we got her as a sponsored MP – we'd had about three previous sponsored MPs and they'd been unable to do much about the tied cottage in the House of Commons. I'm not saying they weren't concerned about the tied cottage, but obviously they hadn't had the drive in the House of Commons to get it through, get the thing going. When Joan got elected I think she felt that now I'm in the place where it's not just campaigning but getting the thing dealt with – onto the statute book. Once she got into the House of Commons she was in the place where it really counts. She did eventually get legislation through with the help of her colleagues; she was not successful in getting everything she wanted, but at least she got the worst evils of the tied cottage done away with. No longer could farm workers and their families be slung out onto the village green or lane because the husband had had a row with the boss the day before.

TWELVE

The earth is honest

The snake was scotch'd. Under the Rent (Agriculture) Act the worst effects of the tied cottage were countered but the system itself remained. The farm cottage as a part of the remuneration, together with the other well-known disadvantageous conditions – isolation, proximity to the employer, lack of opportunity – kept agricultural workers in a weak negotiating position. On 23 April 1987, after eight years in Opposition, Joan made her final speech to the House of Commons. She painted a bleak picture:

> Farm workers continue to exist on low pay, with 12,000 receiving family income supplement. This means that their wages are below the poverty line despite the fact that 21% of farmers who employ labour are still doing very well. The low pay of farm workers represents a subsidy to agriculture and food production, on the backs of farm workers. In 1985 there were 157,000 full-time farm workers according to Ministry of Agriculture figures. They received £40 a week less than the average earnings of industrial workers for a longer working week. If we multiply that £40 a week by 52 weeks for the 157,000 farm workers, the total is £326 million. That is the measure of exploitation of farm workers. The figure also represents the level of subsidy to the industry that their low earnings reflect. I am referring only to permanent full-time workers. If that sum of money was injected into the rural economy via farm workers' pay packets, what a difference that would make to improving the standards of the community in rural areas, not to mention the great impor-

> tance that would have by improving the standard of living of farm workers and their families, which, on the basis of their first-rate production record, they so richly deserve. Working conditions and safety are as vital to farm workers as they are to other workers, but those factors have been very much eroded under this Government. Allowing for the fact that there are fewer farm workers now than in 1979, the accident rate in the industry has become worse. When it comes to fatal accidents, only the construction industry is more dangerous than agriculture. (Hansard, 23 April 1987, col. 830)

As with other issues, Joan had found that the British way of managing consent was most effective in preventing serious disruption to the status quo. As the power of the sea is absorbed by lines of groynes, so radical proposals were worn down in Parliamentary committees, sub-committees, study groups. When it was said by Joan, and others, that farm workers lived under a feudal system, it was of course a rhetorical exaggeration. There was no law that made the farm worker an appurtenance of the farm, but in practice they commonly were, by virtue of the conditions, which reduced them politically and financially. The Union had no illusions about the conditions, even if they equivocated about the solutions. The Labour Party, with its largely urban constituency, and financial support mostly from the industrial unions, was not at the leadership level ready to take radical action.

Joan was clear about the underlying cause of rural poverty. In an electrifying speech to the Labour Party 1972 Annual Conference, she reminded delegates that from the earliest days of the Labour movement public ownership of land had featured prominently in Socialist thinking 'The land originally belonged to the people; then came the Enclosures Acts and of course the Acts were made by the very people who were actually enclosing the land, and under these enclosures the people were robbed. At that time if you stole the duck off the common you were sent to prison, but if you stole the common you were sent to the House of Lords, if you were not already there.'

Political power, economic power, marching in step.

Her solution would be to take back into common ownership the fundamental resource – not farms as such, but land. Farms, as constituted at any particular time, are but expressions of the mode of production. Land itself was the greatest asset of a nation, after its people – the prerequisite for housing, food production, schools, hospitals. Moving the composite resolution she said: 'This Conference believes that all land should be publicly owned. It instructs the National Executive Committee to draw up a plan to bring this about and submit it to the next Annual Conference and, further, include in the next General Election manifesto a pledge that all land will be brought under public ownership'.

The resolution was carried. Land nationalisation had been the policy of the Labour Party in the pre-war period, with Conference in 1926 and again in 1932 having accepted a report recommending it. After the war, the Labour Government passed up the opportunity to carry it through along with other parts of the programme of nationalisation. Instead, the 1947 Agriculture Act was passed.

The intention of the Act was to maintain stability while promoting increase in the crucial area of food production. The strategy was to guarantee prices in assured markets for listed products. The guaranteed minimum prices, reviewed annually, were to be consistent with proper remuneration for farmers and workers. The Minister had powers of supervision to ensure farms practised good management and husbandry. There were also powers to acquire land by agreement, or by compulsory order in respect of neglected land.

In 1952, as Thirsk and Malton's delegate to Labour's Annual Conference in Morecambe, Joan had moved a resolution on land nationalisation submitted by her Divisional Party. Her argument went that food prices, being pushed up on the world markets, needed to be kept low in this country by greater efficiency. The necessary investment was beyond the scope of farmers – only the state could provide it under public ownership.

The following year she continued the debate in the *Land Worker*, recognising that there were problems with the proposal, but determined it should first be accepted in principle within the movement. The editor responded that British agriculture was already more productive per person than that of other European countries, and Joan's proposal would be socially and economically destabilising, 'and in present circumstances, we would prefer that the powers of the Agriculture Act should be more fully utilised'.

Over the following years, reliance on the Agriculture Act was a commonly held position of the Union leadership, as well as of the cautious elements in the Labour Party. Two other positions were articulated within the broad Left movement. The Tribune Group, suggested that all rented lands should be taken into public ownership, whilst the Communist Party advocated bringing estates over 2,000 acres into public ownership. Wilf Page articulated the Communist Party approach:

> Joan and I had differences because she wanted to nationalise everything, all land and I didn't. I said no – let's nationalise the large estates and then divide them into viable working farms so that people who want to go into agriculture can go into agriculture – there would be vacancies on these estates. You could give them financial incentives to form cooperatives so that the biggest estates of, say twenty farms, would have a central depot for machinery so they would have the benefit of the latest equipment on the small farm – hired from the depot. And they'd have a committee governing it. The machinery would be cared for and modernised in the depot and grain and silage would be cooperatively owned. Joan thought the whole of land should be nationalised, even in the towns as well as smallholdings. You'd got to win allies, you've got to get the small farmers on your side, against the big farmers; it's a very important thing.

Joan would certainly have recognised the shrewdness of this. The interests of big and small farmers are often in tension (as was highlighted in 2002, for example, over the issue of vaccination against foot and mouth disease). Big farmers face on to a larger market, enjoy the economies of scale both in selling and in buying. They can make fuller use of more cheaply obtained equipment, dispensing with labour and depressing costs. Small farmers are frequently, increasingly, tenants, squeezed by increasing rents and expensive borrowing, having to buy machinery to compete in increasingly industrialised production.

Since their first meeting at the Cheltenham Biennial Conference in 1954, Joan and Wilf had debated the issue. He clearly remembered her, as only one of two women delegates, taking the rostrum to move:

> This Conference believes that nationalisation of land is essential for any real substantial increase in agricultural production, because the scale of fixed

> capital investment required can only be undertaken by the state. Furthermore, believing Socialism to be a higher and more effective system, we recognise that there can be no advances towards a Socialist system of society unless the land, along with the other means of production, is socially owned.

She called on the next Labour Government, as a start, to take substantial areas of land into public ownership. However, speaking as a member of the Union Executive, Frank Robinson had sought to dilute the motion by moving an amendment to the final part, 'We call upon the next Labour Government to take immediate steps to strengthen the powers of the 1947 Agriculture Act to ensure that increasingly greater areas of the land shall be taken under public control and ownership.' The amendment was carried.

George Dallas, who had been the architect of Labour policy on agriculture before the Second World War, read accounts of Joan's conference speeches and wrote to her from his home in Ayrshire. He deplored the Labour Government for missing the opportunity in 1945 to nationalise land along with the strategic industries, and in line with Party policy; when he resigned from the Executive in 1944 Nye Bevan took his place.

Dallas was scathing about the weakness of the 1947 Act, which only brought under state control the worst-cultivated land, 'and so throws on the community the work and expense of putting things right'. He quoted Sir Daniel Bell, who had been the Chief Scientific Adviser to the Government, and a leading expert in agriculture:

> It is easy to envisage the planning of the land of Great Britain to ensure an increase in productivity and population if it could be treated as a great estate managed by a business corporation with ample capital to enable it to take a long view about development. Such a plan can only be attained under national ownership of the land.

Joan was delighted with the letter and wrote back seeking further advice and information. Dallas provided her with an outline and some of the detail of the pre-war policy on land and concluded: 'You are a grand lass. I am very proud indeed to know we still have young women with their hearts in the cause of Socialism. I trust you will keep on with your good work'.

The 1947 Act was itself simply another condition in which the logic of capitalism worked itself out. Guaranteed prices and markets naturally led to land becoming more expensive with financial institutions increasingly moving into the field. Production concentrated on those products that were privileged in the Act (the only culinary vegetable listed was potato). While the Act talked of fair remuneration for farmers and workers, the workers were actually attended to by the AWB established in 1948.

In spite of the weaknesses of the 1947 Act it continued to be the starting point for the Union leadership as embodied in the policy document *Health and Wealth Under Our Feet*. At the 1956 Biennial (Yarmouth), an amendment was moved calling for a start to land nationalisation by taking into public control selected large estates to be developed as models for the future, and for farms currently under the control of the Coal Board to be transferred to an Agricultural Land Board. (This suggests the influence of Communist members.) In spite of the Executive arguing that Union policy had already been settled, the amendment was carried. It fell short of the total nationalisation Joan advocated, but she voted for it.

Two years later however, the draft Labour policy on agriculture was put before the Labour Party Conference in the document *Prosper the Plough: a Policy for a Sound and Efficient British Agriculture* (June 1958). It contained no reference to land nationalisation. Uncompromisingly it asserted: 'We are convinced that the Agriculture Act of 1947 and the Agriculture (Scotland) Act of 1948 provide the necessary framework within which the next Labour Government can build its agricultural policy, we intend to base our policy on the firm foundations of these Acts.'

The Committee that drew up the policy document was chaired by Edwin Gooch MP, president of the Union, and included the general secretary, Harold Collison. Joan was outraged, as they were flying in the face of their own members' wishes. She moved a resolution instructing the NEC to explicitly accept land nationalisation, and was heavily defeated. It was clear that the leadership was intent on weaning the Party off public ownership, in the belief that fiscal and legislative intervention could determine market forces.

The expansion of the economy in the 1960s brought chronic speculation in property and development land. The Labour Government that came in under Harold Wilson in 1964 introduced Capital Gains Tax the following year, plainly aimed at harnessing the profits that were being made. It also set up a Land Commission to intervene, if necessary, to purchase by compulsory acquisition, and to acquire, manage, dispose and generally deal in land required for development and redevelopment. (The Conservatives abolished it in 1970.) In the countryside, agriculture offered a ghastly analogy with the war in Vietnam, literally so in the instance of the use of the herbicide 245-T, an ingredient of Agent Orange. 'Husbandry' was turning into a techno-chemical war against any life form that did not fit the product profile. For a few years, the battered Massey-Harris could be seen in the same landscape as the sleek new super-combines, but not on the same farm. Small farmers had either to invest in the new methods, or get in contractors, or get out. Whatever route they took, for both farmer and worker the result was alienation. Once love is taken out of the relationship between the farmer and the land, all manner of means can be inserted into the gap, to prise it wider, reducing it to an investment opportunity.

In later years Labour MP Jeremy Corbyn would discuss such changes with Joan:

> We had a lot in common. I grew up in Shropshire in a very rural environment and had worked on a farm and grew up on a farm. We talked about the way farmers treated workers but also, paradoxically, the sense of community that existed in farming communities. In one way you had quite appalling treatment of workers by farmers, but on the other you had quite a closely guarded community. What you now have is actually something worse, which is appalling treatment of people who work by contract, and the community is gone, it is not there because you do not have anyone working on the farm. You have a 500-acre farm and two people, you bring in the ploughman, you bring in the harvesters, you do everything by contract. Cut-throat tendering on contracts, skimming on contracts. There is no sense of community and that is what Joan and I regretted because we both grew up in closely-knit communities. We both admired the skill of farm workers, they were incredibly skilled – tractor driving, animal husbandry, they'd know about plants and soil retention, hedging and ditching. It is tragic; those people did so much for the countryside. I remember an old guy in his late seventies early eighties who had

> never been more than five miles from where he lived in all his life. He had an encyclopaedic knowledge of everything within five miles. Joan really understood that kind of community.

Joan also understood the forces at work, informed by her oft-read copy of *Sharpen the Sickle: The History of the Farm Workers' Union* by Reg Groves. Following a discussion of nineteenth-century changes in the countryside, Groves wrote:

> It was Marx who saw the deeper significance of the changes, of the effect of Capitalist production upon farming and upon the life of man in society. 'Capitalist production... disturbs the circulation of matter between man and the soil, i.e. prevents the return to the soil of its elements consumed by man in the form of food and clothing; it therefore violates the conditions necessary to lasting fertility of the soil. By this action it destroys at the same time the health of the town labourer and the intellectual life of the rural labourer . . . Moreover,' goes on Marx, 'all progress in capitalist agriculture is a progress in the art, not only of robbing the labourer, but of robbing the soil; all progress towards increasing the fertility of the soil for a given time is a progress towards ruining the lasting sources of that fertility . . . Capitalist production, therefore, develops technology, and the combining together of the various processes into a social whole, only by sapping the original sources of all wealth – the soil and the labourer.' (Groves 1949, p. 243 quoting Karl Marx, *Capital*, volume I, pp. 513–514)[1]

This insight encapsulates Joan's understanding, which was the deeper for being grounded in her own experience. If it was true in the 1870s, how much more so a century later, and how much more complete and rapid the process.

At the end of the 1960s, by virtue of her work in the Union and in the Labour Party, Joan had won a reputation for steadfast adherence to her position, for advocacy of workers' rights and for public ownership of land. She was now ready to carry the fight to a higher level of decision-making. In 1970, the NEC Home Policy Committee of the Labour Party, back in Opposition, established an Agricultural Sub-committee. Its remit was to appraise agricultural matters, to consider the import levy proposals being brought in and to look at the working of the 1947 Agriculture Act. Joan and Reg Bottini were appointed to the committee from the NUAAW. Flynn (1989, p. 118) writes:

> As an RD [Research Department] paper pointed out, the appointment of the Sub-Committee was an important departure for agricultural policy formation from the period in government as, 'The NEC had not had a permanent advisory committee on agriculture for many years, although of course it had maintained contact with the NUAW and other interested parties. Policy has developed through such contacts with people of experience.' (39: Sub-committee on agriculture. Draft programme for the Agricultural Sub Cttee, RD96/April 1971.) This seemed to be a diplomatic way of recognising the situation during Wilson's premiership when policy-making had been centralised and the role of the NEC and its sub-committees often played down.

In 1971, the committee was paying close attention to the workings of the Common Agriculture Policy (CAP). Many in the Labour Party, including Joan, opposed accession to the Treaty of Rome as a blank cheque to international companies. They saw the CAP to be the cause of higher food prices, and considered that it exacerbated the problems of the countryside. Land prices were pushed up, and private investment, whether by individuals or companies, diverted land-use more and more towards the interest of profit.

Throughout her life, Joan would remain resolutely opposed to membership of the European Economic Community (EEC) and the CAP. She argued the CAP was a misnomer – it wasn't a well thought-out long term strategy for agriculture. For Joan, the purpose of the EEC was to facilitate the operations of the multinational companies, which are against the interests of working people. She regarded the EEC as the political and economic reflex of the North Atlantic Treaty Organisation (NATO), the military alliance that encircles Western Europe. When accused of being 'anti-foreigner' she replied: 'I am certainly not anti-foreigner. I do not understand the term 'foreigner'. To me, people are people whatever their colour, race or creed.'[2] Unlike so many on the Left who later moderated their views about the EEC – particularly in relation to human rights legislation, for Joan, Britain's membership would remain undeniably, 'an absolute disaster'.

When Joan was elected to the NEC, at Labour's 1972 Annual Conference she had moved the composite resolution that all land should be publicly owned. In over twenty years she had not wavered on this position – and never would. The resolution was passed, but the NEC was tepid in its support, arguing land nationalisation was being studied by the Land Policy Study Group. That group, chaired by John Silkin, had been largely concerned with problems around development land, and was now on the point of turning attention to rural land. After a period of confusion over where the appropriate expertise lay, the Agricultural Sub-committee was asked to submit a paper to the Study Group. Out of the wrangle that followed, it became apparent that majorities in both groups were not in favour of outright nationalisation, and the Study Group was not concerned to nationalise agricultural land (Flynn 1989, p. 122). The recommendation they made was for a rolling programme of tens of years, over which the needs of development would be identified, the development planned, land adopted and compensation paid. Homeowners would be exempted from the scheme.

Joan and other members, from both Groups, favoured a different plan, and drafted a minority report, advocating total public ownership of land, without exception. There was a furious response from David Eversley of the Centre for Environmental Studies and member of the Study Group on Land Policy:

> I cannot question your motives, but if any group had gone out of their way to produce a policy which was bound to lose Labour the next election, and to gladden the heart of any speculator, it would be yours. Your gratuitous threat to the majority of our fellow citizens (and of Labour voters by the next election) who are owner occupiers is a futile gesture which cannot be explained rationally except in a thoroughly disreputable way.[3]

The minority was not dissuaded. Opinion in the Party had moved to the left, disillusioned with the failed ameliorative approach of the previous Labour Government, and they believed the country as a whole was receptive, suffering as it was under the Heath Government.

Oliver Stutchbury told Joan of concerns at Transport House about their report being published as a Minority Report. Joan didn't care whether it was published as a Minority Report or edited as a separate publication contributing to the debate in the Party; the imperative was for the land nationalisation proposals in their report be widely discussed. In September 1973 the Minority Group launched the Campaign for Nationalising Land (CNL), with Oliver Stutchbury as its national organiser, and published their report as a pamphlet *The Case for Nationalising Land.* Its authors were Jack Brocklebank, Joan Maynard, the economists Nicholas Kaldor and Robert Neild, and Oliver Stutchbury, solicitor and alderman of the Greater London Council.

The Case for Nationalising Land – sometimes referred to as the Stutchbury Plan – substantially reiterated the proposal about which George Dallas had advised Joan in the early 1950s. The pamphlet is fifteen pages long, and contains detailed arguments. In summary the proposals are:

> 1. From the 'appointed day' all freeholds should be nationalised, and everyone who before the appointed day owned a freehold would be deemed to be a leaseholder on the terms of a statutory lease from the Crown. There would be no exceptions.
>
> 2. The statutory lease would be of 99 years at peppercorn rent.
>
> 3. A Public Land Management Authority [PLMA] would have the power to end the lease in the event of change of use, or of user; or in the event of the PLMA requiring the land for development or improvement.
>
> 4. Compensation ordinarily payable on the ending of a leaseholder's interest would be the value of the unexpired portion of the statutory lease at existing use value.

As Brocklebank *et al.* (1973) state:

> At the end of the 99 year period all land would be owned and managed by the State on annual (or longer) leaseholds. In this way, speculation would be elim-

> inated and all social needs arising from the use of land could be justly provided. It would in our view be better to concentrate exclusively on the nationalisation of land (at the expense of proposals to nationalise bits of industry) on the grounds that this is the greatest source of power and undeserved gains of ill-directed enterprise and undesirable social pressures; as well as being a source of hardship for the victims of land speculation.

By November 1973, over 3,000 copies of the pamphlet had been bought and 82 people had joined the CNL, including seven MPs. They were a long way from winning over the PLP.

Chair of York Fabian Society and Labour Party activist Hans Breitenbach was impressed with the pamphlet and said of Joan:

> She talked about the theoretical, but she was always very sound on what you might call fundamentals. Her Socialism is quite intellectual. It isn't abstract, it is a real thinking, it isn't a gut reaction, 'I wish the poor weren't poor' sort of thing, or even a reaction against privilege in the sense that some people hate the idea that some people are sitting on a lot of money or land when they've never done anything for it. It's got a much deeper understanding of social structures and economics. I think she probably has a pretty good idea of Marxist historical materialism, theory of value and wage theory and so on.[4]

Tom Gascoyne, 'the greatest teacher of them all', would have been impressed by this assessment of his former student.

In 1974, with a Labour Government back in power and Joan an MP, she was elected chair of the NEC Agricultural Sub-committee. NEC member Frank Allaun said: 'She knew more about agriculture than any man or woman in the Labour Party.' The committee again looked at means by which land could be taken into public ownership and presented an interim report to the Home Policy Committee in September. Its substance was that land could be ceded to the state voluntarily in lieu of Capital Transfer Tax and the proposed Wealth Tax, and that land could also be ceded to the state voluntarily, regardless of tax liability. A number of benefits were held to follow from this, including improvements to the supply and price of food, security of tenure for workers and greater industrial democracy; owner-occupiers would be able to ease their cash flow by a lease-back agreement with the state and prospective farmers would, with more land being made available for rent, be able to make a start.

The narrowness of the Labour majority meant controversial policies were unlikely to go far; the loss of even one by-election would pose a danger. There was, in any case, an inbuilt political reserve in the leadership. Nevertheless, in 1976, the NEC published a statement close to that of the Agricultural Sub-committee's report. After that, in a series of interviews in the farming press Joan sought to clarify the policy. She insisted that the proposal was for voluntary transfer of land, not the public ownership of farming. As free-holder the state would be a better provider of fixed equipment on the farms, leaving much more cash for liquidity. Joan's aim was to stop speculation by financial institutions and to help full-time farmers as well as farm workers. She also wanted a decentralised management – recognising that many nationalised industries were over-bureaucratised – with local controls; those who knew most about the land should manage it.

Frank Allaun recalled Joan's prolific activity on the NEC sub-committees and study groups. In relation to rural issues alone she chaired, or was an active member of, the Agricultural Sub-committee, Environment Study Group, Rural Areas Study Group, Development Land Study Group and Land Policy Study Group. 'She was very vigorous on them and there was no soft-soaping her, she couldn't stand it. She spoke in a forceful way whether she agreed or disagreed and she never missed meetings, she was assiduous in her duties.' In these various groups members discussed intensive livestock production, safety on farms, tourism in rural areas, the acquisition of land for development, rural housing and transport, strategies for hill and marginal land, the reform of the CAP, the use of pesticides and herbicides, nitrates in the soil, the nuclear industry, and the movement of nuclear waste. Joan was a tireless advocate of more labour-intensive farming. Apart from the obvious benefit of creating jobs, it would lead to a general regeneration of rural areas by maintaining population, benefiting schools and shops and renewing the housing stock, as well as combating heavy chemical intervention and loss of wildlife habitat.

The grinding committee work on the NEC, in Parliament and in the Union was only possible because of the constancy of Joan's love of the land

and of those who would work it honestly. Public ownership of land was in her view the only way to secure a just and non-exploitative future, and she was never deterred from presenting that view by the lack of response. All of this indicates a person who was a far cry from the Stalinist as travestied by her enemies in the press.

Joan considered 'good' farming to be environmentally sensitive; it was to intensive farming that she turned the wrath of her criticism – the ways it exploited people, animals and the soil itself. Simply, yet profoundly, she said: 'The soil is honest with you, it gives you back what you put in. Most people do not seem to appreciate that we live off the top eight inches and therefore it is precious. If it erodes, it erodes life itself.'

The Union had a long and impressive history of opposing dangerous chemical additives to the soil; as Joan observed, 'farm workers were always very good on the issue because they were on the sharp end of it'. They were given little if any training in applying chemicals and scant attention was paid to protective clothing.

Retired farm worker John Fry had worked with organophosphates for over twenty years. He described how they affected the central nervous system and the ability to concentrate. Local doctors would laugh at farm workers who complained:

> It came as concentrated stuff in a drum. On the drum was a label saying, dilute so many milligrams, and we used to get a tin can and mix it up and use it on the sheep. Sheep here get blow fly and we used to spray them with a hand spray and the spray blew back on you. We had one bloke with a heart condition and he used to pass out with the stuff. Farm workers with boom sprays, spraying crops, could get a blocked jet and then take it out and blow it with their mouth. When the safety officer would come the farmer'd say, take that machine and hide it down the bottom of the field.

Contaminated clothes were taken home and put in the family washing machine.

Joan was proud of the Union's campaign to ban the use of 245-T. On 28 April 1981 Chris Kaufman, research officer of the NUAAW, told the NEC Agriculture Sub-committee how the campaign against 245-T stemmed from strong grass roots feelings in the Union – something needed to be done about this very dangerous chemical. The NUAAW was backed by other unions and a resolution for a complete ban was passed unanimously at the 1980 TUC. He told the Committee the Government Pesticides Advisory Committee (PAC) had no knowledge of the conditions under which the chemicals were used, therefore its view that 245-T was safe, if used under the recommended conditions, was meaningless. It was simply not possible in field conditions to comply with the recommended conditions. The PAC was placing the onus on the user to prove it was dangerous rather then the manufacturer to prove it was safe. The Agriculture Sub-committee's response was to call for a complete ban on the import, processing, sale and use of 245-T, the winding up of the PAC and transfer of its work to the Health and Safety Executive. Further, it proposed the adoption of policies to minimise use of pesticides, tighter control on pesticide residues in food, and greater access to data about the safety of pesticides.

Farm workers using 245-T reported cancers, other skin diseases, miscarriages, birth malformations and sterility. In 1984, Chris Kaufman described the symptoms as uncannily similar to those of Vietnam War veterans exposed to the US Agent Orange, who had just received $180 million from US chemical firms. Agent Orange defoliant contained dioxin, the most toxic chemical known, which also contaminates 245-T preparations.[5]

Towards the end of her time in Parliament, as a member of the Agriculture Select Committee, Joan worked on an inquiry into the use of pesticides in agriculture. On this issue, as with others related to intensive farming, Joan and the committee's recently appointed Conservative chairman, Sir Richard Body, held firm against the big farming interests. Sir Richard admired and valued Joan's hard work and integrity, 'On agricultural issues Joan and I stood shoulder to shoulder. Joan was a good person. If you divide people into the net givers and the net takers in the world, she was one of the former. She was ahead of her time.' After retiring in June 1987, Joan was delighted when Sir Richard took the brave and highly unusual step as Committee chairman, of publishing a minority report attacking Government complacency on the public health hazards of pesticides.[6] Twenty years previously the Minister of Agriculture, Fisheries and Food had tried to assure Joan, 'the position is that no positive evidence exists to indicate that any pesticide product in use in this country has induced cancer in man'.

The callous treatment of animals under intensive systems of farming was intolerable to Joan. She didn't romanticise animals. Yes, she had cherished her pet cats as a young woman, but she had also witnessed with equanimity the annual slaughter and butchering of the family pig and the sale of young bullocks to market. It was part of farming life. She was a vegetarian but would willingly cook meat for her guests.[7] In 1964 she read Ruth Harrison's seminal work *Animal Machines: The New Factory Farming Industry*. Three years later, when Joan was appointed in a personal capacity to the Ministry of Agriculture's Farm Animal Welfare Advisory Committee, she was delighted to discover that Ruth Harrison was a fellow member. The Committee had been formed as an outcome of the Brambell Committee on Intensive Husbandry. (Joan had respected the work of the Brambell Committee and warmly endorsed its recommendation that farm animals be entitled to five freedoms: stand up, lie down, turn round, groom themselves and stretch their limbs.)

Even with members of the Humane Slaughter Association and the Royal Society for the Prevention of Cruelty to Animals, Joan and Ruth Harrison were in a minority on the fourteen-strong Farm Animal Welfare Advisory Committee. It included a beef and dairy farmer, the vice-chair of the Country Landowners' Association (who owned an intensive poultry unit) and the director of a large intensive poultry and pig breeding group. There was a vet, but no animal behaviourist.

In October 1969 The Farm Animal Welfare Advisory Committee produced codes of practice related to cattle, pigs and domestic fowl; the problem for Joan and Ruth Harrison was that the codes were not mandatory. Although Joan and Ruth Harrison disagreed with some of the Committee proposals they refused to resign – that was never Joan's style; in Ruth Harrison's words, 'We feel the best way to help the animals is to fight on. We regard ourselves as their delegates.'

Corresponding between Lansbury House and Holland Park the two women would agree tactics to influence the work of the Committee. After a visit to Joan in 1971 a prescient Ruth Harrison wrote: 'It is so nice to see the very real esteem in which you are held locally. I'm sure you'd have a very good chance of making Parliament!'

When the chance came, Joan ensured farm animal welfare was placed on the agenda. In August 1982 Compassion in World Farming reported her 'double barrelled attack' in the House of Commons whereby she graphically portrayed intensive farming as cruel to the animals and often dangerous to the people employed in the industry. She challenged the popular assumption that more humane methods would not be viable and would put up prices. 'Stockmen prefer to look after hens out of doors. That is why most of them decide to work in agriculture. It is certainly not for the wages.'

She put questions to ministers on a range of animal welfare issues – vivisection, the removal of antlers in velvet from deer, otter and fox hunting, hare coursing, battery hens and growth hormones in cattle. Her description of force-feeding geese to produce pâté de foie gras was sufficient to put any MP off eating the 'delicacy'.

Joan enjoyed her membership of the Agricultural Select Committee; here there could be 'real discussion of the issues and you did not get the knock-about stuff which goes on in the chamber of the House of Commons, much of which is sham shadow boxing'. The Committee work was not about political point-scoring and the 'debating club' of the chamber. Joan would never refer to herself as a politician; she was a Socialist, convinced that anyone who cares for people must also care for animals and their protection. 'I believe strongly that we are partners on this planet with animals and not their masters.' On Committee fact-finding visits to intensive farm units in France and Holland she and Richard Body shared their distress and disgust at seeing closely confined sows gnawing iron bars, hens crammed in battery units and weeks' old calves exported from Britain incarcerated in 'veal crates'.

Introducing the debate on the report of the Agriculture Select Committee on Animal Welfare, on 19 November 1982, its chairman, Conservative MP Sir William Elliott, singled out Joan's contribution:

> Party politics are transcended and we look at the job in hand. It would be no understatement to suggest that my general political views and those of the hon. Member for Sheffield Brightside are far apart, but during the Committee, Party politics went into the background and the hon. Member for Brightside, with others, gave the Committee the benefit of her considerable knowledge and deep feeling, for which I am grateful.

In the debate Joan spoke movingly and expertly about intensive farming and food production, making connections with animal welfare, the conditions and pay of farm workers and the food requirements of developing countries:

> If people in the developing countries are to have more to meet their basic needs, we must do with less. We must moderate our demands for more and more food. We also need to get rid of codes, which are only guidelines, and bring in regulations. Only in that way shall we be in a position to enforce welfare standards in intensive farming systems in this country.

In her environmental concerns, Joan was well ahead of public opinion. In the 1970s ecology was a word rarely heard and little understood. There were anxieties about this or that loss, or danger; but Joan had a sense of the totality and interconnectedness of life. On the political Left the *soi-disant* rigorous theorists often scorned such greenness as bourgeois, but she had imbibed her Socialism and farming at the same time, and it was essentially a humanist perspective. The social and the environmental were coterminous, all part of the same whole. In November 1984, closing Labour's Annual Conference debate on the environment, Joan paid tribute to the environmental pressure groups but added a cautionary note, 'The pressure groups have a vital role to play, but alone they can't produce the goods. Only a Labour Government can produce the goods and put our resolutions into action.'

She considered the Party had devoted its attention to agricultural policy, rather than rural policy, which affected all the people living in rural areas. It was not until 1977, after the NUAAW called on the NEC to establish a working party, that Labour established the Rural Policy Group with Joan as its chair. Included in the membership were Jack Brocklebank and the Union's progressive new general secretary Jack Boddy (elected in 1978). The purpose of the Group was to recommend policy for the rural areas, which would address the serious problems of transport, employment, access to services and education.

Joan was determined the Group should be 'grass-roots based, not London-dominated'. True to her word, she devoted considerable time and energy to travelling the length and breadth of the country holding 'consultative conferences'. (The term 'focus group' had not been invented.) The aim was to present a statement to Labour's 1979 Annual Conference. The Group decided against a Ministry for Rural Areas for a number of reasons. It didn't want rural areas to be separate and different – farm workers had always been isolated and different with the result that they always lost out. The Group opposed any argument that rural people were a special case; rather they were entitled to the same standard of service as others living in urban and industrial areas. In relation to transport, they were not opposed to such initiatives as postal buses, but the real solution should be along more conventional lines via publicly owned transport. To ensure rural people were not overlooked in a future Labour Government, the Group proposed a coordinating Minister who, whatever service or proposal was being discussed, would have special responsibility to look after the interests of the rural areas.

With Jack Brocklebank and Jack Boddy, Joan remained convinced that more Labour members should fight to get on rural local authorities. She recognised it was still difficult for rural workers to get time off, resulting in a large majority of rural seats being uncontested; 'What price democracy? It is still very much in short supply in rural areas. For too long the prosperous farmers and landowners have been allowed to dominate rural politics.'[8]

At the 1981 Labour Party Conference delegates endorsed the Group's policy blueprint for rural revival *Out of Town, Out of Mind*.

*

The English language is well known for its capacity to generate nuances through context and tone. In the context of conference halls and the Labour movement Joan would inspire her audience. Yet committee minutes and records in Hansard, while they are useful in providing a kind of diagram of the speaker, do not, unless the speaker is particularly skilful, give one a feel for the depth of the person. Joan was not a great Parliamentary orator, though she delivered her ideas clearly and forcefully, and that is in the written record. There is, however, an essential component of her thought that is not there, that other people have commented on, and that emerged in conversations with her, through her sometimes rather lapidary statements. I will give an example.

Two years before she died, Joan was showing me around the places of her childhood, and we arrived at Byland. This is about three miles from Carr Villa. Opposite the ruins of the abbey, we bought apples from a small orchard and stood in the warm sunshine, munching the apples and looking across at the ruins. After some silence Joan said: 'Fruits of the earth, Kristine.'

No irony here, nor any Gradgrind-ish reduction. It was an expression of reverence, for Nature, for the natural world, for human endeavour. I cannot say what were the outer limits of what she meant, and possibly, probably, she did not know either. That does not matter; she knew the centre.

THIRTEEN

Is it good for our class?

Late in June 1977, Joan received a letter from Mildred Pike, whose husband was a member of the NUAAW in Dorset. She wrote to say that she and her husband

> both deplore your action in attending the picket line at the Grunwick factory. You and your fellow MPs should uphold the police in their difficult task of keeping law and order and not try to incite further trouble. Although we often wonder, Miss Maynard, this is still a free country, therefore if a person is satisfied with their working conditions . . . and do not wish to join a trade union, why should you or anyone else make them do so.

Grunwicks was a film-processing plant in Dollis Hill, north-west London, owned by George Ward. He had refused to recognise the Association of Professional, Executive, Clerical and Computer Staffs trade union in the factory, and its members went on strike.

Joan wrote back, thanking Mildred Pike for her letter:

> I went there for two reasons: one to see for myself what was going on, and two, to show my solidarity with the people who are merely trying to get this reactionary employer to recognise that those who wish may join a union. Surely that is a fundamental right of every person, to join a union for his own protection if he so wishes. There is no desire to force people into the union who

> don't wish to join. So far all who have joined the union have been dismissed. Do you and your husband agree with that? I shall not uphold the police while they are aiding and abetting this kind of employer . . . We certainly did not incite any trouble, the trouble was there long before we arrived. Do you realise that this strike for trade union recognition has been going on for 46 weeks? People do not conduct that kind of struggle unless they have very firm convic-tons. It takes courage to stand in a picket line weeks and weeks on end. Most of that time there was no publicity or glamour in Grunwick – only hard slog. Every trade union right that you enjoy has been fought for by people like the wonderful workers at Grunwick. Have you, as farm workers forgotten Tolpuddle and what happened to those brave men?

Mildred Pike replied:

> After reading your letter . . . I must agree with you on most aspects of the case . . . I feel I may have been misled by some T.V., radio and press reports, and I am sorry I criticised you . . . It is sad to think sometimes the fine tradition of the trades unions is abused by a very small minority that may not even be members . . .

In response, Joan thanked her for her kind letter:

> You are certainly entitled to criticise me, and on some occasions you will no doubt be right, but on this occasion I feel I was right and that I should write and explain my point of view. We all learn from each other in life. You are right, sometimes there is a small minority who abuse our traditions in the Labour Movement. The morning we were at Grunwick we saw a few of these people, but they were a very small minority and they were not the people the police were arresting. The majority of people supporting at Grunwick are trades unionists, fellow workers of ours . . . I shall be in Dorset on holiday this summer . . . I also hope to be in Tolpuddle. Will you be there?
> All good wishes to you and your husband.

There are several interesting points about this correspondence. Firstly, the tone, which is frank and open, and comradely at the same time. There is nothing in Joan's replies to indicate what the *Daily Telegraph* called her 'characteristic authoritarianism'.[1] The instance the obituarist cites to support his allegation is a remark Joan made after Neil Kinnock's election to the Labour Party leadership in 1980, in effect warning him publicly not to deviate from Party policy. This certainly was characteristic of her – that she questioned authoritatively the origins and practice of authority. That is a distinction beyond the interest of the *Daily Telegraph*'s journalist, who failed to get right some of the simpler facts of Joan's life.

This leads to a second point from the correspondence, which is the way in which events and people were described in the media, especially during the industrial struggles of the 1970s and 1980s. A crude example would be the soubriquet, 'Stalin's Granny' adopted by the press a number of times to deprecate Joan. It was deployed in a headline position in the *Daily Telegraph*'s obituary – deployed but not owned. The phrase economically couples a patronising sneer at a middle-aged woman with a lie about despotic intentions. Lazy journalists, to coin a small farming metaphor, poke the pig of ideology with the worn stick of prejudice.

Back at Grunwick, the issues were quite clear, viewed from within the framework of the law. The owner, George Ward, had nine-tenths of the law by possession, the workers who wished to work were exercising their freedom within the law, and the police were upholding the law. How could you argue with that?

Joan often used the terms 'our class' and 'the other class'. This is an abbreviated and vernacular version of the social structure that Marx said had emerged under capitalist relations of production: namely, the two great blocks, whose interests were in direct conflict – the proletariat and the bourgeoisie, each produced in dynamic relation to the other. According to Marx, these are objective facts of history, regardless of the perceptions that individuals might have about themselves. The factory foreman, the family with the groceries store, the teacher, the policewoman, the solicitor, the civil servant, are all working out their lives, pursuing happiness, but only within the overarching conditions created by the needs of capital – the hegemonic rule of the bourgeoisie – and by resistance to it. Marx's categories are abstract, the result of analysis.

Joan accepted the analysis, but never used the terminology. She positioned herself within the analysis. 'Our class. The other class.' In furthering their aims 'the other class' necessarily exploited 'our class'. Joan saw this in moral as well as economic terms: by owning and exploiting for profit the resources of life, 'they' limit 'our' capacity for fulfilment. It did not mean that everything under capitalism was evil, but the litmus test which she applied would always be 'Is it good for our class?'.

She was perfectly aware of the complexities and contradictions that arise in lived experience. She could place in the list of lives that do not tidily fit the block model 'daughter of a small farmer'. (Wilf Page commented that she was an unlikely comrade for that reason.) But when the chips were down, at times of clear confrontation, it was for Joan a moral imperative for people to align themselves with the working class, and she was scathing about those who, as she said, 'talked left, but walked right'.

The historian E. P. Thompson, a friend of Joan's from WEA days, has written magisterially of the making of the English working class in the late eighteenth and nineteenth centuries. 'Making,' he says, 'because it is... an active process, which owes as much to agency as to conditioning. The working class did not arise like the sun at an appointed time. It was present at its own making.' (Thompson 1963, p. 9) Tolpuddle is emblematic of exactly that simultaneity. In 1834, six individual farm workers form a trade union, and are sentenced to transportation for taking an oath to the union. In that instant, they are the working class of and for itself, history became History. In the annual gathering to commemorate their courage and oppression, the union of the farm workers, renews its collective consciousness. Politics becomes culture, the culture of 'our class'. This is why Joan made every effort to be at the Tolpuddle Martyrs Rally each July.

At Grunwick, Joan saw a plain parallel with Tolpuddle, as she pointed out to Mildred Pike. Never mind the seedy location, the efforts of some to hijack the conflict, the cameras. The substantive issue was 'our class' and 'the other class'. She went 'to show my solidarity with the people . . . that those who wish may join a union.' Eight Labour MPs visited the picket line. While trying to protect a young Asian woman on the picket from being grabbed by a policeman, Audrey Wise was arrested, and charged with wilful obstruction of the police. Ian Mikardo, with Joan, was crushed against the side of a bus carrying non-union workers. He said he had not seen anything like it since the 1930s, when the police protected, with violence, the march of the fascist Blackshirts. Afterwards, the eight MPs asked the Home Secretary for an immediate inquiry into police methods.

The show of solidarity was not a one-off, and has to be seen in a wider context of change in the Labour Party, which had been simmering for a number of years. The Party was traditionally what Roy Hattersley called a Party of deference[2] – that is, deference of the PLP towards the leader, and deference of the Constituency Labour Parties towards the MPs. MPs elected the leader, who was then the only begetter of preferment, and the deputy leader. There was no accountability downwards from the leader to the Conference, nor of the sitting MPs to the Constituency Party which selected and worked for them. Conference could pass resolutions and propose policies, but the leader, if also Prime Minister, had no obligation to implement them, or, in any case to have them in the manifesto. Following the election defeat in 1970, and with the Constituency Parties increasingly moving to the Left, Left opinion held that defeat was caused by the failure of the Wilson Government to implement Socialist policies.

In 1973, Harold Wilson, in Opposition, was presented by Conference with the Labour Programme, which included a demand for 25 of the leading companies to be taken into public ownership. He decided unilaterally that nothing should be done about it. In exasperation a group of dissident Labour activists in the Constituency Parties formed the Campaign for Labour Party Democracy (CLPD), and were joined by a small group of left-wing MPs. The main aim of the CLPD was, 'to campaign for greater participatory democracy within and between all sections of the Labour Party', and in practice to effect constitutional change in the Party by constitutional means, in order to secure accountability of the PLP to the Party as a whole. The strategies to achieve their aim emerged one by one, and the first was to secure mandatory reselection of the MP by their Constituency Party at least once during each parliament.[3]

Joan had seen enough autonomous leadership in the Union and in the Party to know that radical Socialist policies would not be seriously pursued unless the balance of power was with the rank and file. She joined the CLPD and, following on Frank Allaun, became its president. Chris Mullin, a CLPD activist, said: 'There was real power at stake, and Joan was one of the absolutely reliable people on the National Executive. Because of the heat of that battle, there were so few MPs you could rely on.'

The people who were the organising force of the CLPD were, like Joan, committed to Socialist ideas, but the organisation itself aimed purely at constitutional reform as a first requirement. The right wing of the PLP, knowing the new political tenor of the Constituency Parties, was appalled by the proposal for mandatory reselection. When it came before the NEC, Shirley Williams was sitting alongside Joan. She said, 'This is ridiculous, we'll all be looking over our shoulders the whole time', getting the laconic reply, 'Aye, that's the point'.

It should be emphasised here that while, clearly, the hope was that accountability in the Party would lead to the adoption of a Socialist programme, Joan also believed in accountability for its own sake, as more democratic; in itself educational to those who participate. Showing her commitment to the idea of accountability, in 1974 she led calls for an inquiry into charges of corruption in the Regional Labour Party in the north-east, which many in the Party hierarchy wanted to hush up. The charge was made that there had been a felonious relationship between the architect John Poulson (then in prison) and leaders in the Labour-controlled local government, going back some ten years and involving the handling of Government contracts. The Labour MP for Blyth, Eddie Milne, had asked Wilson for an enquiry as far back as 1965, and had raised the matter with local regional and national officials over the following years but had been stone walled. In February 1974, his Constituency Labour Party refused to adopt him for the coming election. He was generally vilified by the Party, and, because she supported his cause, Joan was accused of 'muckraking'; she retorted: 'The muckraking will not stop until we have got rid of the muck.'[4]

At the 1974 Labour Party Conference, mandatory reselection was defeated, but two million votes were cast in its favour. Heartened by this, the CLPD continued to strengthen its influence in the Constituency Parties, aided by events, in particular the Reg Prentice affair. (Prentice, a Cabinet Minister under Wilson, had come out in support of the Conservative Government's prosecution of the 'Pentonville Five'.[5] His Constituency Party, in any case unhappy with his neglect of the constituency and his right-wing opinions, voted to deselect him under the existing rules. He appealed, but before the appeal could be heard, joined the Conservative Party and became a loyal devotee of Mrs Thatcher, who was to appoint him as a junior Social Security Minister).

Notwithstanding its success in the CLPs, the CLPD recognised that at Conference the constituencies had only 10% of the votes cast. The real power was with the block votes of the unions. Attention was therefore turned to forging links. Kogan and Kogan (1983, p. 36) record the level of engagement:

> In 1974, they had no trade union branches or other trade union institutions affiliated to the campaign. By 1977, thirty-nine trade union branches and other trade union institutions were affiliated, and this figure rose to 161 in 1980 . . . In 1975, the CLPD became involved in trade union mobilisation… once it realised that it was necessary to secure the union block votes it set some of its leading members to work on them.

With these wider developments in the Labour movement in mind one can now return to the picket line at Grunwick, and ask why eight MPs had made it from Westminster to Dollis Hill.

There is no suggestion here that they had in some way been dragooned into the visit. For a start they were not all members of the CLPD, though all were on the Left of the Party. Not all were in favour of mandatory reselection. Many, including Joan, were in the Tribune Group, a purely Parliamentary organisation of MPs of the Left, concerned with Socialist policy. There was now an urgent need for MPs to extend their activities outside the usual arenas of debate. With the culture of deference breaking down, with the shift in grass-roots opinion to the Left, and in the context of increasingly troubled industrial relations, it was vital to consolidate the Labour movement.

For Joan, a heart-and-mind trade unionist, showing solidarity at the factory gates was entirely natural. She had never seen Parliament as the only site of political activity. In any case she said she did not wish to be known as a politician, but as a Socialist. The first requirement in the creation of a Socialist society was the public ownership of resources, operated democratically and she sought to establish alliances with groups inside and outside the Labour Party who had this basic objective, though she may have disagreements with them over strategies and further policies.

*

When Joan had taken her seat in Parliament as a Sheffield MP she knew very little about steel, engineering or indeed the city itself; from the train through Sheffield eastwards to York she had often seen what Taylor, Evans and Fraser (1996, p. 42) describe as the 'jungle of small workshops and engineering works' and the 'quite unforgettable landscape of blazing forges, red-hot furnaces and thundering steel hammers . . . further east, the landscape would thin out into open country of a barren, industrial kind, dotted with the pitheads of the South Yorkshire coalfield and the small colliery villages of the Dearne Valley . . .'

She had been anxious to learn about the industry and there were plenty of people to help her, especially the shop stewards who took her round the factories and arranged meetings with the workers, often at the factory gates. In Sheffield, 'the degree of unity between Communists, Labour Party members and others on the Left, particularly in engineering and steel, is the envy of many other areas in the country'.[6]

Brightside Labour Party activist Bill Eddison worked at Shardlows, where

> all the shop stewards were Communists. Most of the people who worked there were Labour Party members, but the Communist Party members used to do all the running about and we used to let them. Joan must have visited every steel works in Sheffield, she went to learn how people lived and how they worked. Even the local press, after the bad stuff to start with, about her and Lenin's photo, really gave her credit because she fought hard for Sheffield and she spoke up well for Sheffield and the steel workers at the time, they were being decimated. That's why she didn't have any trouble in her second election because she'd done such a lot of work. People were proud of her . . .

George Matthews said:

We had many industrial disputes in Sheffield; there were huge factories, big engineering steel manufacturing companies and a lot of industrial disputes and strikes. Joan would get invitations from shop stewards' committees who were either entering into or embarked on industrial action. She would be full-square behind the strikers. She used to support them, go on platforms with them and support their rights. She used to financially support strikes and she sent me money, after she packed up her seat, for a number of strikers. Her whole life, after all, was geared to representing people she knew were getting a raw deal. The trade union movement was at the heart of her life; she realised the importance of people organising to protect themselves.

The steel industry had been renationalised in 1967 although the more profitable areas remained in private ownership. The immediate cause of the thirteen week steel strike of 1980 was a 2% pay offer. Massive job cuts had been announced but their location was not revealed until 11 December 1979 – four days after the strike was called:

The strike was much more effective than anyone could have envisaged, vividly expressed by one union poster 'The Steelworker – Treated with contempt – Not Ever Again!' Flying pickets were deployed and on St Valentine's Day in March [*sic*] 1980, 1,500 steel pickets, 300 miners and 300 other supporters were mobilised outside Hadfield's plant in Sheffield.[7]

Hadfield's, a private steel company, had a workforce which voted to return to work on 10 February; the St Valentine's Day picket forced them to stop work again.

In January, the Conservative Secretary of State for Industry, Keith Joseph, informed the House of Commons that nationalisation had helped to breed indifference to the customer and competitiveness; the steel industry was a classic example of 'the British disease'.

Joan was incensed, only that Monday she had been with steel workers on the picket line:

How would honourable members react if one-third of them were made redundant and those who remained had their wages frozen? It is not long ago

> that honourable members were clamouring for a much greater wage increase than that sought by the steel workers. There are many factors in the steel industry strike, apart from the workers. For example there is the EEC and all that means to our steel industry. The purpose of the EEC is to facilitate multi-nationals. It is doing exactly that. It is having a bonanza in Sheffield... As we know there is a world-wide steel recession. Virtually all the steel industries in the world are losing money . . . in common with other honourable members I believe that the workers have been set up for the strike and that the BSC is the Government's tool. The corporation is being used by the Government in their attempts to slim down the steel industry.

She blamed the Government's industrial policy for the lack of a home market for steel, in particular its lack of investment in mining, car manufacturing and the railways.

The strike ultimately failed. For 'slim down' Joan might have said 'melt down'. In Sheffield alone 'three-quarters of the 45,000 jobs in existence in Sheffield's steel industry in 1981 had disappeared by 1987' (Taylor, Evans and Fraser 1996, p. 64) and in December 1988 the British Steel Corporation (BSC) was privatised.

*

Whilst Joan developed alliances with the Labour movement outside Parliament she was always keen to bring 'ordinary people' into the Palace of Westminster. As much as she could, she would make the House of Commons, 'open house' – pensioners' action groups, miners from the University of Sheffield's Division of Continuing Education, young unemployed people, family and friends, international peace delegations, human rights activists and representatives of oppressed peoples from every continent. According to Jeremy Corbyn, 'delegations from liberation movements never forgot the experience of meeting Joan'. Human rights activist Rita Maran wrote to her (6 February 1976): 'I would try to convey some glimmer of the deep appreciation and gratitude our Argentinian friends felt at their reception in the Commons on Tuesday. Your interest and dedication shone through, and we were all deeply moved.'

Countless letters of thanks attest to her warm welcome. She was delighted when visitors were not overawed by the Palace of Westminster. In April 1982, after introducing a group of young unemployed people to MPs in the Commons and arranging for them to witness the Falklands debate, their group leader wrote to her: 'Many of the young people felt that during the debate the MPs seem to waste so much time on flowery language and could have made the points a lot more directly.'

She took particular pleasure in welcoming farm workers into the House of Commons on wages lobbies and in showing them around. 'I always enjoyed days at the Commons when our members were lobbying, or other workers, and they spilled all over the Commons, it made it feel a bit more our place.'

As the *Morning Star* reported:

> A tousled haired farm worker in anorak and jeans sat in the hallowed Speaker's chair, while around him dairy hands, tractor drivers, pig handlers and stockmen occupied the two front benches. Escorted by Joan Maynard, they had come to have a look at the Palace of Westminster just before the politicians returned to the Commons fray to hear the Queen's Speech. After getting over their sense of awe and fears of 'presumption' about invading the seat of power, they began to muse about what it would be like if they had a Government which believed in the value of their work and wanted them to be well rewarded. They had brought in a bumper harvest with the help of perfect autumn weather on less than £40 take-home pay a week, so they had every right to dream up phrases in the Queen's Speech which the Speaker was due to read in a couple of hour's time about a big pay rise.[8]

*

As with land nationalisation, Joan's preferred mechanisms for managing agriculture were not centralist, but something closer to syndicalism. Nonetheless, she had friends in the Communist Party, and continued to have discussions with them. She wrote articles for the *Morning Star* throughout her life, visited the USSR on several occasions, went to North Vietnam,[9] favoured détente with Moscow, and was chair of the British Peace Committee, which was organised by the Communist Party.

Given that her views were frankly expressed and her connections outside the Party undisguised, it is not surprising that her opponents inside and outside the Party, and in the press, seized the opportunity to brand her a Communist, and by implication, a traitor; more surprising that some of them thought that she was a covert operator since there was nothing whatever covert about her views.

The charges were of varying degrees of seriousness. The 'Stalin's Granny' attack has been mentioned. Silly though it is, it is also dangerous in that it disables by innuendo serious consideration of the issues Joan raised. Asked how she felt about the title, she drily observed it was unbefitting, as Stalin's grandmother was probably a pillar of the Russian Orthodox Church.

The Social Democratic Alliance (SDA)[10] alleged in July 1975 that Joan was so close to the Communists she shouldn't be a Labour Party candidate. This was because she was chair of the British Peace Committee, which was organised by the Communist Party, and also that she the Organisation of World Youth Festival in East Berlin. Writing to Ron Hayward, general secretary of the Labour Party, the SDA's joint secretaries David Carlton and Stephen Haseler cited an article written by Joan for *Labour Monthly*:

> The courts, the laws, are made by the ruling class for their class, not for my class, the working class. For God's sake, Mr Hayward, what is happening to the Labour Party? Do you not find it a chilling portent when such as Miss Maynard MP, after giving aid and comfort to the newspaper of another (and particularly odious) political party can prosper within the Labour Party?

In a statement supporting Reg Prentice, the SDA named members of Labour's NEC who, it said, had shown sympathy with the Communist Party and East European dictatorships by their writing and visits. Eric Heffer denounced the statement as a McCarthyist witch-hunt. Included in the list with Joan was Michael Foot.

In November 1976, Conservative MP Iain Sproat told a meeting of London Scottish Conservative Graduates in Chelsea that 'the Labour Party has been infiltrated by fifth columnists who aimed at turning Britain into a totalitarian East European state, who tricked decent Labour voters into supporting them'. There were at least thirty MPs, 'perpetrating a massive fraud on the voters by standing for Labour' he said, and he went on to name ten of them.[11] An outraged Arthur Latham told the Speaker Sproat's speech was a disgraceful piece of character assassination implying that thirty Labour MPs were dishonourable frauds, even guilty of treason. Joan and the others named eventually won an apology after threatening group legal action.

Julia Langdon wrote a satirical piece in *Labour Weekly* (17 Dec 1976) which set Joan laughing. It referred to fears of a dangerous fifth column within the Christian movement. Among the worst offenders was St Luke, ('And not one said that ought of the things he possessed was his own but they had all things in common') – other offenders were Saints Augustine and Aquinas.

The SDA attacks continued. In September 1977 it published a statement in advance of the Labour Party Conference accusing Labour MPs and trade unionists of being associated with Communism, and exhorting delegates not to vote them on to the NEC. Joan responded, 'the fact that you write for a newspaper does not mean you necessarily agree with all its editorial comment. This is a bit of a guilt-by-association smear tactic'.[12]

In 1982, as Leader of the Opposition, Michael Foot was supporting Margaret Thatcher's Falklands Task Force. After Joan and thirty-two others voted against the Government, Liberal MP for Rochdale, Cyril Smith, declared on Radio Trent they should all be tried for treason. His accusations were then published in the *Sun*, so a group of those named decided to sue collectively, 'we didn't manage to nail the *Sun* unfortunately but we did get about a hundred pounds apiece; he settled out of court eventually.'

In 1995, Joan's name appeared among a list of five which Rupert Allason, Conservative MP and spy-novelist, planned to name in the House of Commons as helping Soviet intelligence. The allegations had originally been published in Brian Crozier's 'Free Agent' two years previously (Crozier, 1993). Brian Crozier was head of the Institute for the Study of Conflict (ISC). The four others named were Stan Newens, Jo Richardson, Joan Lestor and Frank Allaun.[13]

Neil Fieldhouse wrote in Sheffield's *Star* newspaper how Joan had won respect in Sheffield as a champion of many local causes. Defending her against allegations of assisting Soviet intelligence, he described her as, 'an obvious target for such sensationalist rumour-mongering among novelists who grub about in the remnants of the Cold War.'[14]

Much hilarity in Lansbury House, then, when three years later Rupert

Allason lost his case against the publishers of the *Have I Got News for You Diary*. It had called him a 'conniving little s***'. Joan said the judge obviously agreed. In other litigation Judge Laddie was more polite, merely calling Allason 'a profoundly dishonest man'.[15]

Joan denied all allegations of espionage. Sometimes she wearied of them; at other times she was mildly amused. 'I was involved in nothing so mysterious or interesting.' Yes, she had asked questions in the Commons. 'It didn't mean I was getting information for the Soviet Union.'[16]

Tony Benn records in his unpublished diary that James Callaghan considered Joan to be one of two Communists on the NEC, because she was known to telephone King St (Communist Party HQ). In his published diary (in which the two moles are not named) Benn told Callaghan: 'All that tells me is that MI5 bug their telephones, and that worries me much more'. (Benn 1990, p. 501)

There is no doubt that her political views were closer to those of the Communist Party than they were to those of the right wing of the Labour Party. That did not mean that she was in any way traitorous. The Labour Party was the Party of the trades unions and of the Labour movement, furthermore it was not doctrinaire, and within its so-called broad church, there was room – at least up until then – for many with views similar to hers. She felt that the Party had always included a range of groups of varying opinion, which helped in the development of ideas. As the poet Milton believed, if there is freedom of speech, the truth will take care of itself. An example of her non-doctrinaire approach to Party membership was her opposition, in the early 1980s, to the expulsion of the Militant Tendency. Joan's view on this and earlier attempts to purge the Party (going back to the 1950s) was that the Party would be better directing its efforts towards the real enemy – the policies of the Tory Party. And, she might add, the Tory policies of Labour Governments.

On incomes policies, for example, Dennis Skinner said:

> We were both fighting like Kilkenny cats to get rid of every single one, whichever Government was in power. Incomes policies are devised for trade unionists, you can't put an incomes policy on all those people driving white vans up the motorway – self-employed. You can't have an incomes policy on a

chartered accountant or an estate agent. It's for workers Joan and I saw through that. Joan was clear; she didn't dilute anything at all.

Joan grew accustomed to her name being on lists of people on the Left who were supposed to have transgressed. 'Once there were two lists going round at the same time. Sheffield people would say to me, Are you on both lists, Joan? And I would say yes, and they would say, I should bloody well 'ope so!'

*

The mandatory reselection policy was finally carried in Labour's Conference of 1979. This was seen as a major victory on the Left, and the CLPD now turned their attention to the question of how the Party leader and Deputy were elected. At the conference in 1980, the principle of an electoral college was passed, and in the following January, the Special Conference at Wembley agreed on the division of voting power: unions 40%, Constituency Labour Parties and PLP 30% each. This was the final straw which produced the committee that designed the Social Democrats camel.

Following James Callaghan's resignation as Party Leader after the 1980 Labour Party Conference, 'a new election took place by the old methods, that is to say, by a ballot of the parliamentary party. Tony Benn refused to stand, saying that he preferred to wait until the new method of election had come into operation . . . Foot was elected Leader on 10 November, having won 139 votes in the second ballot to Healey's 129…Denis Healey was elected unopposed as his Deputy'. (Pelling and Reid 1996, p. 163).

Tony Benn had emerged as the leading spokesperson of what can be called the collectivist left of the Party. Joan, his close ally throughout the 1970s, supporting his challenge for the leadership in 1976, now enthusiastically campaigned in support of his bid for the deputy leadership in the aftermath of the Wembley agreement. He stood against Denis Healey on a programme of a non-nuclear defence strategy, withdrawal from the EEC, abolition of the House of Lords, restoration of full employment, and expanded public services. At the September 1981 Labour Party Conference, in the second ballot, he came within 0.8% of winning, and this in the context of a poisonous press campaign, the opposition of the Shadow Cabinet and the tactical abstention of a number of Tribune Group MPs.

Two things were now clear. First, the Tribune Group had become a flag of convenience for career politicians, people who, as Joan said, 'talked left, but walk right' in the new situation of mandatory reselection.[17] Second, the Tribune Group as a leftist discussion group within the PLP did little to promote the ideas where it really mattered – within the trade union movement. Consequently, as *The Times* had it (30 November 1982):

> A number of hard left Labour MPs have indicated they are not prepared to rejoin the leftwing Tribune Group . . . The underlying cause of the split is the perceived failure of the Tribune Group to have any major impact on the Party and its policies, in spite of the fact that Mr Michael Foot, the Party leader, is a group member.

The disaffected Tribunites reformed themselves as the Campaign Group, originally convened by Bob Cryer, and later with Joan as its chair. Its aim was to link up campaigns for Socialism inside and outside parliament, 'in sharp contrast', she said, 'to the majority of the PLP who see themselves as an elite and everyone else as voting fodder'.[18]

Looking back on Tribune, Joan thought it was

> pretty hopeless. They had interesting political discussions, but they never made any real decisions. They never had votes and things and so as a result of that we felt that they weren't very effective. And people like John Prescott were in the Tribune Group then, so I remember discussing this with John and he said he wasn't going to have any group telling him what he should do. There's quite a lot of people like that; they don't want to work in an organised way, they want to work as individuals, probably in order to pursue their own interests.

The General Election in 1983, held in the aftermath of the Falklands War, saw the re-election of Margaret Thatcher and the humiliation of Michael Foot, on whom the press had poured their reserve stocks of bile. The leadership blamed the Left. There had been a catastrophic haemorrhage of support among the skilled working class, particularly in the West Midlands and the south-east. In Joan's view, 'it was not that the policies were too Socialist; they weren't Socialist enough'.

With the ensuing election of Neil Kinnock and Roy Hattersley as leader and deputy, and with the formal rift in the Left of the Party, the policies of the collectivist Socialists were under attack inside the Party and outside. The leadership elections had shown, yet again, that the deciding factor was the block votes of the unions, and the leaders of the unions were not necessarily interested in or persuaded by the members. By 1979, four of the six largest unions were led by right wingers, and the other two leaderships were still operated according to what has been called, 'consensus corporatism'. In practice that means that the leadership acted independently of the members, and came to agreements among themselves, and with the Party leaders. Even a leftward leaning union leader would, from this perspective, see the CLPD activists as seriously rocking their boat; it was time to chuck them overboard.

*

Joan's work on the NEC was prodigious. In comparison with being a backbench MP, as a member of the NEC and chair of its sub-committees, 'you could have some influence on what was going on'. Dennis Skinner said: 'A lot of people who get on to the Executive think, I'd better trim my sails a bit. Joan, like me, never did.' Membership could be a roller-coaster ride with elections held annually at Labour's Annual Conference and success dependent on the union block votes. Within two years of joining the NEC Joan suspected Jack Jones was trying to get her removed. (Benn 1989, p. 615) She was 'saved' in 1979 and the following year increased her vote by 700,000, despite reports she would lose her seat because the leadership of the AUEW hoped to swing the balance to the right. The long knives were out for the Left in 1980, but Joan survived. Despite plans by a reorganised right wing to replace Bennites on the NEC in 1981,[19] Joan was elected and became vice-chair of the Labour Party by virtue of long service on the NEC. But at the following year's Labour Party Conference in Blackpool the right wing finally ousted her, after ten years of trying. *The Times* reported: 'Another potential embarrassment for Mr Foot was removed when the trade union votes denied Miss Maynard re-election to the NEC.'

She was not, of course, to be silenced; chairing the Tribune rally later in the week she poured scorn on Michael Foot's loyal supporter Neil Kinnock, who admitted to being glad he had not voted for Tony Benn in the previous year's deputy leadership contest. The real divisions in the Party, she said, were 'between the Socialists and the non-Socialists'.[20]

She was not the only victim. Panitch and Leys (1997, p. 203) record: 'The new right-wing balance in the union block vote was also applied to clearing out the remaining supporters of the Labour new-left from the trade union section of the NEC. Exactly one month later, at the NEC's first meeting after the conference, Benn, Heffer, Jo Richardson, and Allaun were surgically removed from the key NEC committees...'

Almost everyone saw Joan's 1982 NEC defeat as conspiracy; had she been elected she would have become chair of the Labour Party. According to *The Times*, 'her senior colleagues were afraid that her speeches as chairman would have attracted damaging publicity in what may be a pre-election year.' Joan, however, accepted the cock-up theory, at least at the time:

> Pete Wilson, on the Standing Orders Committee – a lovely chap, a Socialist – was in a hell of a state about me losing my seat. Tom Sawyer and Rodney Bickerstaffe of NUPE had told Pete that because they were new they had given their 600,000 to Anne Davis, a real right-winger. They didn't think she was likely to win, so they felt they could give that vote away. They still voted for me, but the trouble was that the right wing voted for her as well as them. Pete took me to see them. Their statement was that because they were new and they hadn't done it before, they hadn't realised that she was the one who, if anybody was going to unseat me, it was her. And I accepted that statement. I thought, it sounds to me as if what they say is true. But I must say I have wondered since because, you see, Sawyer became a great ally to Kinnock, he's now become an ally of Blair. And of course the other thing that made me wonder was because I would have been Chairman of the Labour Party in that crucial 1983 election, and that would certainly have made the right wing very nervous. They wouldn't have known what I might say. Eric Heffer was vice-chairman when I got knocked off, so he was next in line the year I came back on again. I asked him if he'd stand down. If he'd stood down I think they might have had a job to stop me getting it. He said he wasn't prepared to stand

> down because he felt he'd done a year's apprenticeship for it. So that was that. This was the only time Eric Heffer didn't come up to scratch.[21] Later the devils altered the rules again. Dennis [Skinner] arrived at where he would be chairman so they altered the rules. Normally the chairman would chair the conference but if you notice now they let the chairmanship rotate. It's all skulduggery. When you see what's going on you think, well, no wonder the poor old workers have not got anywhere with that lot always knocking hell out of those who're trying to help them.

As Dennis Skinner put it: 'Enough block votes were whisked away in order that she was off in 1982 and they very kindly put her back on again the following year. Because she had lost her seniority she'd have to start from the bottom rung of the ladder again.'

When Joan announced her retirement from Parliament she emphasised her determination to continue on the NEC. But on 21 September 1987 the TGWU dropped their support. Her position on Ireland and opposition to the expulsions of Militant were too much. 'The executive will now recommend that its delegation meeting on the eve of the Labour Party Conference this weekend should vote for Mrs Ann Clwyd, a sponsored TGWU MP and Chairwoman of the Tribune Group, a staunch supporter of the leadership.'[22]

Tony Benn wrote in his diary (1992, p. 522):

> Went back to the Conference and stood between Joan Maynard and Audrey Wise, both of whom had lost their seats on the NEC and were in tears. Audrey is an MP, so she is all right, but Joan has retired from Parliament and she is such a strong woman that it is very sad to see her upset.

*

When the resolution to implement the mandatory reselection of MPs was finally passed in 1979, Tony Benn's diary records the elation felt now that the balance of power had swung dramatically in favour of the Left. Meanwhile, the newly elected Prime Minister, Margaret Thatcher, was considering the details of a plan which had been drawn up by Nicholas Ridley MP while he was her Shadow Energy Minister in Opposition. With the warning example in mind of the 1973 miners' strike, which had led to the downfall of the Heath Government, the new Tory leadership was convinced that vanquishing the miners was essential before sweeping economic and social changes could be implemented.

In Joan's collection of pictures there are four by Nicholas Ridley the amateur painter. They include landscape scenes of the Cotswolds – where he lived and of which he happened to own a sizeable chunk. It must have given both him and Joan some wry amusement that his most dedicated political foe was also a collector of his art. She judged him a better painter than he was a politician. (One may beg to differ. The plan evinces a ruthless attention to detail. The approach to landscape is similar.)

The Ridley Report was leaked to *The Economist* in 1978. It set out a strategy for confronting the miners at a moment of the Government's choosing, when long-term reserves of coal would be available, and at a time of low consumption. The reserves would be stockpiled by paying the miners productivity bonuses and overtime, and by arranging for foreign imports of coal if necessary. Private hauliers with non-union drivers would be available to transport coal to the power stations. Social security payments to strikers would be reduced. The police were to be well trained and equipped for dealing with mass pickets. (Dorey 1995, p. 189)

The chosen moment was the strike by the National Union of Mineworkers (NUM) over the threatened closure of the Cortonwood colliery in South Yorkshire. The miners' leaders saw a wider objective to the strike – to prevent the planned closure of most pits and the privatisation of those that remained. The Government denied this was the further plan, though subsequent events showed that it was indeed the intention, with the possible loss of 80,000 jobs. The national strike was called in March 1984, without benefit of a pithead ballot, and justified by reference to an earlier resolution at the delegates' conference, which would support a national strike call in the event of widespread pit closures.

During the 1973–1974 miners' strike, Joan had written: 'The symbol of the working class today is the miners. If they go down so do all the workers.' This was the time.

Many of the Nottinghamshire miners, assured that their pits were safe, continued to work, while miners in most other areas came out. The NUM was split, and striking miners turned with fury on their working colleagues. Large numbers of police from 'unsympathetic' areas of the country, such as Gloucestershire and Thames Valley, were drafted in to ensure safe passage for working miners, and to wreak havoc among the pickets. The violence was general. The nightly television pictures of brutal confrontation were reminiscent of the film Culloden. Heffernan and Marqusee (1992, p. 53) say:

> In a further attempt to weaken the strike, opponents of the NUM turned their attention to alleged picket-line violence. The events at Orgreave in the summer of 1984, in which mounted police charged down pickets in a pre-planned attack, became the focus of debate. Years after the conclusion of the strike, it was proved in court that the police attack on the miners had been unprovoked and premeditated. Hundreds of miners arrested at the scene were acquitted and many were paid compensation for injuries suffered at the hands of the police. But at the time the BBC televised edited footage of the fracas that reversed the real sequence of events, implying that the police had reacted to violence by the miners rather than the opposite, which was the case. Though the Labour leadership was apprised of the nature of the police attacks at Orgreave and elsewhere, condemnations of 'picket-line violence' became a Kinnock staple for the rest of the strike.

The failure to hold a ballot was a tactical error in the battle for public opinion. The Government and most of the press portrayed Scargill as a manipulative despot, and the pickets as thugs. For those on the Left, like Joan, the question of the national ballot was of little relevance, because if it had been held and had supported a strike call, the Nottinghamshire coalfield could then have demanded to ballot separately (as they had done previously on the issue of incentive schemes).

Joan campaigned in support of the striking miners, marched in sympathy, appeared on picket lines, along with, especially, members of the Campaign Group. Five months into the strike the Campaign Group called for a debate attacking the Government's economic policies; it was opened by Neil Kinnock, but according to Benn it was a great failure because he, Kinnock, did not want to be associated with Scargill and militancy. Eight months into the strike, the NUM leaders met with the Campaign Group, looking for support for a joint campaign, including fundraising, and coordinating support from the Constituency Labour Parties. On 24 October the NEC passed a resolution committing it to a joint campaign, but it was clear that 'the Front Bench regard the miners' strike as deeply damaging to the Labour Party's prospects, and they think pressing for a settlement is a way of looking reasonable' (Benn 1992, p. 381).

The following day Mr Justice Nicholls sequestered the whole of the NUM funds.

That evening, Joan appeared on TV *Question Time*, chaired by Sir Robin Day. Discussion was mostly around issues of law and order, and the miners' strike. A questioner asked whether sequestration of funds was useful in settling the dispute. In replying Joan said:

> I believe the laws are made by the other class for that class. And I haven't sat on the bench for all the years I've sat without seeing that in operation...The law says to the NUM that we can take all your money . . . but it says to an employer, 'If you break the health and safety laws the only thing you can be fined is a few thousand pounds' . . . there's been plenty of examples in our history that people have thought were unjust and when they have thought they were unjust they have broken those laws, or we wouldn't have made any progress at all.

Those who wished to see it that way complained that she was advocating law-breaking and should therefore be asked to resign as a magistrate. But, as she was obliged to explain in a letter to the Lord Chancellor's office, she was simply stating 'the factual historical position relating to what can sometimes happen in society when laws are broken.'

She continued to raise money and give money to the miners' families. George Matthews recalled:

> Scargill was absolutely crucified by the media, and by the Labour Party; Joan never wavered. She fully appreciated Arthur had got a lot of faults, wasn't perfect, but Joan never wavered. Them lads were on strike and she was going to support them absolutely. She went on platforms all over the country defending them and financially supporting them.

Joan Witham, who has written of the role of Nottinghamshire women in the miners' strike (Witham 1986) recalled:

> Joan came to speak during the miners' strike in Nottinghamshire when things were very bad because of the split, and the men, the miners warmed to her. It wasn't a popular place to come. A lot of Labour politicians were on the fence. They didn't show their allegiance at all. They never came to Nottinghamshire, they avoided it like the plague. She came, and of course Dennis Skinner. Wherever there were working people involved in struggle, she'd be there . . . She always knew the subject, and she went to the heart of it. You were left with a feeling, not of elation, that was not her way of speaking, but a calm sort of understanding. And you went on thinking; it carried you through. If Arthur Scargill came, or Dennis Skinner, they appealed to emotional factors. Joan's emotions were there, there's no question of that, but she went to the fundamentals of the strike . . . Why was it being done? Why was it allowed to happen? Why was it the Government had all the strategies already prepared to break that strike? . . . She could explain why it was – how you had to break the miners because they were the strongest bastions of the unions. And if you were going to go on a union-breaking procedure, which Thatcher was dead set on, you had to start with the strongest. If you broke them you were laughing because all the others went down like ninepins. Joan had no sentimentality about Scargill. Now he was a hate figure but he was also a cult figure among many of the miners and the miners' wives who were on strike. She didn't share in that. She looked at the whole membership, the NUM, that's what she looked at. Not Arthur Scargill . . . We were pulled along, to some extent, in this wonder of this great strong leader. Joan's never been a great believer in leaders, you don't put your faith in leaders but in working people. She admired the strikers, particularly in Nottinghamshire, because they had such a terrible time, and she admired the women because without the women the strike would have collapsed and it's something I think Arthur and the rest of the union leaders just didn't recognise. Joan had this ability to go to the heart of the matter. She had an analysis of politics which enabled her immediately to see the crux of the matter. She doesn't hide behind language ever. She doesn't use words or phrases which are not in common usage.

Without strike funds, without social security, and without support from the trade union movement, the end was in sight. Miners, in desperation, were beginning to go back to work in dribs and drabs until, in March 1985, the NUM delegates voted for a dignified return. Bands played and banners fluttered, but hearts were broken and bitter. Joan said:

> Another and crucial reason why the miners did not win was the lack of industrial action from other workers, particularly electricity workers and the deputies in the pits, who voted 86% for strike action and still managed not to strike. So much for ballots! These two groups were key; the strike would have been won had they come out. All who did not support the miners were traitors to the working class. I can't forgive them.

It is arguable that the failure of the 1984 Miners' strike was not the beginning of the end, but simply the confirmation of a process which had been developing over the previous twenty years – the diminishing sense of the working class of and for itself. The breaking of the strike was a *coup de grâce.*

Psephologists have pointed out that during the 1970s two changes took place that had a profound effect on electoral fortunes. One was that voters of a given class were less likely than hitherto to vote for the party of their traditional class allegiance. In this case it was shown statistically that working-class voters were less likely to vote for the Labour Party than would have been the case in the previous decade. The other effect is that voters of all classes were less likely to vote consistently for a party, and that this was more true of working-class voters than those of other classes. Furthermore, through the 1980s, the traditional working class was shrinking in numbers, with the decline of smokestack industry, the rise of service industries and the sale of council houses. (Dorey 1995, p . 154–159)

All in all, it is argued, the social basis for a party campaigning on Socialist policies was eroded for good, and those who persist in it are due for the dustheap. As J. K. Galbraith has pointed out, governments in electoral democracies need only ensure the contentment of sufficient numbers to guarantee re-election. In the present electoral system, those numbers may be a long way short of a majority of the whole, and the Government need not necessarily be overly concerned with justice or equality.

How does a Socialist respond to these changes? Distinctions need to be made here, as Socialism encompasses a range of attitudes. The liberal Left sees Socialism essentially as a desirable option within the framework of consumer choice and the existing electoral system; if the customer is not buying the product, eventually the product is withdrawn; or 'modernised'. On the other hand, Socialists who draw on Marxism might be disappointed, but not deflected. The power of Marxism is that it claims to make an objective analysis of social forces over the long run of history, and therefore an individual's location in the class structure is an objective fact, not affected by their personal opinion at a particular moment. Psephological spasms, or the mumblings of focus groups, may alter political strategies, but not direction. This sounds rather arrogant and 'we know best', and a platform for tyranny; so one must reiterate here Joan's aspiration, which is for Socialist democracy. That position is beautifully described in a letter to Joan in October 1979, from Roger Fieldhouse, an educationalist and at one time her teacher in the WEA. He refers back to the historian R. H. Tawney:

> I had forgotten how much I owed to Tawney – he believed that political democracy is not just a means of obtaining Socialism, it is part of the Socialist revolution – it is the process by which the working class will free its minds of the falsities of capitalist society 'Here was the forming and energising force which could snap the working class out of mesmerisation by capitalist myths'. Through education, discussion and participation people 'transcend the limitations of their individual perspectives and become partners in a world of interests which they can share with their fellows.' Tawney . . . believed it was necessary to first destroy the attractiveness of the old ways in the minds of the people. This could be done (he argued) not by an elitist or Bolshevik vanguard, but by 'trusting the people' – by taking the people into the heart of the matter, educating them through the processes of democratic participation. Unleash the latent energies of the people – not control or channel them. Socialism is about 'trusting the people', not 'serving the people'. Only then can a Socialist Party hope to create the atmosphere, the confidence, and the belief necessary to bring about genuine democratic Socialism rather than an authoritarian, totalitarian version.

Fieldhouse's letter is worth quoting at length for its clarity (and passion) and also because it suggests a further point; a line can be drawn back in time from Joan Maynard to those who taught her, people like Fieldhouse and EP Thompson, to Tawney, and Lansbury, to William Morris and to the Chartists.

Thompson (1963, p. 803), writing of the 1830s, talks of the

> gigantic, but ephemeral, impulses which caught the enthusiasm of the masses, presenting the vision of a quite different structure which might be built in a matter of years or months, if only people were united or determined enough. A spirit of combination has grown up, Bronterre O'Brien wrote in 1833, whose object, 'is the sublimest that can be conceived, namely – to establish for the productive classes a complete dominion over the fruits of their own industry . . . An entire change in society – a change amounting to a complete subversion of the existing "order of the world" – is contemplated by the working classes. They aspire to be at the top instead of at the bottom of society – or rather that there should be no bottom or top at all.

The development of Socialism in Britain originates in the tradition of radical dissent, dating from the English Revolution in the mid-seventeenth century. Whereas the Marxist theory of dialectical materialism engages the intellect, the energy of the dissenting tradition is moral, part intuition, part lived experience. It comes from the grass roots, like the Levellers and Diggers, communitarian in its ethos, given to acting out beliefs. Joan brought together the moral energy of British Socialism with the theoretical tools of class analysis. Thus, Socialism is a moral objective, which can only be achieved as a result of class struggle, which in turn will only happen by, 'trusting the people' and 'educating them through the processes of democratic participation'.

'We all learn from each other in life.'

*

Class analysis was the lens by which Joan saw all struggles in the world, and she was tireless in support of those she believed in. It was a lens that both facilitated and limited her view. Her response to feminism is a case in point.

As a woman who had achieved political prominence, Joan was often taxed with having a special responsibility to promote the cause of women. Before considering how she answered this call, her achievement should be looked at in the light of feminists' criticism of the Labour movement.

Firstly, there is almost certainly no other example in British politics of a rural working-class woman rising to such prominence, having left school at the age of fourteen. Her background, and especially her education, distinguished her from the majority of women Labour MPs. A photograph in *Labour Weekly* (22 November 1974) shows Joan and the four other newly elected Labour women MPs having lunch with Julia Langdon. Of the three youngest women present Hélène Hayman graduated from Cambridge, where she was president of the Union, Margaret Jackson (Beckett) studied Metallurgy at Manchester College of Science and Technology, and Ann Taylor graduated with a Master's degree from Sheffield. Among Joan's contemporaries in Parliament, Millie Miller attended Dame Alice Owen's Girls' School; Audrey Wise, Rutherford High School; Jo Richardson, South End School for Girls; Maureen Colquhoun, the London School of Economics and Barbara Castle, Oxford University. The earlier generation of women Labour MPs 'were very highly educated, women like Susan Lawrence, Dorothy Jewson, Jennie Lee, and Ellen Wilkinson all had university degrees' (Vallance 1979, p. 64).

Secondly, the trade union movement was very largely a male citadel. Joan served for years as the only woman on the fourteen-strong Executive Committee of the NUAAW. Vallance records that at the 1974 TUC Conference (the year Joan became an MP) there were only 61 women delegates among nearly a thousand men. Melanie Phillips (1980, p. 71). recognised the consequence of women's low participation rate in trade unions:

> The trade union 'A' list also accounts for the dearth of women Labour Candidates, since in 1979 women accounted for only 3% of the names on it. One of the very few women who came to Westminster via the trade union route, Joan Maynard, only became an MP after her union ambitions had been thwarted . . . The tiny number of women who play an active part in trade unions, however, means that few women can follow Joan Maynard's example.

When Joan was elected to Parliament she was one of only eighteen women

Labour MPs, representing just over 5% of the PLP. Analysing the October 1974 General Election, Maeve Denby showed 'the number of Labour women candidates represented only 8% of the total number of candidates'.[23] Suggesting women find it harder to be selected for the safer seats she points to the statistically significant difference between women and men being elected as Labour candidates, Phillips (1980, p. 61) is unequivocal: 'The Labour Party consistently selected women for marginal or even apparently hopeless seats.'

Joan certainly recognised her good fortune in being selected for Sheffield Brightside, one of the safest seats in the country. Looking back on her selection, she said:

> I think there was a tendency in some constituencies, well maybe many, to think in terms of this is a job for a man. But they didn't apply that in Brightside because they were more concerned with the politics rather than if it was a man or woman, and quite rightly in my opinion. I can't ever remember people being against me because I was a woman. If they were against me it was because of my politics. I wasn't conscious of it being rather odd for a woman to go along from a rural constituency to represent a heavily industrial seat because of my commitment to them was as workers, whether they'd worked in Sheffield or wherever they worked. That was the link in my mind. I was bound to them, as I was to farm workers in rural areas. I felt all I had to do was learn about the problems they had and try to represent them in Parliament. I don't remember the men showing any animosity towards me, or prejudice. I can't, honestly.

Hilary Wainwright (1987, p. 113) has written of the Sheffield Labour Group, 'the dominant view of Socialism was on the whole anti-feminist'. And 'feminism was seen as another trendy idea imported from the South'. There was nothing whatever trendy about Joan and she certainly didn't privilege women's issues above those of social class. In contrast to her clear position on class, her approach to feminism was ill-defined. She said:

> In a way I am not very typical. I think that women who are married, or have been married, have different relationships between them and menfolk. I don't

> just mean in the physical sense, I mean in the monetary sense. I never started off with any inhibitions. When I used to let rooms out, here, I can think of some of the wives, probably most of them, having to ask their husbands for money to buy a new pair of tights or to go to the pictures, because they were at home looking after the children and the men were at work. I remember thinking, I wouldn't like that. So I didn't experience it directly. Because of my different experience I didn't set out with any prejudices against men and that is probably one of the reasons why I've never been a very strong feminist. I'm not against it, I mean, I'm in favour of women having equal pay and everything like that – equal opportunities. But I've never been carried away with feminism. I've always thought that the struggle for women for equality is part of the struggle for Socialism against capitalism, which is an exploiter of men, and of course even bigger exploiter of women who are less well organised.

Whilst distancing herself from feminism, she campaigned tirelessly in her Union for equal pay for women. The majority of part-time workers in the 'allied' industries of poultry-packing stations and mushroom units were women who were particularly penalised by the reduction in part-time rates. However, some comrades criticised her for not 'harnessing' Union women together.

Wilf Page said:

> I think it's the last thing Joan would want to do – get a women's movement going. She'd think they've got to fight their way through as she had done – as a result of her activities rather than as a woman. There was no national get-together of women as a result of her efforts. At Biennial Conferences there were a number of women, but I can never remember her deciding, I want to have a discussion with the women tonight to see what we can do. I never remember her saying, I'll get all the women delegates and bring them on. She was with the men and she was fighting with the men – in a man's world. She should have got involved in women's issues because she would have got more support among the women than she got from the men.

Audrey Wise considered Joan to be sceptical, rather than hostile, to feminism, and though she could always be relied on to support a campaign for women's rights she would not take the lead. That said, Joan strongly opposed attempts to limit the right to abortion – provoking angry criticism from Brightside's Catholic constituents – and campaigned against the exploitation of women in the 'gangmaster' system of agricultural employment. She spoke for women's rights at National Conferences of Labour Women and the NCCL, and arranged meetings in the Commons for many women's organisations including the National Assembly of Women, the Women and Peace Movement and the Women's International Democratic Federation; in retirement she addressed meetings of Women's Councils in Yorkshire and actively participated in her own constituency's Socialist Women's Council. Working for Irish prisoners in Britain, she savaged the practice of strip-searching women and in campaigning against the tied cottage system she would often focus on the distress caused to the wives of farm workers.

The issue of women-only shortlists for the selection of Parliamentary candidates highlighted the difference between Joan's approach and that of some of her close associates in the Labour Party. Jeremy Corbyn recalls: 'She was always opposed to what she saw as preferential treatment for women. I would argue for it and she against. Her view would be that you fight the class fight and that the class fight comes first.'[24] Tony Benn (1992, p. 420) describes a discussion at a Campaign Group meeting in Chesterfield where Ann Pettifor of the Women's Action Committee was asking for support for women only short lists:

> Dave Nellist believed selection should be about policy – it shouldn't be about gender alone… I accepted that there was discrimination against women in the Party which men didn't understand because they weren't affected. But enforcing this measure from the centre would take away the power of local parties to choose their candidate. Secondly, the WAC's [Women's Action Committee] demands tended to be constitutional in character without being related to policy, and they might lead to a radical feminist position rather than a Socialist feminist one. Joan Maynard agreed there was discrimination but that policies were what mattered and organisation came second – this is an absolute classic Labour position. Ann Pettifor replied that the rights of constituency parties must be considered but the Party was deeply sexist and

> the NEC should say to C[onstituency] L[abour] P[artie]s, 'You must deal with discrimination.' The policy argument, she said, was a complete red herring. She left, very angrily.

In the event, all-women shortlists were introduced in time for the 1997 General Election, when New Labour swept to power, with 101 women MPs. An early piece of Government legislation cut the benefit paid to single parents – overwhelmingly mothers – and of the new intake of women MPs only one – Ann Cryer – voted against it. Hearing reports of women being in tears as they went through the lobby, Joan exploded angrily: 'I don't know how those women can sleep in their beds at night thinking of those poor people. Never mind crying. Get in the right lobby!'

In retirement Joan enjoyed reviewing Socialist feminist pamphlets and books for the *Morning Star*. She commended the Communist Party of Britain's publication *Women and Class* for 'highlighting the contradictions of the capitalist class in relation to women's place in society'.[25] Yet she displays a naïve view of women occupying, 'equal but different' roles in pre-capitalist societies. In conflating capitalism and patriarchy there is no acknowledgement by Joan of women's subordination in pre-capitalist systems.

In 1994, reviewing Paula Groves's *Reading Labour Women: Women in British Working Class Politics 1918–1939* Joan concluded: 'The struggle is still going on . . . like me they never saw gender issues as separate from class issues – whatever they were campaigning for it was always for their class.'[26]

In the opinion of Audrey Wise, 'Joan certainly would be discriminated against because she was a Socialist – and perhaps in Joan's case mostly because she was a Socialist, but she would have been affected, whether she knew it or not, by the discrimination against women'.

The impetus for writing Joan's biography has been that her ideas, actions and achievements should not be hidden from history, the fate of so many women in so many fields. Though a prominent Socialist throughout the second half of the twentieth century, Joan's name scarcely appears in publications about the Labour movement during the period. In July 1994, Bournemouth's *Evening Echo* carried a photograph of the annual Martyrs Rally at Tolpuddle. There is Joan, marching in the front line, with John

Prescott and Jimmy Knapp on her right, and John Monks and Bill Morris on her left. A reader might wonder, who is the woman in the middle? Only the men are named.

But Joan couldn't see it; like Jennie Lee she considered herself 'a Socialist who just happened to be a woman' (Hollis 1997).

*

One political scribbler has written that Joan was a 'crude materialist'.[27] The record needs to be put straight.

Jack Brocklebank had introduced Joan to Neville Knox in the early 1970s in the context of local government reorganisation in North Yorkshire. She especially asked that he be interviewed for this biography. Knox, a man of impressive presence, is an evangelical Christian preacher, having converted during the Second World War, and was formerly clerk to Harrogate Town Council. Up until her death, he was in regular contact with Joan. He described her, when they first met as 'a country girl, through and through' and 'very poor'. Also, he said, she had 'real discernment in the political field. She knew who were the genuine ones and who were the charlatans'. She and Rowie would go for meals at the Knoxes' and vice versa. They went to religious meetings at his house several times a year and after Rowie died, Joan attended on her own.

Although Neville Knox described her as 'spiritually reborn' this cannot be seen simply as a late conversion, and it would be quite out of character for Joan to maintain her spiritual self as a separate entity from her political self. Since she maintained her politics to the end, to do justice to them we must see how they fitted with her religion.

It was suggested earlier that Joan's politics combined the moral energy of the British Socialist tradition with the theoretical tools of class analysis. This may be a fruitful way of thinking about her religious sensibilities.

To start with factual information, Joan's family were both church- and chapel-goers, and they had taken this seriously (they undertook long journeys on foot to get to Ampleforth, they contributed money to the building of the Methodist chapel in Alne). Secondly, Joan stopped going to church in her teens, because of a moral objection – the hypocrisy of the organisers. Thirdly, she and her father named the home in Sowerby after George Lansbury, which crucially indicates a continuity of thought from her childhood well into the maturity of her political development. Lansbury (1859–1940) was an avowed Christian who wrote, 'Socialism is to me the finest and fullest expression of religion.'

British Socialism is not separable in its origins from Christian Socialism, which criticises capitalism from the standpoint of the New Testament. Not only did Christ say that the poor shall inherit the Earth, but his early followers lived, it is said, communistically (as in the lines from St Luke quoted earlier).

Socialist Christians commonly came from Methodist, evangelical, or low church backgrounds, or were converted to them. They were often socially from the ambivalent territory between capital and labour – the skilled worked and lower middle classes. Self-educated, hard-working, respectable, but no respecter of personages. Lansbury exemplified this: school at fourteen, working on the railways for ten years before emigrating to Australia, started a lumber business on his return, converted to Christianity, became an MP, supported women's suffrage, was a pacifist, and became leader of the Labour Party.

Early Labour Party history is gem-studded with people such as Lansbury. Arthur Henderson (1863–1935), educated in elementary school, worked as an iron moulder, became a Methodist lay preacher, was Party leader, 1931–1932, and won the Nobel Peace Prize 1934. Keir Hardie was another, Philip Snowden another. R. H. Tawney was a Christian Socialist, though with a university education. Beyond the luminaries of the Party were the thousands who shared their ideals, who were witnesses to the crushing effect of capital on the material and spiritual lives of the great mass of people, witnesses to the vacuity of what it offers in place. Christianity has a critique and a vision.

E. P. Thompson (1963) is illuminating about Methodism in particular. He discusses the various and contradictory versions of Methodism that had arisen in the early years of the nineteenth century, and then continues. 'There was one other context in which Methodism of any variety necessarily assumed a more class-conscious form: in the rural areas. The chapel in the agricultural village was inevitably an affront to the vicar and the squire, and a centre in which the labourer gained independence and self-respect.' And he goes on to quote a pamphlet published by 'an irate country parson in 1805' complaining about the seditious opinions of field labourers who were converted to Methodism, 'They say "That Corn and all other fruits of the earth, are grown and intended by Providence, as much for the poor as the rich." They were less content with their wages, less ready, "to work extraordinary hours as the exigencies of their masters might require". Worse, instead of, recouping themselves for the next week's labour they exhausted themselves on Sundays walking several miles to hear a preacher.' (*Ibid.*, p. 397)

Thompson also writes about character. 'The Methodist political rebel carried through into his radical or revolutionary activity a profound moral earnestness, a sense of righteousness, and of "calling", a "Methodist" capacity for sustained organisational dedication and (at its best) a high degree of personal responsibility.' He then names several examples and says: 'We see it in Loveless, the Dorchester labourer and "Tolpuddle Martyr".'(*Ibid.*, p. 394)

This is not intended to collapse Methodism into political radicalism, nor the twentieth century into the nineteenth, but what Thompson says is amazingly evocative of a culture and a character we have met.

Nearly a hundred years after Tolpuddle, a little girl is carried on her dad's shoulder, walking the three miles home from the chapel in Ampleforth. They say rhymes and sing snatches of hymns, as the countryside of childhood slides by.

FOURTEEN

Home ground

> I was looking forward to retirement because I love the countryside. I was looking forward to coming back here to live. I've got involved with quite a lot of things locally since I came back. Too many really.

Joan resolved early in 1985 that she wouldn't stand again for Parliament. She decided for precise personal reasons, not because of rumblings in Sheffield that she could face deselection. Although she felt forces in Sheffield were ganging up against her in quite an organised fashion, she was very confident she would be selected were she to put herself forward. Many Socialist friends tried to persuade her to stand again, but she would not be moved. Her sister Elsie, suffering from Alzheimer's disease, had returned 'home' from the United States to be near her, and Rowie was becoming increasingly frail.[1]

Joan explained:

> What led up to retiring was the hard work being an MP if you do it properly. As soon as I made the decision I told the Brightside people. They were very good, I didn't have much pressure applied there. I think people can see it is hard work if you do it properly. It's a hell of a job. You're there from ten to ten at least, every day, and then you come home on a Friday and you're doing something in your constituency at the weekend. There were some weekends off, but not very many. In my case I might have been travelling somewhere else in the country to speak

as a member of the NEC. It's the sort of thing that wouldn't bother you if you were younger. I think I did the right thing, I knew MPs who were seventy and over who would say after ten o'clock, if it was an all-night sitting, 'Well, I'm going home'. They couldn't cope, which I could understand. I was a few weeks off sixty-six when I retired. I hope you retire before you're sixty-six; you will if you've got any sense. I hung on till I was sixty-five because actuarially the pension wouldn't be paid until I was sixty-five, it's based on men's retirement age. You see, when it was decided, they'd be virtually all men in there; it does need looking into. The other reason was that my brother here needed somebody to be around. He'd done very well up to then but I really felt he needed some help. He had tried to persuade me to retire earlier on the grounds he had sufficient financially to keep us both going. But I didn't fancy that. I didn't fancy being dependent on somebody else, so I didn't accept.

The 'things' Joan got involved in locally included Union meetings and lobbying Parliament to increase farm workers' wages; late at night she would be on the phone to farm workers' leader, Barry Leathwood, giving advice on forthcoming wage negotiations. Through her sister's illness she became involved in the Hambleton branch of the Alzheimer's Society and the Community Care Association. She chaired the Thirsk local Labour Party branch and, in October 1989, she and a group of Socialists established the North Yorkshire Campaign Group, which met in each other's homes on Saturday mornings. Looking at the papers of this group, one is reminded of that small gathering of comrades who met in Thirsk some half a century earlier – Democracy and the Labour Party (March 1990). Expulsions: general dismay expressed at the Party's treatment of Terry Fields and Dave Nellist (December 1991). Is Socialism inseparable from Common Ownership? (January 1996).

Though Joan had chaired the mighty Regional and Local Government Sub-committee of Labour's NEC, she was keen to stand for election to her own parish council – as a young woman she had topped the poll in local elections.

It's essential – to do the job well – to be approachable, anywhere, and at any time, day or night, and to remember that you're there to serve the people. Too many councillors get big-headed. The right kind of humility is essential in life, particularly in public life. Be sincere, be honest with the people and you won't go far wrong.

True to form, she brought her wide experience of politics to bear on local issues. She joined the group REVOLT,[2] which was campaigning against proposals for above-ground power lines, because of their impact on agriculture and the environment.

The 'former MP who swapped her seat at Westminster for a place on Sowerby Parish Council' gave evidence to the public enquiry established to decide on a second east-coast pylon corridor. 'Her contribution to day fifteen of the inquiry was a memorable one. Nowadays Miss Maynard rarely gets the chance to show the oratory which made her the scourge of many a government minister . . . But on Thursday she was back in front of the microphone; hammering those who, in her eyes would seek to put profit before people.'[3]

She joined the Yorkshire Rural Community Council, an independent voluntary organisation which worked with people of all political persuasions and none in support of rural communities, to improve their social and economic environment and influence their own future. She was elected vice-chair. She became a member of the Rural Arts Conservation Committee, giving her the opportunity to promote the arts locally and develop her own appreciation and knowledge. Her friend Hans Breitenbach, chair of the York Fabians, spoke of her 'great interest in the artistic and cultural dimension of Socialism. It is important to her and she regrets we don't do more about it'.

In contrast to her earlier life in Lansbury House, she was now comfortably off and enjoying her beautiful garden, improving the house and choosing locally hand-crafted oak furniture.

She delighted in a wide range of music, from classical to traditional Labour movement songs, and read widely – never the same book twice now; 'there isn't time'. She cheered on Yorkshire during the cricket season – Thomas Lord came from Thirsk[4] – and shared her beloved North Yorkshire countryside with family and friends visiting from Sheffield and London, and Union comrades from Norfolk, Kent and Dorset. She invariably travelled each year to Norfolk in September for the Burston School Strike Rally and to Dorset in July to commemorate the Tolpuddle Martyrs.[5]

In June 1994 her dearest friend and lifetime comrade Jack Brocklebank died. It was Jack who in 1946 had advertised the meeting for anyone interested in forming a Labour Party in Thirsk, and, the following year, invited Joan to join the farm workers' Union; Jack who would warn Joan with a chuckle, 'Now don't get too far ahead of the troops, like'. At his funeral, poignantly, a lone voice sang, 'To Be a Farmer's Boy'.

Her other close comrades in the Union had also died – Jack Bowen, Tom Gascoyne, Bert Waind. But she was mindful of the long haul, and whenever able committed Socialists appeared, she would bring them on and encourage them.[6]

Joan missed Mollie Prendergast and her friends in the Commons but she didn't miss the place itself:

> I was never taken over by the place like a lot of people are. It is easy for people to be taken over, particularly working-class people. People like to be sort of looked up to. I've always said I saw more egotism to the inch down there than anywhere I've ever been. If you sit there in the lobby it's very clear to see. Some people go in with the best intentions, but it can change people. One of the real dangers, and I think we've got it very badly with the Labour Party at the moment, is this acceptance that the system can't be changed, that there isn't any alternative, as Thatcher used to say. I believe people get into positions like MPs and so on and begin to think: 'Yes, well, I used to think like you, but now I realise that it isn't so easy.' It never was easy! They get convinced, either because they want to be convinced, or because they genuinely are convinced, that it is not possible to do the things we want to do as Socialists. I think they get taken over by the place in that way. I'm sure the majority of MPs in the House of Commons do genuinely believe that there isn't any alternative to the rubbish that Blair is putting over about this market economy that we support. I mean, what's so wonderful about it? Honestly love, we have no conception about what some people are putting up with. After I came back here I decided I would help the Union again by collecting the subs. It did me good. I feel that I am committed to working people, but if you look at my lifestyle here it is very different now to the average working-class person. It didn't used to be, but it is now. When I went round the first time collecting the Union subs and started listening to what the members said, and seeing the kind of furnishing that is in their houses, and the problems they were meeting, I thought, 'Well, it's a

> jolly good thing I went round again, it's brought me back to earth.' And that's nothing to what some people have to put up with; I don't know how they carry on at all – high-rise flats, no jobs. I heard recently how children go through infant and junior school and they're full of enthusiasm. But when they get to the secondary schools and through their early teens things change, because they suddenly realise, poor beggars, that there aren't going to be any jobs for them and they get onto drugs and all sorts. It's terrible that young people can't see any prospect and capitalism will never solve it because the technology that's coming in means we won't need as many workers. The other thing is we need to educate people to use their leisure, which we never do. We don't really educate people; I think we just train them to run this complicated society. If you educate people you need small groups of people who you can devote time to, so you can encourage each person to develop their potential to the full and have a critical approach to life. I wouldn't care if it was a Labour or a Socialist Government, I'd still be in favour of encouraging people to look at things critically. Don't just accept what the establishment says – think about it.

Asked if she had considered leaving the Labour Party in 1997 when New Labour was elected, her answer was terse, 'Before the election I did think I would leave but the more I thought about it, I thought, no. It's *our* Labour Party, not theirs. I am not going to leave. I think they've hijacked our Party and they've done it a darn sight more successfully than Militant ever did – the "party of business"! Fancy the Labour Party coming out with that.'

Reflecting on the Labour Government of 1945: 'Most of them weren't really Socialists; they were Labour. Now if you're a Socialist, you've got to believe in people's ability to change society. It's not leaders who are going to do it, it's the people. And I think if you don't believe in that, you can't say you're a Socialist.'

Joan was justly respected among political friends and opponents for her integrity and hard work, for acting according to her beliefs without compromise, though her unremitting demands on herself could make her impatient with those whose capacity or commitment fell short of her own high standard. What also won affection across the spectrum was her warmth, her genuine understanding and sympathy for ordinary people, her ability to relate to people without affectation or pretence.

She loved a good joke, even at her own expense. Bob Cryer, an accomplished mimic, used to take off her low-pitched Yorkshire voice, saying quietly at the end of a Parliamentary Campaign Group meeting: 'Right, now, comrades, it's time to put up the barricade. Are you alright, are you ready, love?' Within the humour is captured exactly her combination of commitment and warmth.

It is the fate of those who challenge privilege and injustice to be called unrealistic, idealistic, perhaps mad. Joan was not spared. She was not alone in this, but as an outspoken woman, she attracted more media spite than most on the Left. With the collapse of the eastern bloc states, and the spreading glow of the politics of contentment, engineered in this country by the sale of public housing and utilities, and across the West by spurious optimism about the 'new technology' in the 1990s, it seemed to many that Socialism was being laid to rest at last. Yet now her views on so many issues would be mainstream. She was right about the impact of agribusiness on food and the environment, serving up side dishes of BSE, *E.Coli*, salmonella, pesticides; right about the CAP; right about the power of trans-national companies; right about economic colonisation.

On Ireland, she saw that the only way to peace was by a political settlement. Gerry Adams has praised her foresight:

> I think it is true to say that if Joan Maynard's position had been acted upon in the 1970s or the 1980s the peace process, difficult though it was, would have been initiated decades before it actually was. She was saying we need dialogue, we need to have inclusivity... Had this been acted upon, we would, hopefully, by now have not just a peace process, but peace; we would have brought the peace process to a democratic conclusion. (Third Annual Joan Maynard Memorial Lecture, 12 October 2001)[7]

She had a Candide-like ability to go to the heart of situations, not tempted by pragmatism, nor deceived by weasel words. She would say 'When I hear a Minister say, he thinks we've got the balance right, I know the workers have lost.' She never let the complexities deflect her vision of where the truth lay. Audrey Wise said: 'If you deal too much in complexities and in shades of grey, you might lose sight of the pure scarlet. Joan never lost sight of the pure scarlet.'

A fighter to the end, Joan struggled with cancer, supported by loving and loyal friends and family. Her house was filled with flowers and cards, the phone rang constantly, visitors from near and far came to see her and say goodbye. Eventually, a little notice was pinned to the front door of Lansbury House – Joan was tired and could no longer see visitors. Days before she died on 28 March 1998, Joan received a letter from Tony Benn. In it he reminded her of their first encounter and their joint campaigns:

> There are so many occasions when I recall your taking a strong stand and getting attacked and holding your ground. And whenever you speak it is always of the importance of the trade unions and their role in protecting the class, and how that class needs socialism if conditions are ever to improve. The deepest footprints in the sands of time are not made by those who leap up and down trying to scramble on the bandwagon. Those are made by the teachers – as you have done – and by those who say what they mean and mean what they say and cannot be deflected.

Joan's funeral in the beautiful village church of St Oswald, just across the road from her house, was a moving celebration of her life. The church was filled to capacity with trade unionists, Labour Party members, MPs, local and national political opponents, neighbours and friends from across the country. Comrades paid tribute to her warmth, kindness and political courage. Joan had chosen the music, beginning with the sublime strains of Mozart's Clarinet Concerto, and closing, resoundingly, with William Blake's *Jerusalem*. Nothing could be more fitting.

Joan is buried in the cemetery of St. Leonard's church in Thornton-le-Street, alongside the graves of her family, and within a few yards of Post Office Farm. Her tombstone is inscribed:

> Steadfast in her beliefs: a True Socialist.

Across the road from Lansbury House in St Oswald's churchyard a young hawthorn, planted in memory of Joan, bears flowers of pure scarlet.

NOTES

One: *The ground on which she stood*

1. Joan's birth certificate gives her date of birth as 5 July 1921. It was always celebrated on 6 July. It may be worth pointing out that Sowerby near Thirsk is not the Sowerby of the West Riding. The North Riding of Yorkshire, where Joan was born now forms part of the county of North Yorkshire, the largest county in England. In this biography the area is referred to as North Yorkshire.
2. Matt's sister Jane was known to all as Jinny. She was married to Herbert Robson. Elsie was a bright sociable young woman who had done well at school. Her experience of the city of York and awareness of her own capabilities determined her to develop a life as far away as possible from shop work, the confines of domestic service and, most of all, the looming poverty of Carr Villa. Elsie saw far beyond these limitations; her ambition was to train as a nurse. She travelled to London, where Effie's sister worked as a housekeeper, and began training at the Royal Free Hospital. Soon after commencing her studies she required an operation, which prevented her from nursing because of its physical demands. For some months she was so ill that Effie, together with the young Edric and Joan, went to London to be near her, staying with Effie's sister. Recovered and undeterred, Elsie undertook secretarial training and secured a job with an American bank in London – until the Wall Street crash of 1926, when the bank closed overnight and everybody was out of a job. With her administrative skills and interest in health work, she was appointed assistant almoner at the West London Hospital in Hammersmith. During this time she qualified as a hospital almoner and studied for a degree in social science at the London School of Economics. Shortly afterwards she returned to the north of England as almoner in charge of the Joint Committees' Venereal Diseases Clinic at Newcastle General Hospital. Seeking further challenge and adventure during the last year of the Second World War she was appointed assistant director of the Soldiers', Sailors' and Airmen's Families Association in Italy. Her letters from Italy to the family in North Yorkshire were to be a source of frivolous entertainment since the censors removed anything of particular interest to a family that read widely, discussed radical ideas and would never miss the news bulletin on the wireless. Her parents had not objected to her plans to leave home – there was very little on offer for such a clever girl. Effie and Elsie were not close as mother and daughter, and Effie's own return from London to marry Matt had not presented much of an example. Joan and her brother Rowie could never forget Elsie's brutal 'I'm getting out, and you're fools if you don't'. Sixty years later, Elsie was to return 'home' to be looked after by Joan after an impressive career as a hospital almoner which saw her winning a travel scholarship to lecture on social services across America – where at the age of 57 she decided to live, work and retire. When she developed Alzheimer's disease and returned to England, Joan took her in and ensured she was cared for in a good hospital. Joan almost forgave but never forgot Elsie's parting words all those years before.
3. The interviews with Joan Maynard for this biography took place over the four years preceding her death in 1998. Short quotations from these interviews are placed within the text in quotation marks.

Where Joan spoke in public or when her views were published, the source, where possible, is given. The main exceptions are when quotations from Joan (and occasionally from other individuals quoted) are contained in unnamed or undated newspaper and journal cuttings or correspondence. With the exception of Labour Party and Union Conference reports, Labour Party National Executive Committee (NEC) minutes and publications in the endnotes and bibliography, the written materials referred to are housed with Joan Maynard's papers.

4. Years later James Hutchinson said to his daughter Doris, 'It's a funny thing, I helped Maynard so much and they soon forgot.' Shortly after her father died in 1977 Doris Hutchinson met up with Joan and mentioned what he had said. Joan responded, 'It's been a very great mistake, Doris, but seeing we didn't do it for Jim we'll do it for you.' Over the next twenty years the two women developed a close friendship.
5. All correspondence housed with Joan Maynard papers.
6. Toc H is an organisation made up of people meeting together and serving their community in worthwhile projects. Begun during the First World War the original Toc H was in Poperinge, Belgium. It was set up to provide basic comforts to the young men going to and from the battle lines of the Western Front, becoming known by its initials 'T.H'., which were Toc H in the signallers' language of the day. T.H. stands for Talbot House, the house in Poperinge whaere the organisation was formed.
7. The source for Edric's activity in London in this paragraph is Tippett (1991).

Two: *Education – breath of life*

1. *Yorkshire Post*, 25 May 1953.
2. *Manchester Guardian*, 7 February 1953.
3. Thompson, E. P. (1950) 'Against "University" standards', *Adult Education Papers* 1(4) 16–39 cited by Roger Fieldhouse in *Sidney Raybould, Fred Sedgwick and the early department* (R. Taylor ed1996 p. 21).
4. Armstrong (1988, p. 128) states: 'Farmers as a body were not conspicuously well-educated, the majority leaving school at fifteen, succeeding to their roles by accident of birth, and having no formal training themselves (Gasson R , 'Resources in Agriculture' p. 113; Newby H, *Green and Pleasant Land?* p. 98). Among 55 Yorkshire farmers surveyed about 1966, Black found a widespread suspicion that trained men would challenge or argue (Black M (1968) 'Agriculture in an Expanding Economy', *Journal of Agricultural Economics* XIX, p. 69).'
5. Roger Fieldhouse negotiated a grant from Balliol College, Oxford to support participants from the NUAAW.
6. *Northern Echo* 25 May 1953.

Three: *The Labour Party from below*

1. Laybourn (1997, pp. 136–137) citing Paul Addison (1975), *The Road to 1945: British Politics and the Second World War*, London, Jonathan Cape. Laybourn continues with Addison's interesting argument that 'the crucial factor in the change (of attitudes) appears to have been the military catastrophe at Dunkirk, which seems to have forced the wartime Government, faced with the need to restore calm and instil unity into the war effort, to offer welfare provisions for all. In the wake of Dunkirk, William Beveridge and many of the Whitehall mandarins began to organise the war effort

and, according to Addison, "The home front organised for war was becoming a model, and an inspiration, for the reorganisation of peace." (Addison P. 1975, p.118)'. (Laybourn K. 1997, p.137)

2. Quoting from G. K. Chesterton's *The Secret People*. The Common Wealth Party put up 23 candidates in the 1945 general election and didn't contest any further elections. Richard Acland had been a Liberal MP from 1935 until forming Common Wealth in September 1942. He joined the Labour Party after being defeated in 1945 and was elected an MP in 1947.
3. Shaw 1996, p. 24 citing S. H. Beer (1965) *Modern British Politics*, p. 134. London, Faber and Faber.
4. Shaw 1996, p. 26 citing A Cairncross (1985) *Years of Recovery: British Economic Policy 1945–51*, p. 494. London, Methuen.
5. *Darlington and Stockton Times* (between Feb 1946 and April 1947) newspaper cutting, Joan Maynard papers.
6. Article by Joan Maynard on the history of the Thirsk and Malton Divisional Labour Party, March 1963, Joan Maynard papers.
7. Unnamed newspaper cutting, Joan Maynard papers.
8. Shaw 1996, p. 23 citing K Morgan (1984) *Labour in Power,1945–1951*, p. 244. Oxford, Clarendon press.
9. Quoted by Hattersley 1997, p. 33.
10. Moeran was elected MP for South Bedfordshire in 1950 and defeated in 1951.
11. *Darlington and Stockton Times* undated.
12. Interview with farm worker John Tubby JP.
13. *Ibid.*

Four: *Joining the union*

1 The National Union of Agricultural Workers (NUAW) was the name adopted by the union in 1920. The union journal the *Land Worker* presents a succinct summary of the changes in nomenclature.
'Milestones in Rural Unionism:
1834 Tolpuddle Martyrs plant seed.
1872 Joseph Arch's National Agricultural Labourers' Union founded. Collapses in the 1890s.
1906 Start of George Edwards' Eastern Counties Agricultural Labourers' and Smallholders' Union.
1910 Name changed to National Agricultural Labourers and Rural Workers Union.
1920 Name changed to National Union of Agricultural Workers (NUAW).
1968 Name changed to National Union of Agricultural and Allied Workers (NUAAW).
1982 Becomes Agricultural and Allied Workers Trade Group of the Transport and General Workers' Union (TGWU).
Ernest Bevin, the power behind the TGWU was fond of saying 'Mergers mean historical strength'.' Armstrong (1988, p. 240) citing F. D. Mills states 'In the early 1960s the proportion of NUAW members in other occupations (notably forestry workers, roadmen, gardens and drainage workers) was of the order of 30–35%. Particular attention was paid to attracting workers in rural food-processing plants . . . From 1968 this policy was reflected in the incorporation of the word Allied into the union's title.' The major problem for the Union was the decline in membership through labour being replaced by new technology and the consequent drift from the land. In 1948 the Union had over 300,000 members, by 1981 it was just over 70,000 (*Guardian* 20 November 1981). Citing Self and Storing, Armstrong (1988, pp. 242–243) writes that the TGWU 'was thought to have about 20,000 farm workers in 1962 . . . At the Biennial Conference of 1980, a resolution to remain independent was carried by only a small majority, and later that year a special conference voted (by 47

against 39) to seek a merger with either the TGWU or one of two other unions . . . By June 1981 it became clear that the Executive favoured the TGWU . . . In November the *Land Worker* . . . set out details of the financial position of the union, whose deficits (notwithstanding regular increases in subscriptions and the implementation of various economies) had mounted to reach £134,458 in 1980, while the value of its investments had tumbled from £485,000 (1962) to £99,000 in 1980 . . . Boddy recommended the terms of the merger with the TGWU, stressing particularly that members need have no fears of being called out on a strike to which they were not a party'. Members were balloted 29,787 for 4,709 against; 50% did not vote. Joan moved the resolution to merge at the 1980 Biennial Conference and at the subsequent special conference led calls for a merger with a stronger union. Referring to the Union's dire finances she argued: 'We have been living on our investments, on the seed corn of the old comrades who built up this Union . . . There is only one way to preserve rural trade unionism and that is to merge this Union. If our Union goes, and it certainly will if we do not merge it, there will be no one in the countryside to organise and help rural workers.' Those arguing to remain independent argued equally passionately to preserve its historical identity and questioned the version of the Union's finances being presented. Developments within the NUA(A)W since 1947 are detailed in Wynn B (1993). Wynn's history includes interviews with union members and Union records and draws extensively on the excellent union journal the *Land Worker*. The journal has provided an invaluable source of information for this biography.

2. Feature on Jack Brocklebank in the *Northern Echo*, 1957.
3. Frank Robinson writing in, the *Land Worker*. For A personal history of a North Yorkshire farm worker see, Harry Walker, *The Story of My Life*, Thirsk, Peat and Son. Harry Walker lived at 46 Front Street, Sowerby for 30 years, 26 of which he was NUAW branch secretary for Thirsk and District.
4. Jack Brocklebank, the *Land Worker* January 1970.
5. Northallerton Branch minutes, January 1949.
6. July 13–15 show brochure, 1954.
7. Barry Leathwood, National Secretary, Rural, Agricultural and Allied Workers, TGWU.
8. Jack Brocklebank the *Land Worker*, August 1969.
9. Examples being Tom Caldwell, JFC Harrison, Roger Fieldhouse.
10. Colin Hands, the *Land Worker*, August 1969.
11. The *Land Worker*, August 1952.
12. The *Land Worker*', May 1954.
13. Northallerton NUAW branch minutes. June, 1960.

Five: *First contest*

1. *Darlington and Stockton Times*, 15 March 1952.
2. Undated unnamed newspaper cutting, Joan Maynard papers.
3. The *Yorkshire Evening Press* headline of Wednesday 7 May 1952 was 'She wins election by 2 votes. Only woman on Thirsk RDC'. At this election Joan defeated the Independent, who had been on the council for fifteen years. The result for South Kilvington was: Joan Maynard (Labour) 64; A. Bird (Independent) 62.
4. Thirsk Labour Party minutes, April 1952.
5. Harold Laski, who had known Lansbury, wrote the introduction to *My Life* by George Lansbury (1928). The introduction was reprinted from the *Daily Herald* (no date).
6. Thirsk and Malton Divisional Labour Party minutes, March 1952. The Government introduced the

Utility scheme during the war to ensure the quality, supply and production (using the minimum of raw materials) of goods at controlled prices. The Utility scheme in relation to furniture, for example, ensured affordable good-quality design. The scheme ended in 1953.

7. Seretse Kahma became the founding president of Botswana (1966–1980). 'South Africa had come under the control of white Afrikaner nationalists in 1948. The British were told that there was no chance of the pro-British opposition party winning the next all-white election in South Africa, if Seretse Khama was allowed to be chief of the Bangwato. The Labour government in Britain desperately needed South African gold and uranium. It agreed to bar Seretse Khama from chieftainship. The Commonwealth Relations minister denied that the government was bowing to racism, and lied about this before the House of Commons. A judicial enquiry was set up to prove Seretse's personal unfitness to rule. However, Justice Harragin concluded that Seretse was eminently fit to rule. His report was therefore suppressed by the British government for 30 years. Seretse and his wife were exiled to England in 1951, and in 1952 the new Conservative government declared the exile permanent.The treatment of Seretse and Ruth Khama by British governments received international press coverage, and outrage was expressed by a wide range of people including human-rights activists, Scottish, West African, Indian and West Indian nationalists, British communists, and conservatives who supported the principle of aristocratic inheritance. Eventually, in 1956, a new Commonwealth Relations minister realised that Britain must distance itself from institutionalized racism in South Africa, and decided to allow Seretse and Ruth home as commoners and private citizens.' (http://ubh.tripod.com/bw/skhama.htm)
8. Joan's opponent was The Reverend J Caesar Dupuis. The previous incumbent, Ben Foggitt, (Independent) did not seek re-election. *Northallerton Times* 7 April 1955.
9. *Darlington and Stockton Times* March 1956.
10. *Darlington and Stockton Times* undated. Joan Maynard papers.
11. Perhaps in recognition of such perceptions its name was changed to the *Morning Star* in 1966.
12. Details of the Len Williams–Edwin Gooch correspondence support this. Union President Edwin Gooch MP writing to Len Williams (24 November 1958): 'In my opinion the NEC acted wisely in deciding that the nomination of Miss Maynard was out of order because she is a part-time Agent. The additional reason for not accepting the nomination is that on some points she does not accept Party decisions. She has campaigned against the Party's Superannuation Scheme… Then there was her attitude to "Prosper the Plough" at Scarborough this year. We are aware of Mr Brocklebank's attitude towards Miss Maynard, but this is not generally held and certainly not by the NEC of the NUAW. We have noted her election as county secretary of the NUAW in Yorks. It is certainly in order, but again, not approved generally.' Mikardo (1988, p. 130) presents a chilling account of the 'vetting' of Labour Party candidates in the 1950s. As a member of a sub-group of NEC members meeting to endorse late candidatures for the 1955 General Election campaign, 'We three met, together with Sara Barker, the National Agent, to look at some late-selected candidates . . . Sara began leafing through two files which she had on the table in front of her, and read some passages from them, most of them consisting of criticisms which Konni (Zilliacus) and Ernie (Roberts) had made of some of the policies and actions of certain of our leaders. I reached across the table and said to Sara, "Give me those files, I want to have a look at them." "Oh no," she said, "you can't do that – they're private." I exploded. "Don't be daft . . . they're the property of the Party." And I grabbed them and went through them. They were an eye-opener. No MI5, no Special Branch, no George Smiley could have compiled more comprehensive dossiers. Not just presscuttings, photographs and document-references but also notes by watchers and eavesdroppers . . . Sara Barker never forgave me . . . Some years later Ron Hayward became National Agent, and the first thing he did on taking office was to tip out all Sara's secret service dossiers and make a bonfire of them.' The Labour Party ended its list of proscribed organisations in 1973.

13. Despite the efforts of the left in the Party and CND (formed in February 1958 with Joan as a member), Shaw (1996, p. 63) states that Gaitskell was able by the following year's Party Conference to have to mobilised the right effectively 'both in the constituencies and the unions and unilateralism was overturned by a large majority. His triumph had profound effects for, as Minkin (1978, p. 287) commented, 'successful confrontation shattered the psychological bonds of the traditional view of Conference authority'. After the Labour Party Conference Angela Tuckett, manager of *Labour Monthly*, wrote to Joan 'I meant to say, by the way, that last evening in Scarborough that if you should at any time and for any reason think of changing your job and coming south – well mind you tell me early! Because I have a little job sitting waiting for you, any when.'

Six: *Cutting blue grass in local government*

1. Extract from transcript of a radio interview in which Joan selected favourite pieces of music. Joan Maynard Papers.
2. *Northern Echo*, 24 May 1971.
3. *Ibid.*
4. *Northern Echo*, 25 May 1971.
5. 'Blunt Speaking.' *Yorkshire Evening Press,* no date. Joan Maynard Papers. Joan remained watchful on such issues. At its meeting in March 1969 a recommendation was made to Thirsk Council that the recently retired council clerk of 32 years' service, Mr W. A. Wilkinson, be reappointed on a year-to-year basis. It was also recommended that the present deputy clerk and financial officer, Mr Eric Forth, be appointed to the post of deputy clerk and chief financial officer. The Finance Committee of the council had learned that Mr Wilkinson 'had expressed his willingness to accept the appointment of Clerk of the council as from April 1 1969 at a salary of £2,400 a year plus a car allowance of £100 on a temporary basis'. (*Yorkshire Evening Press,* 20 March 1969). Brigadier John Walker, chairman of the Finance Committee was confident that the council would confirm its decision. Joan was furious, the posts of clerk and chief financial officer should be publicly advertised: 'I hope that there will be some public debate on this matter on Monday. I object strongly to the fact that, in the past, every time the subject has come up for discussion the council has gone into committee. I am incensed about it.' (*ibid).* Joan considered it wrong for a man on a pension to be appointed to a full-time salaried post, and it was unfair to the younger members of the council staff.
6. *Yorkshire Evening Press,* 25 July 1961.
7. Unnamed newspaper cutting. Joan Maynard papers. Joan said of improvement grants 'the more property you owned, the more money you were going to rake in. And most of the people on the council were property owners.'
8. *Thirsk, Bedale and Northallerton Times*, 23 February 1961.
9. Original letter undated. Joan Maynard papers.
10. *Darlington and Stockton Times*, no date; 1961–1963.
11. *Northern Echo*, 31 May 1963.
12. *Thirsk, Bedale and Northallerton Times*, 29 April 1954.
13. *Ibid.*
14. Letter from St Mary's Hospital, York, 13 July 1961.
15. *Darlington and Stockton Times*, 30 May 1953.
16. *Darlington and Stockton Times*, 5 March 1966.
17. Petition from teachers to Thirsk Grammar School governors, 14 April 1954. Joan maintained

pressure on the Northallerton Trades Council, on the RDC and the county council for a new grammar-modern school to be built in Thirsk. She had no truck with the view of the chairman of Thirsk RDC in 1953 that the council should be thankful for the efforts of the county council in trying to get from the Ministry of Education the first half of the Thirsk school building programme moved from the 1954–1955 reserve programme on to the programme 'proper'. 'Miss Maynard retorted, "we have nothing to be thankful for. We are entitled to a new school and that's all there is to it". (*Thirsk Times*, 30 July 1953) Joan said "In some ways comprehensive education has succeeded more in rural areas than in cities but not usually for the right reasons. It won the day in the first instance on economic grounds, they couldn't justify having a small town grammar school and a secondary modern school, so we in rural North Yorkshire went comprehensive in the early days. Where, however, there is strict streaming, selection has been introduced; they never give up.' In Joan's view the comprehensive school at Thirsk had unified the parents and children in the town in a way that was impossible when there were 'different kinds of schools scattered round the town'. Thirsk School became comprehensive 1962–1964; the grammar-modern school in Thirsk opened Stage 1 1957; Stage 2 1961

18. *Yorkshire Evening Press,* 8 August 1973.
19. Minute PR17 of the Policy and Resources Committee, 25 June 1974, resolved that the headquarters of the council be in Northallerton.
20. Joan's local government election activity may be summarised briefly as follows: after winning South Kilvington by two votes in 1952 she was narrowly defeated at the next election; later that year she won the Sowerby seat at a by-election. Since then she only lost one RDC election and frequently topped the poll. She was elected to the new district council – Hambleton District Council – under reorganisation in 1973; Hambleton, Sowerby: Maynard 657; Potter 624; Dupuis 502; Moore 410. In a speech on 20 January 1978 at the village hall in Purton in Wiltshire Joan said: 'Local authorities in the rural areas have suffered in some ways more than in urban areas from reorganisation. They are now district councils, more remote, more difficult to get at. Like everything else in our modern society they have become bigger, and bigger is not always beautiful, far from it. The danger with the old authorities was parochialism, the danger with the new ones is remoteness.' After her 1955 county council election success Joan lost to Bell in 1958, regaining the seat from him in 1961. In 1964 she retained the seat again for Labour when her opponent was Harry Woodhead (Independent), reported in the local press as a Bradford man who had been a chemist in Thirsk for sixteen years and was well known in the area; his family had farming interests over a wide area in the North Riding. Joan won by a majority of 386. In 1967 Joan lost the county seat and although she contested it each time, never regained it. She was beaten in 1967 by the Conservative candidate Connie Kenworthy who won by nine votes in a year when there was a national swing against Labour. In 1970 Joan was narrowly defeated by Gerald Turton, son of Sir Robin Turton MP (Turton (Conservative) 1,303; Maynard (Labour) 1249; Pallister (Independent) 148. Majority 54). In 1973 Turton again defeated Joan – by 60 votes (Turton (Conservative)1,382; Maynard (Labour) 1,322).

Seven: *The union*

1. *Independent* 30 March 1998.
2. Joan proposed rejecting a contributory scheme in favour of one financed out of direct taxation – this being, 'more in keeping with Socialist principles'.
3. Joan remembered this being when President Gooch MP was present at the Union's Yorkshire

County Conference, where delegates roundly condemned him and the Labour Party for not meeting the pledge to abolish the tied cottage when Labour enjoyed its huge majority.

4. January 1959: Robinson 7,150; Maynard 2,971; January 1961: Robinson 6,304; Maynard 3,957; January 1963: Robinson 5,935; Maynard 4,274: January 1965: Robinson 6,551;Maynard 5,738.In 1964 the press in Yorkshire published accusations of 'ballot rigging'. Joan's Executive Committee election address and nomination papers had not been circulated. John Robinson, secretary of the Northallerton branch of the NUAW (one of the largest in the county with 158 members) said: 'It is not democratic when the sitting candidate (Frank Robinson) has an election address included with the ballot papers and the other candidate has not. I am secretary of one of the biggest North Riding branches but I was not sent Nomination Papers – for one obvious reason – but it won't stop me voting for the person I want in… twenty–five branches nominated Joan Maynard But nomination papers did not come to me, nor did the circular on procedure. Ballot papers arrived on October 15 without an election address by Miss Maynard, but with instructions how to vote plus an election address for the sitting member Mr Frank Robinson. I asked Miss Maynard why there was no election address and she said she had not been notified that she had been nominated, and had never been asked for an election address. A member of the NUAW who asked that his identity should not be disclosed said yesterday, 'Head Office indicate that it is up to the candidates to make sure they knew what was required. They refused to allow her at that late stage to repair the omission and send out her election address.' *Northern Echo,* 9 November 1964. Responding to the allegation the Union Executive told the newspaper: 'So far as we're concerned nomination forms were sent to every branch in the country. But we can't prove they weren't received. If Mr John Robinson says they weren't received, we must accept that. It is not sufficient grounds to accept ballot rigging. We don't know what's happened to them.'
5. Joan would tell of the St Faith's strike and how after 'the sell-out by the leadership the leaders were not voted back in at the next Conference.' The rules were then changed to elections through the branches instead of from the conference floor. Groves (1949) presents an account of the strike.
6. In July 1961 the High Court found the Electrical Trade Union Executive elections had been rigged by the Communists. (Harmer 1999)
7. The minutes of the Staff Conference record how Stan Brumby asked the Executive Committee on behalf of the organisers to, 'kindly withdraw the document that Brother Brocklebank had been asked to sign. Whilst they recognised that they were perfectly entitled to take action against any organiser they failed to understand why they had taken the action on this occasion'. The acting president (Hilton) told the organisers that the agenda for the Staff Conference was 'too long and important' to allow discussion of this matter. They responded by withdrawing all their agenda items and the conference ended. (Conference began Friday 14 May 1965. Staff present: 35 organisers; seven recruiting officers; six Head Office staff; plus Executive Committee members.)
8. These and other Biennial Conference quotations are taken from the Union's verbatim records held in the archives of the Rural Research Centre, University of Reading.
9. Jack Brocklebank, Northallerton Branch minutes, 9 May 1959.
10. Armstrong observes (1988, pp. 227–228). 'The very existence of such a board symbolized the weak market situation of the farm worker, but that is not to deny its value, of which NUAW leaders whose memories extended back to the 1920s were very conscious, in setting a floor to agricultural wages.'
11. Interview with retired farm worker John Fry.
12. *Hull and Yorks Times*,23 January 1970.
13. Undated cutting from *Farmers Weekly* housed with Joan Maynard papers.
14. C. Trinder and S. Winyard (1975) 'A New Deal for Farmworkers: The Case for an Independent Inquiry into the Pay of Farmworkers', Low Pay Paper No. 5. *See also*: M. Brown and S. Winyard (1975) *Low Pay on the Farm*, Low Pay Unit.

15. David Ward in the *Guardian* 20 November 1981 records interviews with farm workers in Lancashire. Gary Dalton: 'You live next door to the boss and you see him every day of the week. It's not like being in a big factory where you don't know who your boss is and you go home at 5 o'clock and switch off... it's like having a row with your wife or children. You can't be at each other all the time. You've got to be quite nice to them.' Graham Humphreys: ' If you put a farm worker into a factory – say a poultry processing plant – he immediately adopts a much more militant attitude than the one he had on the farm the week before.' Ward observes that nice people tend to stay poor and farm workers have never managed to achieve much more than 70% of the average industrial wage.
16. Northallerton NUAW Branch minutes, 9 May 1959.
17 Wages Structure: Craftsmen £17.82; Women £14.26. Grade 1 Men £15.55; Women £15.55. Grade 2 Men £21.06; Women £16.85.
18. Institute for Workers' Control bulletin (1972) No. 10, p. 51. Joan was a leading member of the Institute of Workers' Control, writing for it and chairing its meetings.
19. Joan had been very much looking forward to being in Weymouth where she would stay with friends in Dorset, Gladys and Les Shears, and catch up with other close comrades in the county.
20. Efforts to get the post of vice-president reinstated at the following Biennial Conference were unsuccessful; Joan stood for the presidency against Bert Hazell and lost, with 22 votes to his 78. In 1976 the left vote was split when Wilf Page stood, but again Bert Hazell saw off the opposition: Hazell 68 votes; Maynard 26; Page 4. After Bert Hazell's retirement Joan and John Hose contested the presidency in 1978 with the result: Hose 59 votes; Maynard 29; Pill 4. The closest Joan got to Hose was by 8 votes at the 1980 Biennial: Hose 44 votes; Maynard 36; Aston (a member of the Executive Committee) 12. Voting at the 1980 conference was very tense with a delegate enquiring about the voting slips: 'Do we have a box to put them in instead of passing them from one hand to another? I am not prepared to pass my paper to the next-door neighbour.' In her election attempts Joan was supported by a strong, well-organised campaign group with Roger Fieldhouse, Paul Houldsworth, Tony Gould and Peter Medhurst playing prominent parts. In 1982 the NUAAW merged with the TGWU.

Eight: *Into the national arena*

1. It has been pointed out to the author that Reg Prentice topped the poll because of his opposistion to EEC membership. He was on the Tribune Group Slate for the 1972 Shadow Cabinet elections and his move to the right started later. *See* Crick (1984).
2. A. G. Hughes, 5 July 1974. Cunningham was jailed in April 1974 in the Poulson corruption case.
3. In Lincoln a by-election was held arising from Dick Taverne's resignation in March 1973 protesting against left-wing influence within the Labour Party. He stood as Democratic Labour and won. Phillips (1980, p. 77) quotes Margaret Jackson (later Margaret Beckett): 'Having lost the by-election, and with Taverne having a large majority, they decided they would have to have somebody distinctly different from Taverne, so they went for solid trade unionists or women.' (In Joan's case they would have had both.)
4. Audrey Wise lost her seat, Coventry South West, in 1979 and was out of Parliament for eight years before being elected MP for Preston in 1987. She remained with Joan on the NEC.
5. Unidentified newspaper cutting. Housed with Joan Maynard papers.
6. *Yorkshire Post*, 26 September 1974.
7. The result was: Joan Maynard (Labour) 18,108; Eddie Griffiths (Independent Labour) 10,182; Roy Walker (Conservative) 4,905; Thomas Blades (Liberal) 3,271; majority: 7,926. Joan was Sheffield's

first woman MP. Before the October 1974 general election only four women candidates had ever contested parliamentary seats in the city: Grace Colman (Labour) Hallam 1935; Joan Mellors (Labour) Heeley 1959; Pat Santhouse (Conservative) Attercliffe 1970 and February 1974; Vi Gill (Communist) Brightside February 1974. After staying with Jock and Bett Sturrock for about eighteen months Joan bought a house in Brightside's Bellhouse Road.

Nine: *Not our place – the House of Commons*

1. Article drafted by Joan, 'My advice to new Members of Parliament', Joan Maynard papers.
2. Joan first met Marian Neville in Surrey whilst campaigning to be president of the Union. Marian, a Labour Party activist, and her husband, Union activist Richard Neville, became Joan's close friends. As members of Labour Action for Peace Joan and Marian travelled together on a peace delegation to Bulgaria in 1984, returning with 'warmest greetings' to the women of Greenham Common.
3. Joan was away from the House of Commons between 18 December 1974 and 7 April 1975.
4. Rowie had been widowed since 1966, when his wife Florence died aged 58. He moved to Lansbury House in April 1980. Before becoming too frail, Rowie greatly enjoyed visiting Joan in London, especially accompanying her to the Houses of Parliament.

Ten: *True friend of Ireland*

1. Organized by Liz Curtis, Alastair Renwick, John Lloyd and Frances M. Blake. Tony Benn booked the room. Joan had a photo of Tommy Eccles in the hall of her house. Messages of appreciation were read out from prisoners in the Maze; the messages were written on scraps of toilet paper and smuggled out of the prison.
2. Frank Dolan, *Irish Post*, 23 May 1987.
3. 'Northern Ireland Constitutional Proposals' published 21 March 1973 proposing an 80-member power-sharing assembly.
4 *Guardian*, 31 January 1972.
5 *Guardian*, 12 May 1975.
6. O'Donnell 1997; Cunningham 1991.
7. Stan Thorne, Maureen Colquhoun, Eddie Loyden, Martin Flannery, Jeff Rooker.
8. A. Renwick (1999) 'Something in the air. The rise of the Troops Out Movement. *Troops Out Magazine*, (21) 1.
9. Unlike TOM Joan's position was not for immediate withdrawal (see letter to *The Times*, 20 February 1976). Alastair Renwick felt this was a more logical position but TOM wanted a sharp focus.
10. *The Times*, 23 January 1985.
11. Article by Joan Maynard in *Tribune*, 4 July 1975: 'Ulster: now is the time for change'.
12. *The Times*, 30 September 1975.
13. *The Times*, 21 November 1975.
14. The other MPs were Arthur Latham, Stan Thorne, Ron Thomas and Andrew Bennett. The accused were defended by the NCCL and released.
15. *Labour & Ireland*, October/November 1980, (issue 3).
16. *Labour & Ireland*. May 1980, (issue 1).
17. 'Interim Report of the Northern Ireland Study Group', RD490/July 1980, Museum of Labour History.

18. Mintes of the first meeting of the Northern Ireland Study Group, 30 January 1980, Museum of Labour History.
19. Minutes of 7th meeting of Home Policy Committee, 9 June 1980 at the House of Commons; chair Tony Benn. Museum of Labour History.
20. Elizabeth Sinclair, *Irish Democrat*, July 1980.
21. *TheTimes*, 14 May 1981; *Labour Weekly*, 22 May 1981.
22. Joan was vice-chair of the PLP Northern Ireland Group. At the conference another more radical resolution was defeated by the power of the union block vote. 'On the initial show of hands an overwhelming majority of C[onstituency] L[abour] P[arty] delegates voted for composite 25 which, in cautious tones, sought to underline a commitment to reunification with a repudiation of the Unionist veto and a strategy for withdrawal . . . but the resolution was defeated on a card vote by 708,000 votes to 5,003,000. (*Labour & Ireland)* Joan was always critical of the concept 'by consent' because of its implicit recognition of the power of the inbuilt Protestant majority.
23. *The Times*, 22 July 1983.
24. Reported in the *Sheffield Morning Telegraph*, 21 February 1984.
25. *The Times*, 24 February 1984.
26. In June 1973 Joan wrote to Connie Siefert about a meeting between the Executive of the British Peace Committee and Labour MPs she had chaired at the House of Commons; Jock Stallard and Stan Orme had spoken. 'Jock Stallard was originally the only Labour MP prepared to go to Ireland and speak in support of the Civil Rights Movement. I am glad to say he now seems to have won the support of Stan Orme and Kevin MacNamara.'
27. Northern Ireland Study Group, 31 July 1980.
28. The Birmingham Six were: Hugh Callaghan, Patrick Hill, Gerry Hunter, Richard McIlkenny, William Power, John Walker.
29. The *Irish Times*, 6 June 2000, reported: 'The British Prime Minister (Tony Blair) has apologised to the three men and one woman known as the Guildford Four who were wrongly convicted of IRA bomb attacks in England in 1974.' Each spent fifteen years in prison before the convictions were overturned by the court of Appeal in 1989, when it emerged that the Surrey police had concocted evidence against them and misled the original trial by lying. The apology was sent by Tony Blair to Paul Hill's wife, Ms Courtney Kennedy-Hill, daughter of the assassinated US attorney general Robert Kennedy.
30. Cardinal Hume's introduction to Maguire 1994, p. iv.

Eleven: *House of bondage – the tied cottage*

1. The *Land Worker* October 1951. Meeting in Whitchurch, Hampshire, 16 September arranged by Basingstoke Labour Party in conjunction with the Union's Basingstoke District Committee. Present: Mr A. Carr, prospective Labour candidate for Basingstoke Division and Bro. Holness, editor the *Land Worker*.
2. Joan's report of the Labour Party Annual Conference 1956.
3. The *Land Worker*, January 1965. The Rent Act 1965 stipulated: 'In the case of a tied cottage the court could suspend the execution of a possession order, but must have regard to (a.) whether there is alternative accommodation (b.) whether the efficient management of the farm would be seriously prejudiced unless the cottage were released and (c.) whether greater hardship would be caused by suspending than executing the order. (*See*: Jones 1975)
4. Crossman 1975, Friday 5 March 1965.
5. 'and whether greater hardship would be caused by the suspension of the execution of the order than by its execution without suspension or further suspension'. (See Jones 1975, p. 27)

6. *Darlington and Stockton Times* 24 April 1965.
7. See Chapter 7, Union's Staff Conference at the Grand Atlantic Hotel, Weston-Super-Mare, 4 May 1965).
8. The *Land Worker* August 1965.
9. Unnamed newspaper cutting reporting the Labour Party Conference.
10. *Hull and Yorkshire Times* 23 Oct 1965
11. The *Land Worker* January 1966 summarises the Act. According to Jim Watts Head of the Legal Department, 'the Act consolidates into permanent form the basic protection given in the temporary legislation and to some extent strengthens that protection. We have had virtually 12 months working experience of the 1964 Act, and there is no doubt that evictions from tied farm cottages have declined during this period. At the time of going to press, there have only been three actual evictions among Union members during 1965, a far cry from the position in previous years, when summary eviction was commonplace in the industry. This is due mainly to the clause giving the occupants the right to go back to court with a further application for a suspension of a possession order, should he be unable to remove in the time given. We are not complacent, however, as the basic problem of the tied cottage system remains with us, and we still look to the government to implement its pledge. The working of the new Act will be watched very closely, bearing in mind the words of the minister of housing during the third reading of the Bill 'if the clause does not have the desired effect, and if there is an outcrop of evictions, we shall, as I have said to the agricultural workers, reconsider the position and consider what measures we should take.'
12. R Raimes's letter to the *Yorkshire Evening Press* 7 October 1968.
13. Alwyn Jones (1975, p. 21) succinctly summarises the farmers' case against legislation. 'Fundamental to an understanding of the farmers' case against legislation is the concept that the worker living in a tied cottage "is in the position of a service occupant who is permitted to occupy the dwelling as a term of his employment and for the better performance of his duties; he is not in any shape or form a tenant. Indeed any factor which implies that a tenancy exists is dangerous in the extreme and may well upset the entire concept of service occupancy and leave the man in secure possession of the cottage when his employment has ended, thereby depriving the estate of the inducement with which to replace him."(AR Sarsons (1965) The Tied Cottage and the Future, *Journal of the Chartered Land Agents Society*, (64), 126) The above argument is a circular one and reflects the views of the NFU. It can be summarized as follows: Efficient farming depends on a regular supply of labour. There is a general shortage of housing in the rural areas. Certain key workers, such as herdsmen, must by the nature of their work be housed 'on the spot'. The farm must therefore provide houses for its workers without which it would be impossible to obtain an adequate work force. Should an employee leave it must be possible for the farmer to gain repossession of the house immediately, failing which it could not be used as an inducement to an incoming worker, and the efficiency of the farm would be impaired.'
14. Joan's letter to Anthony Greenwood, Minister of Housing and Local Government 10 March 1970: 'The Yorks County Committee of our Union have considered the new legislation now going through the House on the agricultural tied cottage and they have asked me to write to you and say they find these proposals unacceptable. They do not fulfil the pledge given to our Union by the Party before the 1964 election 'that no farm worker shall be evicted until suitable alternative accommodation has been provided... The Yorkshire Committee are not prepared to accept a compromise on this vital issue, they are prepared to settle for nothing less than the pledge as a step towards total abolition of the tied cottage system.'
15. Letter to the Editor of the *Yorkshire Evening Press* 9 July 1970.
16. Pye-Smith and Rose (1984, p. 23) state,'In 1967 the Maud Committee on Local Government

Reform found that farming was the dominant occupation of rural district councillors, with 35% of all rural district council members in England and Wales being farmers.'

17. Letter from Lord Collison to Joan 12 July 1967.
18. For example, on 7 November 1973 Joan wrote to every member of the NEC Home Policy Committee, 'At Home Policy Committee next Monday you will be considering a letter from my Union the NUAAW about the agricultural tied cottage. The letter from our General Secretary asks for the commitment from the NEC that the pledge to abolish the tied cottage system in agriculture be in the election manifesto... This question, a small matter for most people, is of tremendous importance to farm workers. If you want to help them please support inclusion of the tied cottage pledge in the election manifesto.' As a member of the NEC Clause 5 meeting responsible for drawing up the election manifesto Joan fought for a commitment to get rid of the tied cottage system. The commitment was included in the first draft of the manifesto so Joan was shocked to see, on the eve of publication, its omission in the final draft. Forcefully and passionately she insisted the pledge be reinstated, 'the reason the pledge was in the 1974 manifesto was because I was on the Labour Party NEC and made sure it was in. Only Callaghan, a farmer, opposed it. Had I not been there, those who were not enthusiastic would certainly have stopped it becoming legislation on the floor of the House of Commons and eventually an Act of Parliament.' The pledge was given in both the February and October 1974 Labour Party Manifestos.
19. Official publication of the North Riding and Durham County Branch of the NFU.
20. Joan's Private Member Bill made little progress.
21. Jim Watts summarised the Act in the March 1977 issue of '*The Land Worker*', 'the new act gives security of tenure to agricultural workers who have completed two years continuous service in the industry at the time their job comes to an end. In that event, they become statutory tenants and a possession order can only be obtained against them if their employer can demonstrate to a court that they have unreasonably refused suitable alternative accommodation. Implicit here of course is a situation in which the farm worker has otherwise behaved properly by paying his rent and taking all reasonable care of property etc. There are also provisions for Agricultural Dwelling House Advisory Committee (ADHAC) to issue certificates of agricultural need where they are satisfied that the farmer cannot obtain a replacement worker without having accommodation to offer but even though (sic) the outgoing worker cannot be disturbed until suitable accommodation becomes available to him.' The ADHAC, consisting of a chair and one representative each from the employer's side and the employee's side. A useful account of the workings of the Act is presented by AW Rogers (1992).

Twelve: *The earth is honest*

1. Groves does not give details of the edition quoted but the quotation can be found in Karl Marx (1974) *Capital. A Critical Analysis of Capitalist Production* Volume One pp. 474–475, London, Lawrence & Wishart.
2. *Hansard* 20 March 1980 col 719.
3. Letter to Oliver Stutchbury 6 June 1973.
4. Hans Breitenbach co-authored with Tom Burden and David Coates (1990) *Features of a Viable Socialism*, Harvester, Wheatsheaf.
5. See Cook J and Kaufman C (1982).
6. *Guardian* 18 July 1987.
7. As an MP Joan sought to increase the provision and range of vegetarian meals in the House of

Commons. Conservative MP Sir Charles Irving had a responsibility for catering arrangements and was thrilled when Joan entertained him to a 'fact finding lunch' in Cranks vegetarian restaurant. Joan remembered it fondly as a very jolly occasion.

8. The *Land Worker* May 1979.

Thirteen: *Is it good for our class?*

1. *Daily Telegraph* Obituary 30 March 1998.
2. Cited by Kogan D and Kogan M 1983. (Interestingly, The Leader of the Labour Party was termed the 'Leader of the PLP' until 1978).
3. Discussed by Kogan D and Kogan M pp. 26ff.
4. Hilary Wainwright (1987) records how Milne, 'traced and exposed a web of corruption spun by T Dan Smith, Leader of Newcastle Council between 1966 and 1974, Andy Cunningham, Regional Secretary of the Northern Region of the General and Municipal Workers, and Chairman of the Regional Labour Party, and John Poulson, the Wakefield architect and consultant to the Bovis Construction Company;' (p.23) 'What was the response from Westminster? From Shirley Williams, Roy Hattersley, Michael Foot and others who claim to champion the independence of MPs? Total silence – and probably a good deal of relief among the northern group of MPs who had effectively excommunicated Milne' (26). Milne has acknowledged that among nationally prominent members of the Labour Movement the only support he received was from Joan.
5. The Pentonville Five were five dockers jailed in 1972 for picketing and soon released after mass protests by the Labour movement.
6. Jim Arniston, *Morning Star* 22 March 1978.
7. Grayson (1991 p. 85) cites C Docherty, (1983) 'Steel and Steelworkers – the Sons of Vulcan.' Heinemann.
8. *Morning Star* 6 November 1978.
9. Joan visited North Vietnam in September 1970; the Americans were still bombing North Vietnam. She travelled as a member of a British trade union delegation with Bill Jones, Clive Jenkins, Ken Gill and Dan Duffy. Unlike all the other delegates, Joan had to travel in, 'a personal capacity' as her Union would not permit her to represent the Union, even though she was Vice-President. 'They were damned annoyed that I'd been chosen'. The delegation was the first from Britain. ('The Vietnamese thought we were Russian because we were so tall in comparison to them.') After her visit Joan was absolutely convinced the Vietnamese would win. They were a, 'mixture of gentleness and toughness'. She met with children who were victims of pellet bombs and people burnt by napalm. 'There were other horrifying weapons such as the spider bomb which has threads running out from it and is dropped on the paddy fields to be triggered off when the feet of the peasants touch the threads. There were flechette bombs with sharp edges, which rotate into the body, tearing the flesh.' The delegation took with them £500 worth of drugs and medical equipment. Vietnamese leaders urged them to persuade Britain to withdraw support from the Americans as a step towards peace. Joan and Bill Jones addressed a mass meeting in Hanoi and they all visited the provinces. On their travels they noted that, unlike in Britain, women received equal pay with men. Joan had to return to Britain before the others as she was standing for the NEC at the Labour Party Conference. It was a 27-hour flight stopping twice in India before getting to Moscow; there she was met by a member of the Soviet farm workers' Union. She flew to London the next day and was welcomed at the airport by Colin Sweet, Secretary of the British Peace Committee. 'Clive (Jenkins) was funny, he said, well you'll get there on time Joan. You'll be dead when you get there, but you don't have to be alive to get

elected to the NEC! I said, you're right Clive.' Joan travelled to Russia on several occasions, usually after TUC and Labour Party Conferences. In July 1967 she was one of 300 trade union delegates from around the world invited by the Soviet Farm Workers of the Central Committee of Trade Unions to celebrate the Fiftieth Anniversary of the 1917 Revolution. She was one of only two women in the group from Britain. One state farm she visited had its own school, and wages compared well with industrial wages in Leningrad. A car factory had a kindergarten and many female workers. Russia's largest trade union was for agricultural workers who included both manual and scientific workers. In 1971 Joan arranged for a small 'unofficial' group of farm workers to go to Moscow. She recalled, 'We paid our own fares; which were very reasonable because we went on Russian Aeroflot – about £25 for each of the four of us – Wilf Page was one. About 5 months after the visit I got a letter from Igor Klimov, Labour Attache of the Soviet Embassy, saying could we meet in London. We met at a club in London used by Wilf, for ex- servicemen I think. Klimov bought with him a cheque for £100 to refund the money we'd paid for the fares, he was to give it to me and I'd see the others got their £25. But within about a couple of days – it was one of those occasions when every now and again the British Government would descend on the Soviet Embassy and expel so many people, forty or so spies. And this was one of those occasions. They decided to expel so many, of which he was one. But he had said to me when he gave me the £100 would I give him a receipt, which is quite reasonable. So I'd given him a receipt which said, "received from Igor Klimov one hundred pounds sterling", signed and dated it. When he was picked up I had visions of talk about Moscow Gold. I thought, oh dear. They didn't find it I don't think, or I didn't hear anything about it.' (Laughs). On a more serious note, Joan did have concerns she might be set up by the Central Intelligence Agency (CIA). She was befriended by a young American woman; friends warned her that she could be CIA and Joan dropped her. The young woman had stayed with Joan in Sowerby with her boyfriend. A union friend of Joan said, 'I am sure that the CIA and people like that tried to set her up at times because she would get funny stuff coming through the post and I am sure it could be constructed as secret and they would watch what she would do with it.'

10. The Social Democratic Alliance, 'formed in June 1975 by right-wing Labour Party members to work against what they saw as growing left-wing influence and to further the aims of social democracy. Alliance attacks in October 1975 on NEC members who spoke on platforms for the Communist *Morning Star* led to the group's denunciation by Labour leader Wilson as 'anti-Party.' (Harmer 1999, p. 282)
11. *Labour Weekly* 19 November 1976.
12. *The Times* 2 September 1977.
13. Before he became an MP Chris Mullin had developed an interest in the ISC. An enormous pile of ISC internal documents had been dumped on the doorstep of *Time Out*. The documents showed 'where their money was coming from and all sorts of things, all sorts of interesting things. And their contacts with various people in the Ministry of Defence and the Cabinet Office, and *Time Out* showed me and gave me the documents, and I saw lots of possibilities there so from that time drafted a lot of Parliamentary Questions and then Joan and Jo Richardson, and Frank Allaun probably, put them down, and actually it's me that got them all into trouble I think really, over that.'
14. *Star* 12 January 1995.
15. *The Times* October 17 2001.
16. *Star* 12 January 1995.
17. Eric Heffer writes of the Deputy Leadership contest and Tribune (1993, p. 178) 'Some of the Tribune group urged me to stand... I became suspicious of the motives of some of the Tribunites and it became very clear that they wanted to use me as a fall-guy. Robert Kilroy-Silk reveals in his book 'Hard Labour', "I can remember we were urging Heffer to stand for the deputy leadership...

against Denis Healey and Tony Benn. We actually didn't want to support him, although he thought we did. We just wanted someone on whom we could waste our vote instead of being forced to vote for Benn." I realised people like Kilroy-Silk, John Silkin and Frank Field had joined Tribune not out of Socialist conviction but because they felt it might advance them in Labour politics. That really sickened me.'

18. Heffer (1993, p. 207) quotes from the concluding lines of a Campaign Group pamphlet on the Thatcher Government, issued after the 1983 General Election: *Tory Government Policy – a threat to Democracy* (The Radical Right in Power). These lines capture, succinctly, Campaign Group thinking, 'Freedom and democracy, then, belong to Socialism. They are the spiritual property of the labour movement. In our campaigns around specific issues, be they peace, jobs, the defence of the welfare state, or local government, or the trade unions, we must present people with the common thread. Whether it is at Greenham Common, or on a trade union picket line, or in the many other struggles with which the Labour movement is associated, it is the aim and purpose of Socialism to defend freedom, and to further democracy. We believe it is that message which we need to present in a convincing manner to the public, before this monetarist Government runs off with our freedoms and subverts our democracy.'
19. *The Times* 5 April 1981.
20. *The Times* 30 September 1982.
21. Joan challenged right-winger Alan Hadden (who had the longest unbroken service) for the Vice-Chair post in October 1983. Hadden was chosen by 13 votes to 11.
22. *The Times* 22 September 1987
23. Maeve Denby in Lucy Middleton (1977, p. 186)
24. On the issue of all-women shortlists Roy Hattersley told John Humphrys, *On the Record*, 'David Blunkett, was the heir apparent to the seat he now occupies. Everybody knew the constituency wanted him, he was the local boy, he was the leader of the council, he was the star in Sheffield, they believed he'd become a star in Westminster and they turned out to be right. How absurd it would have been if when Joan Maynard gave up the seat that constituency had been told, "You can't have David Blunkett, we're going to find you three women, two from Birmingham, one from Newcastle, I don't know where".'
25. *Morning Star* 3 July 1990.
26. *Morning Star* 7 March 1994.
27. Andrew Roth's (1984) *Parliamentary Portraits.*

Fourteen: *Home ground*

1. Elsie Maynard died 25 February 1990. Rowie Maynard died 6 May 1993 – 'A Yorkshire Tyke' is inscribed on his tombstone.
2. Rural England Versus Overhead Line Transmission.
3. *Darlington and Stockton Times* 13 June 1992.
4. Wynn (1993, p.278).
5. Burston Strike School – The longest strike in history. Following the dismissal of their two radical Socialist teachers, Kitty and Tom Higdon, on trumped up charges, the children of Burston School went on strike in April 1914. 'As the Higdons were handing over the keys of the school house, the sound of children marching and singing was heard… the children, bearing cards aloft and around their necks, proclaiming, "We want our teachers back." Sixty-six of the school's seventy-two

children continued their education with the Higdons on the village green. After being accommodated in a carpenter's shop sufficient funds were raised by the labour movement nationally to purchase and equip a building in the centre of the village. The Strike School continued until 1939 with the death of Tom Higdon by which time Kitty Higdon was in her seventies. Kitty Higdon died in 1946. ('The Burston Strike School. The Story of the Longest Strike in History'. Published by the Trustees of Burston Strike School. Undated. ISBN 0 9514688 0 4). Joan would speak at the annual rally – it was one of the highlights of her year. The Tolpuddle Martyrs: George Loveless, James Loveless, James Hammett, Thomas Standfield, John Standfield, James Brine were brought to trial at Dorchester in March 1834 and sentenced to 7 years transportation. Their 'crime' was establishing a Friendly Society of Agricultural Labourers, 'to preserve ourselves, our wives, and our children from utter degradation and starvation'. The men were charged with administering illegal oaths because combinations were not in themselves unlawful (*Tolpuddle. An historical account through the eyes of George Loveless* compiled by Graham Padden for the TUC 1984). Paradoxically Joan's radical views excluded her from being invited to speak on the platform at the annual rally. 'I spoke just once. It was a tremendous struggle to get the right to speak there. They would always have right-wing speakers. They would have me on the platform but they wouldn't let me speak you see. The crowd would be shouting, so eventually they gave way.'

6. Examples in the Union being Tony Gould, Paul Houldsworth, Peter Medhurst.
7. At the last moment the organisers Carol Cartridge, Don Cartridge, Bob Duffy and Helen Hepburn (Joan's great niece) arranged for the lecture to be transferred to the Cleveland Trade Unionists and Unemployed Workers Resource Centre in Middlesbrough after the Management Committee of Thirsk Town Hall banned Gerry Adams from speaking there. The President of Sinn Fein arrived in Middlesbrough to speak on his way to Dublin after talks with Nelson Mandela in South Africa and Tony Blair in Downing Street.

REFERENCES

Armstrong, Alan (1988) *Farmworkers. A Social and Political History 1770–1980*, London, BT Batsford Ltd.

Ashcroft, MY, (ed) (1974) *A History of the North Riding County Council 1889–1974*, North Yorkshire County Council.

Benn, Tony (1989) *Against the Tide. Diaries 1973–76*, London, Hutchinson.

Benn, Tony (1990) *Conflicts of Interest. Diaries 1977–80*, London, Hutchinson.

Benn, Tony (1992) *The End of an Era. Diaries 1980–1990*, London, Hutchinson.

Bogg, Edmund (1906) *Richmondshire and the Vale of Mowbray*, London, Elliott Stock (Reprinted, 1982 G H Smith and Son Easingwold York).

Bogg, Edmund (1926) *The Charm of the Hambletons*, Thirsk, Z Wright and Sons.

Breitenbach, Hans; Burden, Tom and Coates, David (1990) *Features of a Viable Socialism*, Harvester, Wheatsheaf.

Brocklebank, Jack; Kaldor, Nicolas; Maynard, Joan; Neild, Robert and Stutchbury, Oliver (1973) *The Case for Nationalising the Land*, CNL 139 Old Church Street, London.

Brown, M and Winyard, S (1975) *Low Pay on the Farm*, Low Pay Unit.

Butler, David (1995) *British General Elections Since 1945*, Oxford, Blackwell.

Clarke, Sister Sarah (1995) *No Faith in the System*, Cork, Ireland, Mercier Press.

Connolly, Michael (1990) *Politics and Policy Making in Northern Ireland*, Hemel Hempstead, Philip Allan.

Cook, J and Kaufman, C (1982) *Portrait of a Poison. The 2,4,5-T Story*, Pluto Press.

Crick, Michael (1984) *Militant*, London, Faber.

Crossman, Richard (1975) *The Diaries of a Cabinet Minister. Volume One Minister of Housing 1964–66*, London, Hamilton Cape.

Cunningham, Michael J (1991) *British Government Policy in Northern Ireland 1969–89: Its Nature and Execution*, Manchester University Press.

Dale, Iain (ed) (2000) *Labour Party General Election Manifestos 1990–1997*, London, Routledge/Politico's Publishing.

Dorey, Peter (1995) *British Politics since 1945*, Oxford, Blackwell.

Elliot, Sydney and Flackes, WD (1999) *Northern Ireland. A Political Directory 1968–1999*, Belfast, The Blackstaff Press Ltd.

Fieldhouse, Roger (1996)'Sidney Raybould, Fred Sedgwick and the Early Department', in Taylor R (ed) *1996 Beyond the Walls*, The University of Leeds.

Fieldhouse, Roger (ed) (c1977) *Jack Bowen. Life Member of the NUAAW*, Bedale, WF Vasey and Son Ltd.

Fielding, Steven (1997) *The Labour Party. 'Socialism' and Society Since 1951*, Manchester, Manchester University Press.

Flynn, AC (1989) *Rural Working Class Interests in Party Policy–Making in Post–war England*, PhD Thesis, University College London.

Grayson, John (1991) *Solid Labour. A Short History of the Yorkshire Regional Council of the Labour Party 1941–1991*, Wakefield, Yorkshire Regional Council of the Labour Party.

Groves, Reg (1949) *Sharpen the Sickle! The History of the Farm Workers' Union*, London, The Porcupine Press.

Harmer, Harry (1999) *The Longman Companion to The Labour Party 1900–1998*, London, Longman.

Harrison, JFC (1995) *Scholarship Boy. A Personal History of the Mid-Twentieth Century*, London, Rivers Oram Press.

Harrison, Ruth (1964) *Animal Machines: The New Factory Farming Industry*, London, Vincent Stuart.

Hattersley, Roy (1997) *Fifty Years On. A Prejudiced History of Britain Since the War*, London, Little, Brown and Company.

Hatfield, Michael (1978) *The House the Left Built. Inside Labour Policy Making 1970–1975*, London, Victor Gollancz.

Heffer, Eric (1993) *Never a Yes Man. The Life and Politics of an Adopted Liverpudlian*, London, Verso.

Heffernan, Richard and Marqusee, Mike (1992) *Defeat from the Jaws of Victory. Inside Kinnock's Labour Party*, London. Verso.

Hoggart, Richard (1958) *The Uses of Literacy*, Harmondsworth, Pelican Books.

Hollis, Patricia (1997) *Jennie Lee. A Life*, Oxford, Oxford University Press.

Jones, Alwyn (1975) *Rural Housing: The Agricultural Tied Cottage*, Occasional Papers on Social Administration, no 56, London, G Bell and Sons.

Jones, Mervyn (1994) *Michael Foot*, London, Victor Gollancz.

Kogan, David and Kogan, Maurice (1983) *The Battle for the Labour Party*, London, Kogan Page.

Labour Party (1981) *Out of Town Out of Mind*, London, Labour Party.

Lansbury, George (1928) *My Life*, London, Constable & Co Ltd.

Laybourn, Keith (1997) *The Rise of Socialism in Britain c1881–1951*, Stroud, Sutton Publishing Ltd.

Maguire, Anne with Gallagher, Jim (1994) *Miscarriage of Justice. An Irish Family's Story Of Wrongful Conviction as IRA Terrorists*, Harper Collins.

Mason, Roy (1999) *Paying the Price,* London, Robert Hale.

Marx, Karl (1974) *Capital. A Critical Analysis of Capitalist Production: Volume 1*, London, Lawrence & Wishart.

Maynard, Joan (ed) (c1974) *100 Years of the Farm Workers' Struggle.*, Institute for Workers' Control Pamphlet no 44.

McSmith, Andy (1996) *Faces of Labour. The Inside Story*, London, Verso.

Middleton, Lucy (ed) (1977) *Women in the Labour Movement*, London, Croom Helm.

Mikardo, Ian (1988) *Back-bencher*, London Weidenfeld and Nicolson.

Minkin, L (1978) *The Labour Party Conference: A Study in the Politics of Intra-party Democracy*, Manchester, Manchester University Press.

Mullin, Chris (1997) *Error of Judgement. The Truth about the Birmingham Bombings*, (Revised Edition) Dublin, Poolbeg Press Ltd.

Newby, Howard (c1974) 'Agricultural Trade Unionism and Structural Change', in Maynard J (ed), *100 Years of the Farm Workers Struggle*, Institute for Workers' Control Pamphlet no 44.

O'Donnell M. (1997) *Analysis of the Development of the British Labour Movement's Policies and Attitudes Towards the Northern Ireland Problem 1979–1997*, PhD Thesis, University of Surrey.

Panitch, Leo and Leys, Colin (1997) *The End of Parliamentary Socialism. From New Left to New Labour*, London, Verso.

Pelling, Henry and Reid, Alastair J (1996) *A Short History of the Labour Party*, Hampshire and London, Macmillan Press.

Phillips, Melanie (1980) *The Divided House. Women at Westminster*, London, Sidgwick and Jackson.

Pye-Smith, Charlie and Rose, Chris (1984) *Crisis and Conservation: Conflict in the British Countryside*, Harmondsworth Penguin.

Rogers, AW (1992) *Legislating for the Tied Cottage: A Study of the Rent (Agriculture) Act 1976 Journal of the Royal Agricultural Society of England*, (153) 81–88.

Seyd, Patrick (1987) *The Rise and Fall of the Labour Left*, Basingstoke, Macmillan Education.

Shaw, Eric (1988) *Discipline and Discord in the Labour Party. The Politics of Managerial Control in the Labour Party 1951– 1987*, Manchester, Manchester University Press.

Shaw, Eric (1996) *The Labour Party since 1945*, Oxford, Blackwell.

Taylor, Ian, Evans, Karen and Fraser, Penny (1996) *A Tale of Two Cities. A Study in Manchester and Sheffield*, London, Routledge.

Taylor, Richard (ed) (1996) *Beyond the Walls. 50 Years of Adult and Continuing Education at the University of Leeds 1946–1996*, The University of Leeds.

Thompson, EP (1963) *The Making of the English Working Class*, London, Victor Gollancz.

Tippett, Michael (1991) *Those Twentieth Century Blues. An Autobiography*, London, Hutchinson.

Trinder, C and Winyard, S (1975) *A New Deal for Farmworkers: The Case for an Independent Inquiry into the Pay of Farmworkers*, Low Pay Paper No. 5.

Vallance, Elizabeth (1979) *Women in the House. A Study of Women Members of Parliament*, London, The Athlone Press.

Wainwright, Hilary (1987) *Labour: a Tale of Two Parties*, London, Hogarth Press.

Witham, Joan (1986) *Hearts and Minds: The Story of the Women of Nottinghamshire in the Miners Strike 1984-1985*, London, Canary.

Wynn, Bob (1993) *Skilled at All Trades. The History of the Farmworkers' Union 1947–1984,* London, Transport and General Workers' Union, Frontline.

INDEX

Joan Maynard